THE ATLANTIC COMMUNITY
A Complex Imbalance

by
ROBERT L. PFALTZGRAFF, JR.
University of Pennsylvania

NEW PERSPECTIVES
IN
POLITICAL SCIENCE

A foreign Policy Research Institute Book. This volume is the 22nd of a series of studies published under the auspices of the Foreign Policy Research Institute, University of Pennsylvania.

VAN NOSTRAND REINHOLD COMPANY
NEW YORK CINCINNATI TORONTO
LONDON MELBOURNE

To
Diane

Van Nostrand Reinhold Company Regional Offices:
Cincinnati, New York, Chicago, Millbrae, Dallas

Van Nostrand Reinhold Company Foreign Offices:
London, Toronto, Melbourne

Published by Van Nostrand Reinhold Company
450 West 33rd Street, New York, N. Y. 10001

Published simultaneously in Canada by
D. Van Nostrand Company (Canada), Ltd.
15 14 13 12 11 10 9 8 7 6 5 4 3 2 1

Preface

A GENERATION AFTER THE FOUNDING OF THE ATLANTIC ALLIANCE, THE United States faces a new set of problems in its relations with Western Europe. The early postwar European dependence upon the United States in the aftermath of war has given way to new forms of dependence as a result of transatlantic technological, military and political disparities. Apprehensive of U.S. hegemony, the European peoples have been unable thus far to muster the resources, the will, or the organizational skills to transcend prevailing structural limitations upon the European environment. Although Western Europe forms potentially a partner in the attainment of common foreign policy goals, the United States has been unable to enlist European support, especially outside the North Atlantic area. The perceived decline in threat from the Soviet Union, the quest of the United States for improved relations with the Soviet Union, and the revival of tensions among Atlantic countries have contributed to the crisis of NATO. The optimism of the early 1960's about the prospects for the creation of an Atlantic Partnership, linking North America and an integrating Europe in the pursuit of commonly held objectives, has been superseded by doubts about the future of the Atlantic Alliance.

A study of U.S.–West European relations is illustrative of several problems confronting the major national units of the international system: the reconciliation of diverse, and often divergent, foreign policy goals; the impact upon alliance members of policies by the dominant member to improve relations with the adversary nation against whom the alliance was originally directed; the effect upon the alliance of declining perception of threat by alliance members from the adversary power; the impact of major technological change upon the alliance; and, in particular, the credibility of military guarantees provided by the alliance. This book addresses itself to these problems confronting the Atlantic Community of nations.

Since its founding in 1955, the Foreign Policy Research Institute has made the study of the problems of U.S.–West European relations one of its major concerns. This focal point of interest reflects the continuing importance of Western Europe to the security of the United States. Yet, more fully than any other region, the North Atlantic area has experienced the kinds of change which have preoccupied the students of contemporary politics. The most "highly developed" political systems of the world are to be found in the North Atlantic area. Political development and modernization are not only Western concepts; they are also processes which occurred in the West long before they occurred elsewhere in the world. If models based exclusively on the development and modernization processes as they unfolded in the North Atlantic area cannot be imposed upon the study of other regions, the experience of the West is instructive at least for the hypotheses, paradigms, and models which it can generate.

In another problem of contemporary concern, namely integration, Western Europe furnishes a rich data base. The patterns and problems of integration beyond the nation-state which evolved in Western Europe are without parallel elsewhere in the world. Finally, in the development of an understanding of alliance processes, the North Atlantic area supplies an abundance of experiences. Historically, the alliances of the international system were, for the most part, alliances formed among countries within the North Atlantic area. Although the study of NATO by itself is not sufficient to explain alliance behavior in general, propositions on alliance behavior may be generated from the NATO experience and tested in other contexts.

The Foreign Policy Research Institute has produced several studies of problems related to Atlantic affairs. In 1959, the Institute prepared a study on "United States Policy toward Western Europe" for the United States Senate Foreign Relations Committee. This study, published together with twelve other reports on U.S. foreign policy by the U.S. Government Printing Office in 1961, focused upon the major military, political and economic problems facing the United States in its relations with Western Europe in the 1960's.

In 1963, *Building the Atlantic World* was published under the imprimatur of the Foreign Policy Research Institute. The objective of this book was to set forth a framework for the achievement of partnership between North America and Western Europe in political, military and economic affairs. The book contained a detailed examination of the political history of NATO, the problems of Atlantic defense, Atlantic economic relationships, the arguments for and against—and the political framework for—nuclear sharing, and proposals for the reform of NATO.

In 1957 and 1967, the Foreign Policy Research Institute initiated conferences on problems of concern to Atlantic peoples. In September, 1967, the Institute, together with the College of Europe, co-sponsored a Conference on North Atlantic Community in Bruges, Belgium. This meeting brought together more than one hundred leading Americans and Europeans to discuss the intellectual and cultural basis of the Atlantic Community, and to explore the fundamental intellectual and cultural problems of Atlantic cooperation. From this conference came the idea of an Atlantic Institute, founded in 1961 and located in Paris, for the promotion of scholarly and cultural exchanges within the North Atlantic area.

A decade later, in May, 1967, the Foreign Policy Research Institute, in cooperation with the Scientific-Technological Committee of the

North Atlantic Assembly, co-sponsored a Conference on Atlantic Technological Imbalance and Collaboration in Deauville, France. Supported by the Ford Foundation, the Rockefeller Brothers Fund and others, this conference brought together forty European and thirty U.S. and Canadian participants, from academic, industrial, scientific and governmental backgrounds. Among the recommendations of the Conference was the creation of a European Institute of Science and Technology with an international faculty and students in all subjects concerned with technical progress, ranging from scientific subjects to their industrial application and including the basic sciences, economics, sociology, and psychology.

The present book has had the generous support of the A. W. Mellon Educational and Charitable Trust. A grant to the Foreign Policy Research Institute has made possible not only the completion of this study but the preparation of articles which have been published in ORBIS, *The Atlantic Community Quarterly, The New Republic, European Review* (London), *Freedom and Union,* and the *Journal of Common Market Studies* (Oxford).

In the preparation of this book, the author has benefited from discussions with the following Associates, and former Associates, of the Foreign Policy Research Institute: Dr. James E. Dougherty, Executive Vice President and Professor of Political Science, Saint Joseph's College, Philadelphia, Pa.; Dr. Hans Kohn, Professor Emeritus of History, City College of New York; Dr. Laurence Krause, Brookings Institution; Dr. Philip E. Mosely, Director, European Institute, Columbia University; Dr. Norman D. Palmer, Professor of Political Science, University of Pennsylvania; Dr. Stefan T. Possony, Director of International Studies, Hoover Institution of Peace, War, and Revolution, Stanford University; and Dr. Arthur P. Whitaker, Professor Emeritus of History, University of Pennsylvania. The author is indebted to the following Institute staff members for insights and guidance: Dr. Morton Gorden; Dr. Wolfgang Klaiber, Dr. Diane Kressler Pfaltzgraff; Dr. David C. Schwartz; and Dr. Edward G. Janosik, now Professor and Chairman, Department of Political Science, New York State University, Genesee, New York. The author had the benefit of research conducted for this study by the following graduate students: Mr. Charles Ashton; Mr. Daniel Dolan; Mr. Jeffrey Hahn; and Mr. Chander Rajaratnam.

The author received valuable insights as a result of conversations with, or comments on parts of this study from, the following persons: Mr. Alastair Buchan, Director, Institute for Strategic Studies, London; the Hon. Frederick W. Mulley, Minister of State, the Foreign Office, London; Admiral Anthony Buzzard, Vickers-Armstrong Corporation; Francois Duchene, the *Economist* (London); Lt. Col. Otto Ferdinand Miksche (France); Colonel Marc Geneste (France); M. Pierre Emmanuelli, French North Atlantic Treaty Association; Senator George Portman, Conseil de la Republique (France); Dr. h.c. Kurt Birrenbach, MdB, Member, Foreign Affairs Committee, Bundestag, Federal

Republic of Germany; Mr. Aurelio Peccei, President, Olivetti Corporation; Mr. Michael Palmer, Member of the Secretariat, Western European Union Assembly; the Honorable Dean Acheson; Mr. Henry Owen, Chairman, Policy Planning Council, Department of State; the Honorable Eugene Rostow, Under Secretary of State for Political Affairs, Department of State; the Honorable Paul Findley, Chairman, House Republican Committee on NATO and the Atlantic Community; Mr. Adolph W. Schmidt, T. Mellon and Sons; Dr. Edward Teller, Lawrence Radiation Laboratory, University of California (Berkeley); Mr. Francis C. Hoeber, The Rand Corporation; Dr. L. F. Audrieth, Professor Emeritus of Chemistry, University of Illinois; Dr. Arnold Wolfers, the Washington Center of Foreign Policy Research; Mr. James Huntley, the Atlantic Council; Ambassador Walter Dowling, Director-General, the Atlantic Institute (Paris); Mr. Joseph Harned, the Atlantic Institute; M. Pierre Uri, the Atlantic Institute; Dr. Gerhard Mally, University of Virginia; Major General W. W. Stromberg, former U.S. Standing Group Representative, NATO Council; Dr. George A. Contos, Scientific Advisor to *SACEUR*; and the following members of Radio Free Europe, Munich: Mr. Zygmunt Michalowski, Polish Broadcasting Desk; Mrs. Dorothy Miller, German Broadcasting Department; Mr. J. F. Brown, Chief of Analysis, Office of the Policy Director; Mr. Herbert Reed, Deputy Director for East European Research and Analysis; Mr. Harry Trend, Economist; Mr. Noel Bernard, Chief, Romanian Desk, Broadcasting Department; and Mr. Fritz Ermarth, Research Analyst on Problems of the Warsaw Treaty Organization.

In the preparation of the manuscript, the author received editorial assistance from Mrs. Margaret Capotrio and Mr. Robert C. Herber, respectively Assistant Editor and Managing Editor, ORBIS.

In the typing of drafts of the manuscript, Mrs. Lynne Koch and Mrs. Marie Burke performed invaluable service.

Finally, the author owes special gratitude to Professor Robert Strausz-Hupé, Director, and Professor William R. Kintner, Deputy Director, of the Foreign Policy Research Institute for their insightful critique and unfailing encouragement from which this work has greatly benefited.

Contents

Introduction

Robert Strausz-Hupé

THE UNIVERSE OF HISTORICAL ALLIANCES CONSISTS OF TWO classes: those that were put to the test and those that were not. The military alliances of World War I were put to the test of war: the Entente prevailed over the coalition of the Central Powers and thus achieved its purpose; the coalition of the Central Powers suffered defeat. However, the gains and losses of the individual members were not proportionate to the collective outcome for the respective alliances. As a member of the winning coalition, Russia received a payoff which, at the end of the war, seemed indistinguishable from defeat. Among the members of the losing coalition, Germany was penalized far less than Austria-Hungary and the Ottoman Empire. Yet, *grosso modo,* the Entente could claim to have furthered the interests of its members, who under any then conceivable circumstances could neither have stood up singly to the Central Powers nor have saved themselves by withdrawal into neutrality. In all likelihood, even Russia would have fared infinitely worse had the defeat of Germany not saved her from foreign subjugation. Thus, by summing up the returns of the individual members it is possible to declare the Entente a winning coalition. Yet who can argue that the international system, if not humanity at large, would not have been immeasurably better off had this particular alliance not been put to the test of war?

The Entente, an alliance loosely joined, inexplicit in its purpose, and lacking salient military superiority, did not deter the aggressors. Strategic parity did not prevent war. To the contrary, it encouraged (as it always has in history) the challenger of the status quo, more dynamic than the defenders. The failure of deterrence resulted in 20 million dead and another 20 million killed off by disease and starvation. It also sparked a series of revolutionary catastrophies which culminated in World War II. The returns from NATO have been infinitely less spectacular—and infinitely more rewarding by virtue of battles that were not fought, lives that were not lost, property that was not destroyed, and an international order that was not upset by dynamic aggressors.

Since retrospective scenarios can be made even more selective than futuristic ones, the ifs of history are far more intriguing and immeasurably less ambiguous than that mixed bag of tricks, real history. Since NATO has never been put to the test of war, it is easy to argue that the threat of war never existed. In theory, especially in vulgarized Hegelian theory, it is possible to assert that what has not happened in history could not have happened anyway. In the last resort, the ethical justification and practical usefulness of NATO stand and fall with the West's perception of the Soviet threat to Europe. If the West, after World War II, perceived that threat correctly, then the decision to create NATO flowed logically from historical objective reality. Since no one has yet been able to fully understand objective historical reality, a degree of uncertainty remains. This degree of uncertainty has gnawed at the vitals of NATO ever since its inception. During the first decade of NATO's existence, its members could live with it, and they relied upon the original model rather than speculating on alternative security schemes. Of late, that degree of uncertainty about Soviet purpose has been growing mightily, and revisionism is now threatening to overwhelm the orthodoxies of NATO. The question is now what is left of these orthodoxies and what doctrines are taking their place. In the present book, Professor Pfaltzgraff seeks to answer these questions.

Foreign policy making, like any other rational activity, proceeds by simplification. If it did not, rational decisions could not be made. In democratic societies, the problem of how to present this process to the average citizen, presumed to be knowledgeable but not knowledgeable enough to do without professional expertise, is fraught with many technical difficulties and moral dilemmas. In the present age of public-relations technology, all very large organizations, national and international, tend to develop their particular mythologies. It is these mythologies, rather than the record of performance, which vest the organization with legitimacy —and help sell the product. In certain cases, as for example that of the United Nations, the gap between myths and metaphors on the one hand and operational realities on the other hand is perilously wide.

The gap between myth and substance is far narrower in NATO. Even so it was quite natural that the participating governments should endow NATO with reductionist myths. One of these was the ever-present danger of an all-out military attack against Western Europe—the Soviet tanks filling their radiators with water from the Loire and the Tiber. True, this specter of a Soviet attack, like most myths, was rooted in the haunting memory of historical transactions. In World War II, the Soviets displayed the traditional Russian propensity for the use of crude manpower. In France and Italy the Communist Party rode the tide of antifascist, anticollaborationist sentiment and widespread economic distress. In communist parlance, the revolutionary situation seemed "ripe." Who can now prove beyond a shadow of a doubt that Stalin, particularly after his 1948 squeeze on Berlin, could have resisted the temptation to exploit Europe's military vacuum, had NATO not begun to fill it? Or prove that Stalin was unlikely to stake the "sure thing," i.e., control of East-Central Europe, on an all-European gamble? Although massive Western war aid, enormous war booty, and plentiful slave labor had sped the recovery of the Soviet Union, the Soviets had not yet been able to reequip their hard-used military forces, and the battered Soviet economy could hardly have sustained the logistics of a large-scale offensive. But such an offensive might not have been needed against a largely disarmed Western Europe. Perhaps, because of the American atomic monopoly, the Soviets deemed the odds too heavily weighted against them. Yet, undoubtedly, the specter of the Red Army sweeping over Europe strengthened popular support for NATO.

It is just possible that Western statesmen did not contrive this and other myths about Soviet purpose in order to rouse their peoples' sense of urgency. It appears that the Western governments themselves had only the foggiest notion of communist conflict techniques, and hence of Soviet strategy. Indeed, what is past is prologue: NATO is rooted in conflict situations which, despite significant variations, have shaped the enduring pattern of West-East confrontation to this day.

NATO was created in the wake of the Greek civil war and the Czechoslovak coup d'état of 1948. These events belong to the category of the Strategy of the Indirect Approach. They set the standard for communist subversion, directed and supported (as in the case of Czechoslovakia) from nearby Soviet control posts, or (as in the case of Greece) from an allied communist state, Yugoslavia. Soviet operations against West Berlin and in Cuba are classic examples of the Strategy of the Indirect Approach which, from the outset, should have been a primary concern of NATO. Scanning the presently available evidence, one cannot now argue convincingly that the Western governments ever grasped the complex interaction between insurgent forces operating locally and Soviet-supplied materiel, between formal diplomacy and political warfare, between the uses of low-level violence and strategic blackmail. It is not clear that the Western governments understand the "system" even now.

As now can be seen, NATO has suffered grievously from its success—and from this success being taken for granted. It has suffered even more from that lack of sophistication which reduces the public discourse of Western statecraft to hardened platitudes. The masses of the Western peoples cannot be blamed for ignoring the real threats to the Atlantic Alliance and, hence, its real usefulness. Myths have taken the place of sober explanations. Since the political leaders of the West are content to live with myths, and since no one is more myth-receptive than the West's opinion-making elite, no one now speaks for NATO—except the logic of events. Unfortunately, the logic of events speaks with a small voice, and the cacophony of pseudo-events is apt to drown it out.

As the striking power of the strategic air command shifted from bombers to missiles, the mission of the American nuclear deterrent became to forestall a Soviet nuclear attack against the United States. But only within the political and strategic environment created by NATO can the American deterrent be said to have contained the expansion of Soviet power in Europe. Insofar as NATO has thwarted the Strategy of the Indirect Approach and has prevented the release of tensions within the communist bloc into foreign conquest, NATO has helped to cause the disintegrative process which has loosened the Soviet grip on the satellite states and weakened the hold of individual communist regimes upon their respective peoples. Again, we are forced back upon the perilous terrain of conjecture. The progress of industrialization and organization and the conflict of generations might have set in motion, unaided by external pressures, those changes in the communist world which have slackened the dogmatic zeal of communism and thus "relaxed tensions." Yet, it is not recommended to read history out of context. The real and putative changes in the communist world have occurred within an international environment of which NATO was a part. Indeed, in the perception of communist leadership, it was a major part.

Innumerable communist statements have been addressed to NATO. Indisputably, the communists have always seen NATO as the obstacle to the kind of world they want. Hence, if many of the changes which we deem beneficial to our security and the well-being of mankind are deemed undesirable by communist leadership, it follows that NATO looms large in the communist assessment of the present state of affairs. It also follows that the present state of affairs might not persist, if NATO ceased to matter in the international environment. While we can guess at the consequences of NATO's demise, no one can now predict what these consequences actually will be. In brief, no one knows whether the kind of European settlement which we deem to be conducive to human freedom and world peace can be achieved in a world without NATO.

From the outset, an underlying rationale of NATO was the expectation that the pooled power of the West could induce the Soviets to accede to a European settlement conducive to individual freedom and world peace. Thus, NATO was conceived as a stage in international evolution, not as an end in itself. Semantic novelties do not necessarily help us to understand better the real world as it is and as it has been for a long time. The idea of NATO as a bargaining instrument is not novel, though the words for it might be. From the beginning, NATO was designed to open "bridges" towards the East. At that time it was thought that the bridging arc had to rest upon two equally stable platforms, namely, a powerful united West and a stable East likely to be powerful, but also (so it was hoped) prepared to restore the civil liberties and national freedoms which as a result of World War II had been ground down by Soviet power. In the more distant future, Western statesmen could then perceive the prospect of profound political and social changes in the Soviet Union itself: the Soviet people, wearied by the exactions and contradictions of communism, would enter the community of the free peoples. Were these assumptions and contingent expectations altogether unreasonable? Of course they were not. In the wake of de-Stalinization, political and social change swept the East. Cracks have opened in the once monolithic empire. The fundamental assumptions stood the test of time: the Atlantic Alliance created that framework of security within which the West achieved unprecedented levels of widely distributed prosperity, a fact that has done more to expose the fallacies of communist doctrine and to weaken the authority of communist rulers than any other. Whatever else NATO did or did not accomplish, it provided the psychological ambiance of European economic recovery.

By restoring the balance of power in Europe, NATO laid the basis for negotiation leading towards a European settlement. The overarching issue of such a European settlement is now, as it has been during the last twenty years, the unification of Germany. For reasons explored in this book, a European settlement has to this day eluded the West. Ever since the early 1960's, United States diplomacy has sought to bypass this and related political issues and to bridge the chasm of the Cold War by arms-control agreements, bilaterally negotiated with the Soviet Union. The wisdom and efficacy of this approach stand and fall with one assumption, namely, that the political issues which gave rise to the East-West confrontation can be healed or at least painted over by agreements which reduce the danger of war between the two superpowers. Although historically the danger of war has been proportionate to the intensity of unresolved political conflicts between nations rather than to the quantity of arms possessed by the contending parties, I will not seek here to test the validity of the assumption which underlines the contemporary dialogue between the United States and the Soviet Union.

This book traces the consequences flowing from the shift of emphasis in American policy. So massive has been their impact upon the cohesiveness of the Atlantic Alliance as to suggest more than a casual relationship between the vicissitudes of alliance cohesiveness and the fundamental change in priorities of United States foreign policy. It would have been surprising if NATO could have survived unaltered the United States' change of preferences. Without prejudicing the case for this change, it is legitimate to question here a widely held view, namely, that Western Europe's perception of the decrease in the Soviet threat has weakened the cohesiveness of the Alliance. An alternative hypothesis needs to be tested: the relaxation of Western Europe's posture in NATO is a function of American perceptions and policy preferences.

In foreign policy, as in everything one does, timing is of the essence. A strong and cohesive Atlantic Alliance might well have served as the diplomatic means—the "bridge"—for reaching a European settlement. Once that settlement had been achieved, NATO *qua* military alliance could be dissolved and America and Europe, if they were so minded, could move towards other forms of cooperation. It is, however, difficult to see how the disintegration of NATO, in anticipation of a settlement yet to be concluded, will strengthen the bargaining power of the West. Viewed from this perspective, United States foreign policy is tantamount to a gamble on disintegration: the loosening up of the communist bloc is expected to compensate for the disintegration of NATO. Even if this were the direction in which events are moving, this extrapolation leads us far away from the conception of NATO as a functioning military alliance or "crisis manager"—indeed so far that what is left of NATO is unlikely to find its way back home.

Not the least stake of this gamble on the mutuality of dissolution is the future of Germany. NATO created the framework for the integration of the German Federal Republic into the community of Western Europe. West Germany has progressed from membership in the North Atlantic Treaty Organization and the West European Union to membership in the European Economic Community. The analogy of NATO as a lever of change in the East holds for West Germany. We do not know how Germany would have fared in the hypothetical NATO-less world; we do know that the political and economic development of the Federal Republic unfolded within an international environment of which NATO formed part. The importance of NATO to West Germany has been reciprocated by the importance of West Germany to NATO. The awareness of this community in fate has been an indispensable element in the evolution of a democratic Germany. If it were only for this consideration (and not for others such as the strategic geography of Europe), the dissolution of NATO would be fraught with incalculable consequences for the future of Germany and Europe. No one knows what a neutralized, demilitarized Germany, united or divided, would be like. There is no dearth of scenarios such as the Rapacki Plan and its many variants. At the risk of appearing a hardened foe of innovation, I suggest that at present no one has the foggiest notion about the kind of Germany which would issue from the crucible of an "All-

European-Security Arrangement," a synonym for the withdrawal of the United States from NATO Europe.

Alliances consisting of more than two members confront two related problems, namely, the one of size and the other of motion—how large the membership of the alliance should be, and how the alliance should proceed towards its goal.

Too small a coalition might not be strong enough to accomplish its purpose and might suffer defeat; too large a coalition might be unwieldy and riven by factional differences. In theory, it is possible to define the "optimality" of an alliance; in practice, the leaders of an alliance are apt to bid for all likely adherents in sight, and alliances, once they have been put together, develop a bandwagon effect: some of the states who did not join the alliance when it was formed or when it was still weak now "want in," either to share in the gains of the alliance or to divert from themselves the retribution which the founding members might mete out to the latecomer, the trimmer, or simply the weak.

Alliances are formed for a specific purpose: to upset the status quo, or to maintain it by deterring the likely aggressor or by defeating him in war. Sooner or later the specific purpose is either accomplished or defeated, depriving the alliance of its raison d'être—if no other common concerns have taken the place of the original purpose. Even while the ostensible purpose of the alliance still enlists the pledged collaborative efforts of the members, more or less subtle changes in the allies' perceptions of that common purpose impinge upon the behavior of the alliance: the "personality" of the alliance changes—and the attrition of time and other variables alters the very purpose of the alliance. In this respect, alliances do not differ from other things: we can step into the same river, and yet that same river is never the same; I am I, and yet I am never the same man; and so forth and so on *ad infinitum*. No matter how constant its purpose, an alliance must adapt itself to changes of the international environment of which its members as well as nations that are not its members are parts.

Not that everything in the international environment changes as significantly or as quickly as some revolutionary or pseudo-revolutionary doctrines will have it! A good many things do not. The inertia of the international system is much greater than historical pragmatism allows. Alliances which have existed for a long time and were intended to be permanent, have always reached a critical threshold: on this side of it lies stagnation and ultimately dissolution; beyond it lies another evolutionary stage—the creation of a new unitary institution. In brief, alliances among sovereign nations either disintegrate or grow into federations—closer unions. The choice is between moving forward or backwards, and not between either of these alternatives and standing still.

The organismic analogy is as obvious as it is tempting. Indeed, contemporary research in international relations has sought to adapt models developed by economics—the behavior of large organizations, such as giant corporations—and biology—the evolution of organisms—to the building of theories about alliance behavior. Thus far, this endeavor has yielded some interesting hypotheses about the life cycle of alliances; it has not added significantly to the fund of knowledge accumulated by traditional historiography. The story of the Delian League, for example, or the Thirteen American States or the Entente of World War I or the United Nations of World War II provides the sensitive student who knows how to pursue historical analogies, and when not to press on, with the best framework of analysis now available. Still, no one should be stopped from trying to devise a better one. This book points in new directions; it does not gainsay the difficulties along the path of exploration.

No doubt the Atlantic Alliance has not been on every count an "optimal" alliance. Confined, let us say, to "les Anglo-Saxons," together with the Netherlands, Belgium, Denmark, and Norway, it might have been a more congenial one in political consensus, and hence a more cohesive one. The inclusion of France, Germany, and Italy burdened the Alliance with divergencies of domestic political structures, and in the case of Germany and Italy, the haunting memories of aberrant political ideologies. Thus, it impeded the growth of that "belonging together" feeling which, especially during periods of diminished external threat, keeps the alliance pledge from fading into public indifference.

The contribution of Portugal to the Alliance, namely, bases in the Azores, has not sufficed to mute the critics of her regime and policies toward her overseas territories. No doubt the Scandinavian members would have preferred to keep Portugal out. Greece and Turkey have never found universal acceptance as bona fide members of an alliance purporting to be both Atlantic and a repository of individual liberty. In fact, geographical-strategic considerations weighed heavily upon the composition of the Atlantic Alliance. That they did not entirely dominate it reflects a reconciliation of principle and expediency which has harmed the cohesiveness of the alliance less than subsequent, more suspect compromises. Alternatives to NATO, if they are to be found in more selective groupings, will have to satisfy the criteria of strategic-geographical sufficiency. By the vote of "optimality," NATO may have been too large; yet the price of exclusiveness might be the balkanization of what is now still NATO Europe.

The Atlantic Alliance has not crossed the critical threshold: the standing military treaty organization has not developed into a political union. To the contrary, its *political* cohesiveness has diminished, and its military establishment has deteriorated apace. In no other country has the case for international collaboration and all kinds of "integration" found more forceful and persuasive spokesmen than in the United States. European integration has been an explicit desideratum of United States foreign policy; so has been general and complete disarmament, a measure inconceivable without the allocation of powers now vested in national sovereignty to the United Nations. Yet, as this book shows, at every major turn in NATO's history, the United States has shunned supranational solutions. Whether this was or was not the wise course, and whether the United States rose to the "necessity of choice," are questions which this book seeks, if not to answer, at least to pose concisely. They need be stated clearly, for the alternatives are fraught with considerable finality—for us, for Europe and for the rest of the world. The systemic revolution of our times is pregnant with new political formations. The future fortunes of the Atlantic Alliance—dissolution or evolution—will determine the shape of the new world order.

I. The Crisis of the West

FOR MORE THAN FIVE HUNDRED YEARS, SINCE THE EARLIEST European explorations overseas, Western civilization has been the incubator of the dynamic forces which have transformed the world. From the North Atlantic area have come modernizing influences which have galvanized dormant societies around the world and spurred them to the formidable tasks of political and economic development. The industrial and technological revolutions, which had their origins in the West, have made possible for the first time in history the emergence of a global international system and consequently have had a profound impact upon international politics. If the human race is moving toward a world civilization, it is because of the Promethean impact of the West upon all mankind.

The revolutionary influences of the West have far from run their course. By the end of this century, the increase in transactions among political units of the world and the exploration of outer space—both results of the development and exploitation of advanced technology—will have a major impact upon political systems at both the national and international levels. In the shaping of this new world, the peoples of the North Atlantic area will play a role of decisive importance. The West was the birthplace not only of advanced technology and economic systems, but of modern political institutions once, but no longer, adequate to the demands placed upon them.

An ever-accelerating pace of change has affected international relationships. Within just one generation the once-great empires of Western European powers have given way to new states, most of which face difficult problems of political, social, and economic modernization. As a result of increasing political, economic, military, and technological interdependence, patterns of collaboration and integrative institutions at the international level have replaced the rivalries and conflict of earlier periods. But disintegrative tendencies still grip the West. Since World War II, a "new Europe" has emerged which differs in many ways—in levels of economic growth, prosperity, and mobility—from the Europe of previous generations. The changes which have occurred within the West itself have been no less rapid and far-reaching than those which have transformed regions outside the North Atlantic area as a result of stimuli from the West.

U.S.-EUROPEAN DISCORD

For generations the peoples of the North Atlantic area have been linked by bonds of kinship and culture, as well as political, economic, and strategic interests, despite the great conflicts which historically have pitted their countries against each other. In spite of these Atlantic links, the cohesiveness of Atlantic peoples has come to be measured largely by the cohesiveness of the chiefly military Atlantic Alliance.

In two world wars the United States intervened upon the assumption that the domination of Europe by a hostile power would menace North America. In joining NATO, the United States, in contrast to its earlier policy, committed itself in advance to prevent hostile encroachment in Western Europe. NATO stemmed from the belief of its founders, in North America and Western Europe, that the security interests of peoples on both sides of the Atlantic coincided. The utility of NATO can only be deduced from a non-event, namely that the Soviet Union did not attack or conquer Western Europe. NATO provided the security which enabled Western Europe to rebuild shattered economies and to experiment with a variety of forms of international integration. The alliance however has not yet achieved one of the objectives of its founders, a general European political settlement.

The Atlantic consensus was based not only upon generally shared objectives, but also upon specific national interests of its members. For the German Federal Republic, NATO contributed to the attainment of a position of greater equality and respectability within the West. Moreover, German policy makers saw in NATO an important avenue to the eventual achievement of reunification. Membership in the Atlantic Alliance accorded not only with Britain's security needs, but also with her interest in preserving a strong link with both the United States and continental Western Europe. NATO permitted the Scandinavian and the Benelux countries to reconcile earlier policies of neutrality with the need to develop security arrangements at the international level. For

Canada, participation in NATO, which included the European countries with which Canada has links of kinship, was preferable to a bilateral defense arrangement with the colossus to the south. For the United States, the Atlantic Alliance affirmed the long-standing U.S. recognition that the defense of Europe is vital to the defense of the United States. In short, each member believed that it derived specific as well as general gains, which exceeded the cost of NATO membership.

Alliances are creatures of the contemporary political environment. Seldom does an alliance outlive the conditions which prompt its formation. The diplomatic history of the nation-state system abounds with examples of shifting coalitions—*le renversment des alliances*. Erstwhile allies may find themselves, after the passage of several years—or even several months—members of opposing alliance systems. An alliance system created to meet the security requirements of its member states at a given moment in history is eventually subject to defections, for the relationships among its members are unlikely to remain stable.[1] NATO has not experienced the *renversement des alliances* which has confronted other alliance systems. Whatever their difficulties, for the most part the nations of the West have evolved patterns of interaction in which resort to military conflict or formation of opposing alliances is considered unthinkable. Even though organizations may live on even after they have lost their *raison d'etre,* their membership is likely to decline with the passage of time, and those who remain members may find increasingly burdensome an organization whose importance is deemed marginal. A generation after its formation, NATO faces such a prospect.

The problems which beset NATO can be traced to many causes. Changes in technology over the past generation have contributed to the disarray. Conceivably, the impact of technology has been such as to reduce the utility of alliance systems for the attainment of national security objectives. The advent and spread of nuclear weapons have aggravated the ancient problem of achieving in foreign policy a balance between interest and risk, between the objective of a given course of action and the cost of achieving it. In particular the development by the Soviet Union of nuclear capabilities aroused doubt that NATO in its existing form can ensure the national security of its members. West European allies were apprehensive that the United States would not be prepared to risk its own destruction in defense of Western Europe.[2] Changes in U.S. strategic doctrine reinforced such European doubts and contributed to the growth of European interest in acquiring physical control of nuclear weapons.

Having assisted Western Europe to achieve a remarkable post-war recovery and prosperity, the United States has been unable to develop a policy which will enable Western Europe to reduce its dependence upon the United States. In fact, the United States' policies in Western Europe have contributed to the perpetuation of Western Europe's dependence, even though U.S. policymakers a generation ago did not intend that the United States should assume a permanent tutelage over Western Europe. The U.S. imposition upon NATO of strategic concepts to which official opposition exists in Western Europe, and the U.S. disparagement of European efforts to develop modern defense capabilities, have fueled European opposition to NATO and affected adversely the European contributions, within the Alliance, to the defense of the North Atlantic area.

Especially since 1964, U.S. interest in the Atlantic Alliance has waned as a result of the official U.S. preoccupation with Asian affairs, together with growing U.S. interest in the subordination of foreign policy to formidable domestic problems. To an extent without precedent since World War II, the idea that a divided, rather than integrated, Western Europe might serve U.S. interests has gained currency, at least in unofficial circles. As a result of shifting U.S. policy concerns and the reorientation of European foreign policy, the assumption that there is a harmony of interest between the United States and its Atlantic allies has been questioned. The United States has found it increasingly difficult to reconcile a policy of detente with the Soviet Union with the preservation of Alliance cohesion. Forced to choose between these two policy objectives, Americans have been prepared since 1963—the year of the signing of the Test Ban Treaty—to subordinate the strengthening of U.S.-West European relationships to the quest for a U.S.-Soviet agreement. Even at a time when the forging of transatlantic security links and the formation of an Atlantic partnership were of central concern, the United States adopted policies which did not always accord with the strengthening of Atlantic relationships. Although U.S. policymakers repeatedly expressed fidelity to the Atlantic Alliance, which they deemed crucial to American security, the

United States pursued a variety of other foreign policy objectives: the containment of communism in Asia, the improvement of U.S.-Soviet relationships, the emancipation of subject peoples from colonial rule, the reconciliation of Alliance strategy with U.S. strategic doctrine, and the conclusion of arms control agreements with the Soviet Union. Whatever the intrinsic merits of each of these policy objectives, in their pursuit the United States contributed to doubts in Europe about both the consistency of U.S. foreign policy and the relative importance of NATO in U.S. policy calculations. The NATO experience is indicative of the potentially disintegrative impact upon an alliance of policies pursued by one of its members —especially the leading member—toward outside powers.

The efforts of the United States to develop new patterns of collaboration with the Soviet Union have affected the Atlantic Alliance. Not only has the U.S. subordination of Atlantic relationships to other foreign policy objectives served to weaken Alliance cohesion, but it has also contributed to a reassessment among other members of the importance of the Alliance to their own security. Fearful that the United States and the Soviet Union might reach an accord detrimental to European interests,[3] they have reconsidered and reshaped their own policies toward both the Soviet Union and the Atlantic Alliance. In placing reduced emphasis upon the Alliance, European members have adopted policies toward the Soviet Union in many ways similar to those of the United States. Like the United States, they have chosen to subordinate Alliance cohesion to East-West relations.

U.S. policy in Southeast Asia, whatever its justification, contributed to tensions within the Alliance and especially between the United States and France. Dissatisfaction with U.S. policy in regions where France no longer has interests deemed vital to her security affected the French decision to withdraw from the integrated command structure of NATO. Outside NATO, France could avoid involvement where interests not specifically those of France were at stake and where France had not been consulted.[4] French foreign policy regarding the extension of European support to the United States in regions beyond the geographic perimeter of NATO bears great similarity to U.S. policy just a decade ago. In calling for a broadening of the alliance to extra-Atlantic affairs, the proponents and the opponents have changed more than the substance of the argument.

A decade ago, the United States refused to accede to French requests for the coordination of the foreign policies of Britain, France, and the United States in regions where the three major powers of NATO had common interests. In recent years, however, a curious change has occurred in NATO. Having assumed commitments in regions where European powers were once predominant, the United States has sought to obtain from European NATO countries a greater contribution to the resolution of problems outside the North Atlantic Area. European governments have become increasingly reluctant, and even unwilling, to assume new burdens outside the North Atlantic Area, and instead have become preoccupied with strictly European problems.[5] This focus upon Europe of European energies helps to explain the growth in the 1960's of West European interest in the "normalization" of relations between Eastern and Western Europe.

More than any other Alliance member, France under the Fifth Republic has developed foreign policies which do not accord with the Alliance as presently constituted. According to official French thought, if France and her neighbors in Western Europe are to safeguard their interests and gain a greater measure of international influence, they must strengthen their technological, economic, and military capabilities. French policy is based upon two assumptions: that the Soviet threat has diminished and that the development of a rift between China and the Soviet Union and the apparent increase in initiatives open to leaders in Eastern Europe present Western nations, France in particular, with new opportunities. No longer "subordinated" to the United States in NATO, whose structure and strategic concepts do not conform to official French perceptions of the international environment, France has sought and obtained new maneuverability in foreign policy. French policy under De Gaulle is the amalgam of several factors, including the French President's long-standing distrust of the "Anglo-Saxon" powers and his design for a more independent and modernized France. But policies which the United States adopted undoubtedly influenced De Gaulle's decisions vis-à-vis the Atlantic Alliance. Like the United States, France strove to develop and to control the means to assure her own military security. She was no less willing than the United States to subordinate herself to another power within an alliance system or to restrict her freedom of action in foreign policy. In pressing either for nuclear capabilities or for greater influence in strategic decisions, West European governments have attempted to obtain for themselves only what the United States sought for itself. No less than the United States was France prepared to place the defense of its own territory in the hands of another power. No less than the United States was France willing to adopt a strategy which left doubt about her willingness to use nuclear weapons in the defense of her national territory. In seeking to expand contacts with communist states, West European governments have embarked upon policies not greatly different from those of the United States. In refusing to accede to U.S. requests for greater European assistance in regions outside the North Atlantic area, West European governments have adopted policies similar to those which just a decade ago the United States held. In effect, the United States, as the leader of the Alliance, claimed for itself rights which it was not prepared to extend to lesser members. As they recovered from the devastation of war, West European governments were not willing to acquiesce in such subordination to the United States.

Although France has been the principal recipient of criticism for her policies, other European countries have contributed to the disarray in NATO. Britain has undertaken periodically to reduce her military commitment to the Alliance. British efforts to preserve a "special relationship" with the United States long after the postwar recovery of continental Western Europe, increased European apprehensions about excessive Anglo-American influence in the Alliance. Most European members of NATO, with the notable exception of the German Federal Republic, have not maintained force levels at sufficient strength to permit the United States to reduce greatly its share of the burden of European defense. In many cases, European interest in gaining increased influence within the Atlantic Alliance has not been matched by a greater willingness to assume a greater portion of the costs of defense. Nor has the U.S. interest in obtaining a greater European commitment to defense been matched by a U.S. willingness either to develop strategic doctrines which accord with European perceptions or to accede to European requests for major influence in the command and control of nuclear weapons.

THE "NEW EUROPE" AND ATLANTIC IMBALANCE

It is widely acknowledged that a "New Europe" has sprung from the destruction of the Second World War.[6] The emergence of this "new Europe" has contributed to discord within the Alliance, because it is no longer so willing as in the first decade after World War II to acquiesce in U.S. leadership, especially a U.S. leadership not sufficiently responsive to European interests. While this new Europe may assume one day major new international burdens and responsibilities, it is easy to overestimate its capacity to take such steps at the present time. Conceivably, a post-Gaullist regime in France will face conditions of political instability which will set drastic limits on its foreign policy and will even affect its capacity for sustained domestic growth. Both Germany and Italy lack a long tradition of representative government, and Germany faces pressures for reunification which could strain the political fabric of the Federal Republic. In addition to political instability in major European countries, the political and economic complexion of the "new Europe" rests upon uncertain foundations, with the existentialism of the early postwar period having given way to a form of nihilism and materialism which, to be sure, does not augur well for the assumption of vast new international burdens. Student and industrial unrest, most pronounced in France, erupted elsewhere in Europe in 1968. Such manifestations of dissatisfaction with archaic educational systems, employer-employee relations, and wage levels are likely to limit resources available to European countries for defense and foreign policy.

Nor is the "new Europe" unified in the goals which it seeks to attain. Under De Gaulle's leadership, France evoked that spirit of independence which once before animated Europeans. Yet the "new Europe" is still a Europe based upon the old national political units. Despite the development of the European Community, the locus of decision-making in Western Europe remains the nation-state. However impressive its achievements, the "new Europe" has taken shape at a period in history when only vast political units, such as the United States and the Soviet Union, possess the resources needed for the maximization of the potential inherent in science and technology, for the attainment of economies of vast scale, and for the provision of defense.

Although Western Europe has regained a measure of confidence in its future that could hardly have been foreseen a generation ago, it remains heavily dependent upon the United States. As the perception of Soviet threat has declined, the apprehension about U.S. hegemony in Atlantic relationships has risen. NATO has represented U.S. hegemony in Atlantic military relationships. Despite its remarkable postwar recovery and growth, Western Europe seems unable to escape American dominance in other fields as well. As a result of changes in technology, the European national units are likely to find themselves less and less able over the next generation to reduce the widening disparity between their own achievements and capabilities and those of the United States. The increasing U.S. dominance is fraught with considerable danger to Atlantic relationships, for the Europeans face the prospect of becoming ever more tied—economically, technologically, and militarily—to the United States, but less willing psychologically to accept U.S. hegemony.[7]

The perpetuation and extension of U.S. hegemony holds implications of considerable importance for Atlantic relationships. To be sure, a status-quo in which decisions affecting the future of European economic life, technology, and military affairs are taken in the United States may not be totally without appeal in Western Europe. For instance, the influx of U.S.-developed technology via the European affiliates of American corporations would enable Western Europe to gain access to advanced knowhow, but at the expense of greater dependence upon the United States. Although not a few in Western Europe find unobjectionable the assumption by the United States of even greater responsibility for decisions about the defense of Europe, the extension of U.S. hegemony in other fields would give rise to European opposition to the perpetuation of West European subordination to the United States. European apprehension about the widely publicized Atlantic "technological imbalance" stems from a belief that in fields vital to its future, Europe will become excessively dependent upon technologies developed in the United States. French objections to NATO issue from the unwillingness of France to permit decisions about its own future—and the future of Europe—to be taken by the United States.

The problems facing the United States in its relations with Western Europe are novel in Atlantic affairs. To be sure, a generation ago, the gap between the United States and Western Europe was wide. At the time of the Marshall Plan, European inferiority to the United States stemmed in part from the devastation of World War II. Then, the Soviet Union as well was inferior to the United States. A generation after the Second World War, however, the West Europeans have become inferior in many fields, especially in advanced technology, to *both* the United States and the Soviet Union, and the gap between the United States and the Soviet Union has narrowed. In certain cases, moreover, the disparities separating Western Europe from the superpowers have increased rather than diminished. The existing Atlantic imbalance can no longer be attributed to the devastation of war.

A generation ago, Europe faced the immediate task of postwar recovery. The success which Europe experienced in achieving reconstruction, together with the impressive economic growth of the past decade, has contributed to the development of European aspirations toward greater equality with the United States. In fact, the problems of importance to Atlantic countries in their relations with each other include trading policy, the future of the international monetary system, the balance of payments of major Atlantic countries, U.S. investment patterns in Western Europe, and the so-called Atlantic technological imbalance. As a result of increasing Atlantic economic interdependence, such issues have assumed even greater importance, in some cases, than the external threat which once gave cohesiveness to the Alliance. Unlike the perception of external threat, however, new intra-Atlantic problems have had a divisive, rather than a unifying, effect upon Atlantic peoples.

In two world wars, but especially in World War II, the importance of the U.S. contribution to the victory of the allied cause was indicative of the disparities between the United States and the countries of Western Europe in industrial growth, economic productivity, and population. But however decisive the U.S. military contribution in two wars, the leading European national units retained vast commitments and responsibilities in the non-Western World.

Earlier in this century, Europeans could take comfort from the belief that in many fields they remained in advance of the United States. In cultural attainments and basic science, Europeans could view with pride their superiority to the U.S. Whatever the remaining disparity between U.S. and European cultural attainments, Western Europe has over the past generation been the object of massive cultural influences from the United States, largely as a result of the great increase in communications. In turn, the United States continues to be the recipient of great cultural influence from

Western Europe. In the future, though, the development of advanced technologies for global communications systems by the United States and the Soviet Union, rather than by Western Europe, will give the superpowers the edge in the vital field of public information. Given the growth of the already great Atlantic imbalance in military affairs, technology, economic capabilities, and political influence, the United States will face in Western Europe a situation in some respects comparable to the U.S. relationship with Canada: a heightening sense of domination by American culture, American industry, American technology, and other things American. Less than ever before will it be possible for Europeans to take comfort from the fact that at least in some fields they are without rival.

It has been widely assumed that in European integration lies in part the key to the reduction of the Atlantic imbalance. Over the next decade the United States will face at best a Europe beset with the difficult problems of integration but at the same time subject to U.S. hegemony in many important fields. Hence, the 1970's are likely to be a period of considerable difficulty, as well as opportunity, for the United States in its transatlantic relationships.

In not all sectors, however, does the United States convey the image of superiority. Racial conflict in U.S. cities has reinforced European apprehension about the cohesiveness of the American social system. Many in Europe have seen the United States on the verge of a large-scale civil conflict which the U.S. government seems unable to avert. To an extent unparalleled since World War II, the United States has been forced to turn inward to the solution of complex domestic problems while continuing to bear massive international burdens. The growth of unrest in U.S. cities, together with the increasing importance of urban areas in the American political system, places new demands upon the federal government which compete with national security and foreign policy for attention. Despite the fabulous economic growth of the American economy, the United States seems unable to respond effectively to the barrage of demands placed upon it. In fact, unprecedented economic growth has contributed to rising expectations and frustrations among disadvantaged groups, whose members live for the most part in the politically important urban complexes. Thus there is a connection of increasing importance between domestic and foreign policy in the United States. Demands for increased spending—for domestic programs, national security, and foreign policy—create for the United States formidable economic problems upon whose solution depends not only the future of the U.S. economy itself, but the orderly evolution of the international monetary system to whose operation the United States is crucial.

Despite the military and technological imbalances which favor the United States, domestic, racial, and economic problems give rise to doubt about the effectiveness of American leadership. Fear and resentment of American hegemony in certain Atlantic relationships are matched by apprehension that other U.S. policies, in economics and urban questions, will have adverse effects upon the international system, and Western Europe itself. In fact, French policy is apparently motivated not only by a desire to reduce U.S. hegemony in Atlantic military and technological relationships, but by the belief that certain U.S. economic and foreign policies bode ill for Europe. By opposing the United States, France may not only reduce U.S. hegemony but force upon the United States needed changes in its policies. Failing this, it may even increase French influence at the expense of the United States. U.S. hegemony in technological and military affairs has not been sufficient to quiet West European misgivings about U.S. policy. Uncertainty about the consistency of U.S. policy both at home and abroad contributes to dissatisfaction with U.S. leadership in the Alliance. It has tempted France, in fact to exploit U.S. vulnerabilities.[8]

U.S. INTERESTS AND THE ATLANTIC ALLIANCE

Despite U.S. preoccupation with other problems—in Asia and at home—the preservation of a military link with Western Europe continues to hold great importance for the United States. From a strictly U.S. standpoint, the preservation of NATO even without basic changes would serve short-term interests. In fact, the United States has attempted to maintain NATO in essentially its existing form: (1) to assure the United States a major voice in any future European political settlement; (2) to provide a multilateral framework for the conduct of relations with the German Federal Republic; (3) to ensure that the German Federal Republic will not one day enter bilateral negotiations with the Soviet Union for German reunification on terms unsatisfactory to other West European countries or the United States; (4) to keep in Western Europe a

U.S. military presence in order to minimize the likelihood of Soviet miscalculation about the U.S. determination to counter the communist use of military force; and (5) to retain U.S. command and control of the vast bulk of the nuclear capabilities of the West.

However, the United States is not likely to have the option of preserving NATO in its existing form. By the early 1970's several factors will give new impetus to change in the Alliance. Even in the absence of major commitments in Asia, domestic opposition to the permanent stationing of U.S. troops in Western Europe can be expected to increase, especially if France continues to adopt policies in opposition to those of the United States. The assumption of new U.S. military commitments outside Western Europe will hasten the withdrawal of U.S. forces from the continent, of course. But even more, pressure by European members for changes in the Alliance (including continued European unwillingness to commit ground forces to the defense of Europe), is likely to fuel domestic U.S. opposition to the retention of large numbers of American troops on the continent. In the presence of a diminishing West European perception of Soviet threat, together with a rising fear of U.S. hegemony, interest in Western Europe in the basing of U.S. forces on the continent will be reduced. Thus the willingness of either Western Europe or the U.S. to bear the burden of large-scale U.S. troop commitments on the continent will decline. Within Europe, pressures for the reorganization of the Alliance will increase. Efforts by the United States to preserve the status quo in the Alliance will be viewed, even more than now, as a thinly disguised attempt to perpetuate U.S. hegemony in Atlantic military and political affairs. In this event, the Alliance will be less than ever a useful framework for the attainment of U.S. policy objectives in Europe.

The deepening of the Atlantic cleavage holds implications of great importance not only for the United States and Western Europe, but for the future of the international political system. The circumstances which led to the formation of NATO have not changed completely. Moreover, there are new problems, in the solution of which collaborative action among the peoples of the North Atlantic area is essential. Upon a recognition of the existence of a series of new problems, as well as the persistence of certain older ones, the Atlantic consensus of the 1970's will be built, if it is built at all.

NATO AND THE EAST-WEST MILITARY BALANCE

The growth of common interests between the Soviet Union and the West has been the theme of numerous analyses of East-West relations in recent years. The Test Ban Treaty, the "hot-line" tele-communications link between Washington and Moscow, the Draft Treaty on the Exploration and Use of Outer Space, the Consular Agreement, and the Non-Proliferation Treaty have been presented as tangible evidence of detente between the United States and the Soviet Union. Despite these accords, however, the Soviets and the West remain in profound disagreement on the fundamental issues which have divided them over the past generation: the re-unification of Germany, the future of Europe, the taking of major steps towards arms control and disarmament, and the resolution of major problems in regions outside the North Atlantic area, in particular, Southeast Asia and the Middle East.

Even though the Western perception of the Soviet threat has been altered, the Soviet Union possesses even more formidable military forces than at the founding of NATO, capable of inflicting severe damage upon Western Europe. Since the Cuban missile crisis of 1962, the Soviet Union has made a major effort to surpass the United States in the development and deployment of both offensive and defensive weapons systems. Much of the Soviet nuclear capability remains targeted against Western Europe. For the first time in its history the Soviet Union has deployed major naval forces in the Mediterranean. The effect of this action is to provide the Soviets with greater military mobility on NATO's southern flank. Moreover, the military forces of the Warsaw Pact, especially those of the so-called northern tier countries—Poland, Hungary, and Czechoslovakia—are equipped with advanced weapons, and have achieved levels of integration unmatched in NATO. In marked contrast to the discord over strategy within NATO, Warsaw Pact members have accepted Soviet strategic doctrine, which calls for the use of nuclear weapons at an early stage of a European conflict. By virtue of their nuclear and conventional capabilities, the Soviets possess a force posture in Europe which permits greater flexibility than that of NATO. As a result of communist military capabilities, Western Europe, deprived of the NATO guarantee, would become a hostage.

Given the preponderance of Soviet military power vis-à-vis

Western Europe, the removal of the formal U.S. security guarantee embodied in NATO would call U.S. intentions in Europe into question. Conceivably, the Soviets have never intended to conquer Europe militarily, but the threat remains sufficiently real that it must be a concern of central importance to U.S. and West European policymakers. The further erosion, or the dissolution, of NATO, in the absence of a mutually satisfactory alternative scheme for assuring European security, would have a destabilizing effect upon Europe.

The revival of West European self-confidence, together with the growth of European interest in greater independence from the United States and doubts about U.S. policy, has provided the Soviet Union with opportunities which the Soviets have sought to exploit. Soviet strategy toward Western Europe has taken the form of a major diplomatic effort to exacerbate divisions between the United States and its NATO allies.[9] An examination of diplomatic traffic in recent years reveals a widening and thickening web of visits by ranking Soviet officials to Western Europe and visits by West European leaders to Moscow. During the discussions occasioned by such visits, the Soviets have proffered increased trade, cultural exchanges, and technological collaboration. Sensing the importance attached in Europe to the Atlantic technological imbalance, the Soviets have offered collaboration in technology between the Soviet Union and Western Europe. Together, the Soviets have suggested, Europeans—East and West—might remove whatever gap separates them from the United States.[10] Such a ploy permits the Soviets to emphasize the importance which the Soviet Union allegedly attaches to increased collaboration among European countries and thus to the creation of a "wider Europe," a concept which, especially before the Soviet invasion of Czechoslovakia in August 1968, attracted widespread attention in Western Europe.

The idea of a "European" Europe, of which President de Gaulle has been the most eloquent spokesman, has given the Soviets yet another opportunity which Moscow has not been loath to exploit. In such a Europe, American influence would be greatly reduced, even to the extent perhaps of excluding the United States from a peace conference for a general European settlement. This theme is to be found in Soviet statements, for example, during President de Gaulle's visit of June 1966 to the Soviet Union, and in the declaration issued at the end of the conference of the Warsaw Pact members held in Bucharest in July 1966.

Finally, the Soviet Union has directed its propaganda against the German Federal Republic. From its founding the object of Soviet propaganda, the Bonn Government has been the recipient of intensified verbal attacks from the Soviet Union since the departure of France from the integrated structure of NATO. Undoubtedly, the Soviets realize that the withdrawal of France has enhanced the position of the Federal Republic as the principal U.S. ally in continental Western Europe, for Germany is even more vital to the Atlantic Alliance than it was so long as France remained a full member of NATO.

GERMANY BETWEEN EAST AND WEST

Since the formation of the Federal Republic in 1949, the principal goal of German policy has been the harmonization of Bonn's objectives with those of her Western allies. In NATO and the European integration movement, the Federal Republic found a principal outlet for German national energies. Membership in the Atlantic Alliance and the European Community gave the Federal Republic an alternative to the narrow nationalism which once gripped German minds.

A generation after the Second World War, Germany is entering a new phase. Despite great strides in the postwar period toward the development of representative government, it is by no means certain that Germany's alienation from modern Western political thought and practice has been ended. In the Adenauer era, Germany became an economic giant while remaining a political pygmy. Once content to subordinate herself to Western allies in atonement for the excesses of the Hitler regime, Germans now are prepared, more than at any time since the founding of the Federal Republic, to seek solutions, unilaterally if necessary, to pressing problems, and have begun to question the assumptions which have guided the policy of the Federal Republic. A generation after World War II, Germany is entering a period which may be crucial to both her future internal political development and her foreign policy orientation. Whatever the causal nexus, if any, the shift in German policy occurred at a time when U.S. interest in NATO and the European integration movement had waned. Policies based upon the Atlantic Alliance and European integration found greatest support in Germany when the United States itself placed great emphasis upon such policies. Changes in U.S. foreign policy preceded changes in German domestic affairs and foreign relations. Both the Atlantic Alliance and European integration appealed to the Federal Republic because they offered the only real prospects for assuring German defense; for enabling Germany to regain a position of international respectability; for providing, in the form of markets, outlets for German economic dynamism; and, last but not least, for holding out the hope of eventual German reunification through Western strength.[11] At the very least, Germany's West European and Atlantic relationships provided the Federal Republic with some measure of non-territorial compensation for losses to the East.

Twice in the twentieth century, in the Rapallo Pact agreement and the Molotov-Ribbentrop Pact of 1939, Germany has concluded far-reaching agreements with the Soviet Union. To be sure, in its foreign policy, in the degree that its political system, despite the rise of the National Democratic Party, is accepted by the German people, and in its economic achievements, the Federal Republic differs fundamentally from the Weimar Republic. But the issue of reunification, once subordinated to other foreign policies, would gain greatly in importance if German ties with the West were weakened. At the same time, the prospects for eventual reunification on terms satisfactory to Germany's Western allies would be adversely affected.

The Soviet Union holds the key to German reunification. The Soviets would exact important concessions from the Federal Republic in return for the settlement of the German question. In all likelihood, the reunification of Germany on terms set by Bonn and Moscow would not satisfy the security interests of other Western countries, including the United States. Moreover, a settlement of the German question which detached Germany from military relationships with other Western countries would reduce German interest in the European Community and the development of a West European political unit capable of playing a greater role in world affairs.

Since the founding of NATO, German potential for making an effective contribution to European defense has increased substantially. Therefore, even in the absence of NATO, the United States would seek to maintain bilateral military links with Germany. Without the Atlantic Alliance, the defense of the Federal Republic would depend upon the supply of U.S. military aid by air or North Sea ports, thus presenting awkward logistical problems. But a German-American alliance would present other problems as well. It would deepen cleavages between the Germans and their West European neighbors, especially France. In all likelihood, it would lessen the prospects for European integration, and thus for the development of units more adequate than the nation-state for the solution of many of the problems facing Europe.[12]

THE WEST AND THE LESS DEVELOPED AREAS

Historically, periods of political instability have attended the collapse of empires. There is little evidence to suggest that the world in the post Western-colonial era will be exempt from revolutionary violence. Well before the year 2000, the potential for instability in many regions outside the North Atlantic area may increase dramatically. Especially in Latin America, India, and China, population growth which outstrips increases in industrial and agricultural productivity may contribute to instability. Moreover, political disputes based upon conflicting ideologies and foreign policy objectives can be expected to contribute to political instability in less developed areas. The peoples of the West possess about 60 percent of the world's wealth. The Soviets and other East European communist countries, with a total population of 350 million, own 20 percent. The two billion Africans, Asians, and Latin Americans who, by the end of this century, will have increased to at least 3.3 billion, control the remaining 20 percent. Of the West's 60 percent, 200 million Americans possess 30 percent, i.e., 6 percent of the world's population holds nearly one-third of the total. The 450 million West Europeans and their kin outside Europe own another one-third.

It is by no means inevitable that the industrialized West and the less developed areas will find themselves locked one day in North-South conflict, or even that the peoples of less developed areas will be pitted against each other. In fact, the peoples of the Southern Hemisphere may face problems so formidable as to preclude the development of capabilities sufficient to enable the rural regions of the world to mount a successful attack against the industrialized, urban West. To be sure, technologies developed in the West may be diffused to peoples elsewhere in the world, but the ability of the West to exploit the potential inherent in science and technology may serve only to widen the gap between the West and the less developed areas. Moreover, the dependence of the West upon outside resources of raw materials may decline as a result of technological advances. In the period since World War II, trade among industrialized countries has increased at a more rapid rate than trade between the developed and less developed areas. Such trends, which reduce the dependence of the West upon less developed areas, have already had adverse repercussions upon countries in the Southern Hemisphere. The inability to achieve rising levels of productivity, industrialization, and income could breed intense frustration and further alienation from the West. The potential for the development and manipulation of revolutionary forces in such an environment would be considerable. At the very least, the West would find less than satisfactory an international system divided largely on the basis of race and income. Hence the peoples of the North Atlantic area have a long-term interest in guiding the process of modernization in less developed areas. It is questionable whether they have the means, or the will, to utilize their resources most effectively in the modernization of regions in the Southern Hemisphere—unless new organizational forms and patterns of political behavior are evolved in the West itself.

Over the next generation, the tasks confronting the United States in the less developed countries can be expected to grow, rather than diminish, both in bulk and complexity. Nevertheless, given existing tendencies in European policy, the former colonial powers of Europe will become less willing to divert resources from Western Europe to assist new states in the attainment of economic modernization, political development, and a modicum of regional stability. Within Western Europe and the United States, pressures have mounted for reductions in foreign aid programs in favor of efforts to achieve higher levels of domestic growth. A greater European reluctance to share responsibilities outside the North Atlantic area could accelerate such trends in the United States.

The problems which beset U.S.-European relations are not only greater, they are far more complex than those which faced the United States and Western Europe at the founding of NATO. The existence of an Atlantic imbalance in several important fields, the future of East-West European relations, the role of Atlantic countries in other regions of the world, disagreement about the strategic concepts appropriate for the defense of the West, and the future of Atlantic economic relationships pose problems of major importance both to Western Europe and the United States. How such problems will be solved, if they are solved at all, is uncertain. But the ability of Atlantic countries to find common solutions, where necessary, depends upon Atlantic collaboration. It depends as well upon the ability of Western Europe, by its own efforts, but with the assistance of the United States, to take effective steps to minimize the adverse impact of the various Atlantic imbalances on U.S.-European relations, and even to contribute to the resolution of major problems which give rise to them. Most of all, the responsibility for the shaping of a new Atlantic consensus rests with the United States, for given the existing and emergent Atlantic imbalances, the U.S. weight in Atlantic relationships is enormous.

NOTES

1. For a theoretically oriented discussion about alliances and coalitions, see George F. Liska, *Nations in Alliance: The Limits of Interdependence*. Baltimore: Johns Hopkins Press, 1962; William H. Riker, *The Theory of Political Coalitions*. New Haven: Yale University Press, 1962.

2. See, for example, Pierre Gallois, *The Balance of Terror*. Boston: Houghton Mifflin, 1961, Chapter I.

3. For example, as early as November 10, 1959, President de Gaulle suggested during the course of his Press Conference of that date: "Who can say whether, in the future, if basic political facts should change completely, as has already occurred on the earth, the two powers that would have a monopoly on nuclear weapons might not make a deal to divide the world between them? Who can say whether, should the occasion arise—while each side might follow a policy of not hurling its devices at the principal adversary, so as not to be threatened by it—who can say whether the two rivals might not crush others?" General Charles de Gaulle, *Major Addresses, Statements, Press Conferences, May 19, 1958—January 31, 1964,* New York French Embassy, Press and Information Division, 1964, p. 61.

4. But it may also be argued that West European membership in NATO provides a restraint on U.S. policy outside the North Atlantic area. Western Europe is a Soviet hostage against the possibility of U.S. action intolerable to the Soviet Union in areas of the world less accessible to the Soviet Union.

5. In December 1966, in response to a request from Belgian Foreign Minister Pierre Harmel, the NATO Council formed a Committee to study the future of NATO. The Harmel Committee's report

was approved by all members of the NATO Council, including France, on December 14, 1967. Referring to extra-European problems, the report contained the following passage: "The North Atlantic Treaty area cannot be treated in isolation from the rest of the world. Crises and conflicts arising outside the area may impair its security either directly or by affecting the global balance. Allied countries contribute individually within the United Nations and other international organizations to the maintenance of international peace and security and to the solution of important international problems. In accordance with established usage, the Allies, or such of them as wish to do so, will also continue to consult on such problems without commitment and as the case may demand." Thus the report reflected the general willingness of European powers to make specific defense commitments in non-European areas. Text of Harmel Report. Reprinted in *Atlantic Community Quarterly,* Vol. 6, No. 1 (Spring 1968), p. 117.

6. For a detailed examination of basic trends in Western Europe since World War II, see Stephen Graubard (ed.), *A New Europe?* Boston: Houghton Mifflin, 1964.

7. See Jean-Jacques Servan-Schreiber, *The American Challenge.* New York: Atheneum, 1968.

8. See Harold Kaplan, "De Gaulle and America: The New Cold War." The *New Leader,* January 1, 1968.

9. Marshall D. Shulman, "'Europe' versus 'Detente'?" *Foreign Affairs,* Vol. 45, No. 3 (April 1967), pp. 399-401.

10. In his speech of April 24, 1967 to a meeting of European communist parties at Karlovy Vary, Czechoslovakia, Brezhnev declared: "During the period of NATO's existence, the European states belonging to this bloc have spent over 300 billion dollars on military preparations. These expenses strike painfully at the interests of the working people, slow down economic development, and retard the progress of science and culture. Taking advantage of the situation, the United States has taken many talented scientists out of Europe. In many countries this phenomenon has been aptly termed "the brain drain." . . . The developing scientific and technological revolution, the increasing efforts to consolidate national independence and liberation from the dollar diktat, suggest to the European states many ways and projects in a great variety of fields—from the construction of a gas pipeline crossing the continent to the introduction of a unified color television system for all Europe."

—"The Soviet Union of NATO." Speech by Leonid I. Brezhnev, April 24, 1967. Prepared for the use of the Subcommittee on National Security and International Operations, Committee on Government Operations, United States Senate. Washington: U.S. Government Printing Office, 1967, pp. 7, 11.

11. See Konrad Adenauer, *Memoirs 1945-53.* London: Weidenfeld and Nicolson Ltd., 1966, p. 298.

12. See Robert Strausz-Hupé, "The World Without NATO." ORBIS, Vol. X, No. 1, Spring 1966, pp. 86-87.

II. The Strategic "Dissensus"

WHEN NATO WAS CREATED, FEW FORESAW THAT THE ADVENT OF nuclear weapons would challenge the *raison d'etre* of alliances. NATO was formed before the detonation of a nuclear device by the Soviet Union or the perfection of intercontinental ballistic missiles by both superpowers. Today the United States is the predominant member of an alliance in which two other members possess national nuclear forces. Nuclear weapons have revolutionized the strategy of every nation possessing them. To an even greater extent, they have made more complex the task of collaboration among allies and, in the case of NATO, have contributed to disintegrative forces in the alliance.

The strategic discord which besets NATO, together with diminished Western perception of external threat, does not augur well for the restoration of a military consensus. The exit from the NATO command structure of France, the chief opponent of prevailing Alliance strategic doctrine, provided a temporary solution, although a negative one, to the vexing problem of strategic discord.[1] With the departure of France, the remaining NATO members in 1967 affirmed their adherence to a strategy of flexible response, similar to that advocated by the United States. But the official NATO strategy is clearly inadequate. NATO is not likely to retain the confidence of remaining members or to contribute to the resolution of disagreement with France unless a new consensus on strategy can be created. In the absence of such a consensus, NATO members will view the Alliance as decreasingly relevant to their security needs and hence unworthy of their continued support.

Just as the strategic controversy which has rent the Alliance over the past decade arose from the technological break-throughs in weaponry of the 1950's, future innovations in technology—in the Soviet Union and the United States—can be expected to produce important modifications in prevailing strategic doctrine. By 1975 advances in technology will have altered the range of weapons available to West European countries. The cost of producing nuclear weapons will decline as the technology of nuclear weapons and delivery systems becomes more widely diffused.

At the same time, however, the cost of developing and producing a new generation of weapons systems will rise. As the weapons systems which in the 1960's were the preserve of the United States and the Soviet Union become available to other countries, the two superpowers will have developed a new generation of weapons systems.[2] According to the experience of the past generation, the cost of military R & D will become even more prohibitive to European national units in the 1970's than it was in the 1960's. Thus the imbalance which favors the United States and the Soviet Union in the development and deployment of the most advanced military technologies is likely to increase.

CONFLICTING STRATEGIC DOCTRINES

Until 1957, when the Soviet Union launched its first sputnik and thus provided vivid evidence of its capacity to inflict nuclear destruction upon the United States, the U.S. military guarantee appeared to provide adequate protection to Western Europe. The advent of the intercontinental ballistic missile drastically altered the East-West strategic confrontation. European confidence in the willingness of the United States to employ nuclear weapons to defend Western Europe waned once the United States itself became vulnerable to attack by intercontinental missiles. In Europe the question was raised whether the United States would risk its own destruction in order to defend Western Europe. The very utility of alliance systems was cast into doubt, since alliance membership might commit a nation, to an extent unprecedented, to the defense of interests which could not be safeguarded without the risk of national destruction.

European apprehensions were sharpened as a result of the strategic doctrine adopted by the Kennedy Administration. In particular, the emphasis placed on conventional rather than nuclear weapons, the introduction of the "pause" concept, and the attention devoted to a highly centralized system of command and control over nuclear weapons,[3] contributed to European apprehensions about the willingness of the United States to employ nuclear weapons, if necessary, in the defense of Western Europe. In fact, the centralization of command and control in the hands of the U.S. President, by reducing decision-making authority available to local commanders, underscored the dependence of NATO allies upon major decisions taken in Washington.

The Administration opposed the proliferation of national nuclear capabilities in Western Europe.[4] The United States did not give active support to the building of the French nuclear force, for fear that such a force would impede the centralization of command, control, and communication of nuclear capabilities within NATO, and contribute to the proliferation of atomic weapons.[5] Within the U.S. defense establishment itself, the Administration sought to reduce the dangers of an accidental or undesired war by developing and introducing more sophisticated technical means for detailed civilian command and control over military forces.

The strategic doctrine adopted by the Kennedy Administration provided for greater flexibility in response than had the strategy of "massive retaliation" of the Eisenhower Administration. Initially at least, the United States might respond to a major Soviet attack against Western Europe with conventional rather than nuclear weapons. It was the objective of the U.S. government to have available in Western Europe conventional forces adequate to provide the United States with options other than a nuclear response or no response to a major enemy strike westward. In the event of a Soviet attack, for example, against the German Federal Republic, both sides would be given the opportunity to re-evaluate their actions before nuclear arms were committed to battle. Conceivably, a Soviet attack might be halted, initially at least, with NATO conventional rather than nuclear forces. In short, by providing a series of non-nuclear options, the United States attempted to raise the threshold of nuclear war.

The U.S. strategic doctrine of flexible response as it applied to Europe contrasted sharply with Soviet strategy. According to Soviet strategic doctrine, nuclear weapons would be used both in a strategic and tactical mode at an early stage of a conflict.[6] Unlike NATO, there is no apparent strategic divergence within the Warsaw Pact, whose members are in basic agreement that nuclear weapons would be used at an early stage in a future war in Europe. In keeping with this feature of Warsaw Pact military doctrine, East European military units are equipped with tactical nuclear weapons, with the warheads remaining under Soviet control.[7] Moreover, the Soviet Union has made available sophisticated radar systems, high-speed fighter interceptors, and surface-to-air missiles. In order to improve their combat effectiveness, Warsaw Pact countries in recent years have conducted a series of joint maneuvers. The so-called northern tier members of the Warsaw Pact, Poland, Czechoslovakia, and East Germany, whose military forces are probably the most effective of all Warsaw Pact countries, except for the Soviet Union itself, have received frontline attack aircraft and short-range tactical rockets which could be armed with nuclear warheads, high explosives, or chemical charges.[8]

It is difficult to assess the potential effectiveness of Warsaw Pact forces. Their effectiveness would depend as much upon the morale of officers and troops as upon the quality of weapons available to them. Although the measurement of morale in advance of combat is difficult, several factors provide an indication of this variable as it affects East European armies. The East German, Polish, and Czechoslovak officer corps are members of their respective communist parties. Troops are said to receive constant indoctrination, especially against the "revanchist" German Federal Republic. Because of the high levels of integration within the Warsaw Pact, the Soviets would probably be able, as they were during World War II, to incorporate allied units into Soviet army groups in order to assure their loyalty.

The Warsaw Pact deploys formidable forces in Europe. The Soviet Union is said to have stationed some twenty divisions in East Germany, two divisions in Poland, four in Hungary,[9] and, after August 1968, fourteen in Czechoslovakia. Poland, East Germany, and Czechoslovakia together have about 35 divisions. Although their effectiveness is less certain than that of the Northern tier countries, the other members of the Warsaw Pact possess a total of 28 divisions, which could be quickly reinforced by Soviet forces deployed in western Russia.

At the time of the invasion of Czechoslovakia in August 1968, the Soviet Union gave evidence of its ability to deploy major military forces rapidly. Although the invading force consisted of regular army units, the Soviet Union was able quickly to move reserves and home guard units into support positions. With the arrival in Czechoslovakia of communist bloc forces, primarily from the Soviet Union, the Warsaw Pact troop strength was increased from about 960,000 troops to 1.3 million. In fact, the efficiency with which the Soviet Union was able to move several hundred thousand troops to battle positions for the occupation of

Czechoslovakia reinforced fears about the stability of the prevailing military balance in Europe. After the invasion, the Soviet Union stationed major military forces on the Czech-West German frontier, heightening apprehension within the Federal Republic about both the adequacy of NATO capabilities and the intentions of the Soviet Union.

The Warsaw Pact armies, together with the formidable Soviet strategic capabilities targeted against Western Europe, provide a military force in the communist half of Europe of which West European countries, collectively or individually, have no equivalent. By comparison with the Warsaw Pact, twenty-five divisions have been assigned to the NATO Central European Command. Of these forces, the six U.S. divisions are best prepared for combat. The German Federal Republic, with its twelve-division army, has made the largest single national commitment of manpower to NATO. Yet there is uncertainty about the potential effectiveness of German forces because of a shortage of non-commissioned officers and officers of field and staff rank. Moreover, the Federal Republic has experienced repeated failures with its Star-Fighter, in part because of a shortage of trained technicians for the maintenance of such sophisticated fighter-bomber aircraft. The military forces of other European members of NATO are deficient in the most advanced equipment. In contrast to the Warsaw Pact, NATO achieved little standardization of military equipment, and has not pooled the logistical support facilities of its members. In the event of conflict, the problems of interchange of units and equipment, as well as the lack of modern weapons systems in certain armies, would reduce the effectiveness of NATO forces.

According to U.S. spokesmen, the French decision to withdraw from NATO commands, announced formally in an *aide memoire* on March 11, 1966, contributed to the "rejuvenation" of the Alliance.[10] Nevertheless, the French withdrawal cast doubt upon the effectiveness of NATO structure and strategy. As a result of the French action, the defense of Western Europe without the early resort to nuclear weapons would be difficult, and perhaps even impossible. The Low Countries and the Federal Republic provide but a narrow, densely populated belt of territory which must be supplied from ports on the North Sea or the Channel. As a result of the French withdrawal, NATO has been divided geographically between its northern and southern sectors. Supply lines run dangerously close to the front lines and would be subject to attack in the event of war. The most modern forces, those of the United States, are based in southern Germany, in the region which once was under U.S. military occupation. The North, with its flat terrain, is a suitable invasion route, being held by understrength British forces. In a communist thrust westward, the United States would risk the isolation and encirclement of its forces at an early stage in the conflict. So far as the defense of Western Europe is concerned, NATO as it exists is scarcely more satisfactory militarily than a bilateral German-American alliance. The effect of the French withdrawal has been to increase the gap between NATO resources and strategy and thus to cast doubt upon either the credibility or utility of prevailing strategic doctrine.

EUROPEAN CRITIQUES OF U.S. STRATEGY

By and large, European strategic doctrines have not placed great emphasis on the use of conventional forces against a Soviet attack in Europe. Instead, European strategic doctrines have either (a) stressed the need, as in the case of France, for a national nuclear force capable of deterring a Soviet attack or (b) placed heavy reliance upon the U.S. strategic capability, as in the case of smaller West European countries and the German Federal Republic.

U.S. strategic doctrine has proven unacceptable to France and, to a lesser extent, Germany, for several reasons: Not unnaturally, there is an overriding concern in Western Europe that, in a future conflict, the Continent would become, for the third time in the twentieth century, a major battlefield. While U.S. officials could view such a conflict as a "limited war," to Europeans it would approximate an "all-out" conflict.[11] The United States might be willing to sacrifice West European territory for the sake of avoiding a nuclear exchange with the Soviet Union. Both the Soviet Union and the United States might even be prepared to confine the use of nuclear weapons to targets in Western Europe and East-Central Europe, respectively, thus making their own territories sanctuaries from nuclear attack.[12] Given the widespread destruction to which Western Europe would be subjected in future warfare, military strategy must be designed, according to official French thought, more to prevent war from ever breaking out than to fight a conflict which has already begun.[13]

According to the official French critique, the military doctrine which the United States has urged on NATO embodies many features of military strategy of previous wars. The massing of conventional armies, as in the two world wars and the Korean conflict, is not appropriate to the needs of the future. Massed armies present targets for nuclear attack. Hence changes in warfare brought about by the introduction of advanced military technologies make deterrence of war the principal objective not only of France, but of all other governments in Western Europe. The presence of large-scale armies, together with an American strategic doctrine which stresses a conventional response to even a sizable communist ground attack, may not deter, but may even tempt the Soviet Union to strike Western Europe in the expectation of winning a non-nuclear victory. According to French as well as German official strategic thought, such a contingency can be avoided only if the certainty exists that nuclear weapons will be used without delay in response to a Soviet thrust westward. French strategy, it has been pointed out in Paris, does not differ greatly from the U.S. strategy for the defense of the United States. In official U.S. circles, there is no disagreement that a Soviet thrust against the United States would be met with a nuclear response. In contrast to U.S. strategy for Western Europe, the Soviets must calculate that beyond a doubt a Soviet strike against the United States will be met with nuclear retaliation. If the United States held that the defense of Paris was as vital as the defense of New York, the United States would not be prepared to use nuclear weapons in defense of its own territory while adopting a strategic doctrine which emphasizes conventional forces for the defense of Western Europe.

Official French strategic doctrine posits that the possibilty of a Soviet attack may be reduced by the development, under French national control, of a highly mobile nuclear force.[14] Undoubtedly, De Gaulle's thinking on the role of the French nuclear force was influenced by the views on strategy which he held in the 1930's, for the rationale for the *force de dissuasion* is similar in many respects to De Gaulle's thinking on strategy more than a generation ago. At that time De Gaulle saw in the highly mobile army, the *armée de métier,* equipped with the most modern weapons, the means by which France might assure her national survival. Nazi Germany, not France, built a military machine which embodied many of the features set forth in De Gaulle's writings, while France, with its large land armies, clung to outmoded strategic concepts.[15] Had France possessed a mobile military force with advanced weapons, she might have averted the disastrous defeat of 1940. Moreover, France's allies were unable, or unwilling, to commit the military resources which would have been needed in order to defeat Nazi Germany. Can France be certain, it is asked in French strategic thought, that France's allies would not once again be unable, or unwilling, to come to her aid and rescue?

In the late 1960's French strategy began to stress the deterrence of attack from all directions. The late General Ailleret was the author of the so-called "all-azimuth" strategy, designed to enable France either "to escape certain major wars or, if we did not escape them, to take part in them under the best conditions."[16] Implicit in this strategy was the assumption that alliance membership could not provide a full security guarantee "since it is practically impossible to foretell what might one day cause a serious conflict or how the powers would be divided between the opposing camps or what hold any particular power might have over the territory of any other power, with or without the latter's consent."

As outlined by Ailleret, the all-azimuth strategy called for the development of nuclear forces with global range, which could eventually be converted into a space force. Naval forces and tactical forces would be equipped with nuclear weapons. In the event of an invasion, France would have the capability for resistance "on our soil, at least in regions that lend themselves to such resistance."

It is by no means certain that the French *force de dissuasion* would suffice to deter the Soviets or their Warsaw Pact allies from an attack against Western Europe even if interests clearly vital to France were at stake, nor is it likely that France alone has the ability to provide an all azimuth defense for her national territory. However, at the very least, the existence of an independent French national deterrent increases the uncertainties facing Soviet strategic planners. Moreover, the French national nuclear program helps to sustain a French quest for advanced technologies in aerospace, electronics, nuclear energy, and other defense-related sectors where an Atlantic technological imbalance exists. As a result of the French atomic effort, France is developing scientific and technological resources which place her, in certain fields, in the forefront of West European nations. Given her scientific-technological position, as well as her nuclear capability, France would play a leading role in a European technological-political-defense community. Thus the French nuclear program is at least as important for the technological and political opportunities which it affords as for its purely military implications.

Much of the French criticism of NATO has been focused upon the integrated command structure which the Alliance developed in the decade after its founding. According to official French strategic thought, the war of the future would be fought with nuclear weapons. So long as such capabilities remain in the hands of national governments, the leaders of nation-states must make the decisions about their use. During the course of his press conference of September 9, 1965, President de Gaulle declared:

> . . . It is true that, in many areas we have the best reasons for associating with others. But on condition of retaining our self-determination. Thus, so long as the solidarity of the Western peoples appears to us necessary for the eventual defense of Europe, our country will remain the ally of her allies but, upon the expiration of the commitments formerly taken—that is, in 1969, by the latest—the subordination known as "integration" which is provided for by NATO and which hands our fate over to foreign authority shall cease, as far as we are concerned. Thus, while working to unite the states on both sides of the Rhine and the Alps, from the economic, political, cultural and strategic viewpoints, we are making sure that this organization does not deprive us of our free will. . . .[17]

The North Atlantic Treaty, as negotiated in 1949, provided in Article 9 for a permanent Council, on which each member was to be represented "to consider matters concerning the implementation of this treaty." In Article 9, the Council was empowered to "set up such subsidiary bodies as may be necessary for the security of the geographical region covered by the treaty."

In the years immediately after its founding the Alliance acquired an integrated command system and supply infrastructure. The North Atlantic Treaty contains no specific provision for SHAPE or for the integrated commands. Hence the French drew a distinction between the Treaty as an expression of the basic identity of interest which binds nations of the North Atlantic area and the organizational structure which allegedly enhances U.S. hegemony over Western Europe. Under the Fifth Republic, France, however much she continued to see her destiny linked to that of other

Atlantic nations, questioned the necessity for, and rejected, institutions developed within NATO since 1949.

According to French spokesmen, military integration as practiced in NATO subjected France to U.S. hegemony. The NATO integration to which France took exception has been nowhere more pronounced than in the nuclear field. To the extent that it has been international, NATO nuclear planning has been primarily in the hands of the United States and Britain.[18] Therefore, France opposed an integrated military structure which, in the capabilities of primary importance—nuclear weapons—did not accord France a satisfactory voice.

The nuclear arsenals of both Britain and France have contained almost exclusively offensive weapons designed to inflict damage upon the Soviet Union. Such emphasis is logically consistent with a strategic doctrine which seeks to deter an opponent from taking military action against the vital interests of the West European nuclear powers. By contrast, West European strategists have not been preoccupied with active or passive defensive strategic systems. The effect of the Soviet deployment of such systems on the West European ability to inflict damage upon the Soviet Union is problematical. Thus far, there has been little concern in Western Europe that the Soviet deployment of an ABM system and other defensive strategic capabilities will seriously downgrade the British and French offensive capabilities. So long as the view prevails that West European nuclear forces can penetrate Soviet defenses, West European interest in an ABM system is likely to remain minimal. Should the Soviets achieve a demonstrable defensive capability to neutralize West European nuclear forces, interest in the development and deployment of defensive strategic systems in Western Europe would probably increase. Similarly, the deployment of an ABM system by the United States, together with the development of a generation of demonstrably effective ABM systems, is likely to lead to greater West European interest in defensive strategic capabilities.

Undoubtedly, the French decision to withdraw from the integrated NATO structure was prompted in part by the strategic discord in the Alliance. Paradoxically, this decision, to the extent that it increases the problems of conducting a conventional conflict in Europe, presses the remaining NATO countries toward a strategic doctrine more akin to that favored by Paris. Moreover, the commitments of the United States outside Western Europe, together with U.S. domestic pressure to reduce force levels in Europe because of balance of payments problems, increase the likelihood that the United States will be pushed, by a combination of circumstances, toward a strategic doctrine which places greater emphasis than prevailing U.S. strategic concepts upon nuclear weapons. The more the United States withdraws troops from Western Europe, the less likely it becomes that nuclear weapons, at least at the tactical level, can be withheld for long in a major European conflict. In making force reductions in Western Europe, the United States has responded more to economic pressures and military requirements elsewhere in the world than to a carefully conceived strategy responsive to West European defense needs and long-range U.S. interests in Western Europe. Clearly, it would serve the interests of both the United States and Western Europe to evolve a strategic doctrine which both reflects the present military-political environment and preserves military stability in Europe.

Although the withdrawal of France deprived NATO of logistical facilities and terrain for maneuverability and increased the problems associated with the employment of a flexible response strategy, without France the other Alliance members regained formally at least a level of strategic consensus not possible so long as the French remained. In December 1967, the NATO defense ministers adopted a strategic doctrine based on a three-step flexible response. Non-nuclear forces are to be available in order to permit NATO to respond, initially at least, to a variety of potential challenges. In the second and third stages, respectively, tactical and strategic nuclear weapons would be employed.[19]

In an address to the North Atlantic Assembly on November 20, 1967, General Lemnitzer, Supreme Allied Commander in Europe, declared that France's withdrawal from the NATO integrated command "increased the possibility" that nuclear weapons would be used at an earlier stage of a conflict than previously anticipated. General Lemnitzer expressed concern that member governments of the Alliance planned military reductions that would "directly and adversely affect the readiness and level of forces available."[20] The thinning of conventional forces reduces the chance that NATO could defend Western Europe without early resort to nuclear weapons. Reliance on the flexible response strategy, especially if that strategy is not backed by adequate conventional capabilities, would make necessary the sacrifice of German territory at an early stage in a European conflict. Thus the remaining NATO members have not bridged the gap between strategic doctrine and political-military trends in member countries.

AREAS OF STRATEGIC ACCORD

Whatever Western strategic differences there may be, there is is an area of agreement about the strategic doctrine appropriate to the North Atlantic area. Few deny the need to retain tactical nuclear weapons and to assure close control over their use. There is general accord that in future conflict conventional forces would have at least some role. Few dispute the need to ensure the credibility of the Western deterrent while maintaining some conventional forces. Even those who hold to the need for independent European national nuclear forces acknowledge the importance of Western strategic coordination. For the most part, agreement exists that the U.S. monopoly over nuclear weapons should be replaced by arrangements in which Europeans would gain a greater voice in the Alliance.[21] Yet this is easier said than done. The central question is who would be authorized to take a decision to employ nuclear weapons in a conflict situation. As the leading nuclear power, the United States does not wish to remove its finger from the nuclear trigger. Nor does a supranational authority exist either in Western Europe or the North Atlantic area to replace it.

It is conceivable, although unlikely, that the United States would initiate the use of nuclear weapons to meet a threat against NATO without the consent of the country in which the weapons are located and would be employed. It is less likely that the United States would authorize the launching of nuclear weapons to meet an ambiguous probe against NATO members without prior consultation with major allies. It is conceivable, although again unlikely, that NATO members possessing their own national nuclear forces would initiate the use of nuclear weapons in most crisis situations if the United States was not also prepared to use them. If such weapons were employed, however, the United States, because of the large-scale presence of U.S. forces in Western Europe, would almost certainly be drawn into the conflict. Conversely, it would be difficult, if not impossible, for the United States to embark upon a general war without involving its NATO allies, and vice versa. By extricating herself from NATO, however, France sought to avoid being drawn into a general conflict in which her perceived interests were not in harmony with those of the United States. In particular, French policy is designed to prevent French involvement in a general conflict resulting from the escalation of a war outside Europe, such as Vietnam.

In the control of nuclear weapons, NATO clearly faces a dilemma: The United States does not wish to yield or share fully the control of its nuclear weapons; at the same time, there is doubt in Western Europe that the United States will come to Europe's defense. Both U.S. and West European policymakers recognize that neither would be likely to go to war without consulting the other; however, there is a range of possible threats which might not necessarily produce an agreed response. The complexity and duration of consultations required to reach decisions among Atlantic countries on possible military action would probably increase according to the ambiguity of the enemy thrust. It is not possible to construct a hypothetical model, or series of models, to include agreed NATO responses for all possible contingencies. Yet the Alliance is in need of machinery for more effective political and military planning and consultation on problems which, in one contingency or another, might confront the West. Two examples of such problems will suffice.

A Soviet invasion of Finland, or northern Scandinavia, could pose an immediate threat to two NATO members, Norway and Denmark. Yet it is conceivable that an attack upon Finland would meet with no effective NATO action, even though the United States might act unilaterally or in combination with some other NATO power. It is possible to envisage an ambiguous communist attempt to seize West Berlin which included, for example, increased interference with the land and air corridors. Such a probe might be resisted only by U.S. and *Bundeswehr* forces, perhaps backed by France. In contrast, in the event of strong Soviet forces deployed against West Berlin, all of the Western occupying powers could be expected to respond.

The outbreak of a "war of national liberation" in Greece or Turkey, supported by communist "volunteers," might not produce an effective NATO response. "Wars of national liberation" are not likely to break out in most NATO countries, although the potential exists for this type of conflict on the southeastern flank of the Alliance. Hence NATO, or its successor organization, is in need of machinery for consultation and planning to assure collaborative action in response to a broad range of threats to the security of one or more Alliance members.

STRUCTURE AND STRATEGY

The resolution of U.S.-European differences on strategic doctrine and the restructuring of NATO are closely related. Like U.S. strategic doctrine, the organizational changes which the United States proposed for the Atlantic Alliance proved unacceptable in Western Europe. The U.S. proposal for an Atlantic partnership stemmed from U.S. recognition of the need to broaden the process of decision-making within NATO even though the United States continued to possess the preponderance of the nuclear power of the West. The prospects for an Atlantic partnership would have been enhanced if the United States and West European countries had been able to speed the movement toward European integration, including the formation of a European political executive. The entry of Britain into the Common Market would have enhanced the prospects for building a European nuclear force based initially upon the coordination, and eventually the pooling, of British-French atomic capabilities. If Britain had shown a preference for defense agreement with France, especially in the nuclear field, instead of signing the Nassau Agreement with the United States, the British might have proven themselves sufficiently Europe-oriented to gain De Gaulle's consent to Britain's entry into the Common Market.

With the failure of the Brussels negotiations of 1961-63 for British Common Market membership, the United States sought alternative schemes to achieve greater European participation in NATO. The Multilateral Force represented an effort by the United States to accord Europeans a greater voice in NATO while retaining for the United States a decisive role in the Alliance. The MLF, it was hoped in Washington, would enable the United States to reconcile European nuclear aspirations with the U.S. interest in retaining the centralized command and control of NATO nuclear forces and a growing U.S. interest in preventing the proliferation of nuclear capabilities. Whereas national nuclear forces would split an already weakened NATO into several parts, the MLF, its proponents in Washington claimed, would contribute to the restoration of cohesion in the alliance.

Far from helping to resolve problems confronting the Atlantic Alliance, the MLF contributed to a deepening of the cleavage in NATO. Discussions for the MLF were conducted between the United States and individual NATO allies and within the MLF working group which, technically, was not a part of the NATO structure.[22] The manner in which discussions were conducted helped to dampen European interest in the MLF. In pressing for the MLF, the United States undoubtedly reinforced French suspicions about the U.S. unwillingness to grant Europeans a greatly enhanced role in NATO nuclear matters, for the MLF, whatever the ultimate objective of the United States in advancing it, appeared as little more than a gimmick designed to divert Europeans from allocating their resources to the development of nuclear capabilities over which they would have full control. Although U.S.-policymakers viewed the MLF as an alternative to national European nuclear forces, they undoubtedly foresaw that such a force would provide technical knowledge and experience, as well as a framework within which Western Europe, if it so desired, could eventually achieve a European nuclear deterrent.[23]

The United States failed to make proposals for the control of nuclear weapons acceptable to its major European allies. The MLF solution, in particular, did not attract widespread support in Western Europe.[24] In Britain, for example, opinion on the MLF was divided, but political leaders, in both the Conservative and Labour Parties, were opposed to this solution to NATO's nuclear problem. Nor did the British government look with favor upon the building of a NATO nuclear force in which decisions would be taken by majority vote.[25]

Given its opposition to the MLF, Britain, shortly after the return of the Labour Government to office in October 1964, proposed the creation of an Atlantic Nuclear Force (ANF) designed to divert attention from the MLF. The British proposal differed from the MLF as envisaged by the Johnson Administration. Britain was prepared to assign her nuclear force to NATO, including most of her fleet of supersonic Vulcan bombers, as well as four nuclear submarines then under construction. Yet the British proposal provided for a NATO nuclear force composed of national contingents, thus preserving the British national nuclear force. Moreover, the British proposal provided only modest scope for German participation and thus would have made unlikely a substantially greater German voice in the formulation of Western strategy. The ANF did not find favor in Bonn. The Germans were quick to note that Germany would be only one among several continental European participants, and would not have a voice in the ANF comparable to that of Britain. Undoubtedly, the ANF would have been less objectionable than the MLF to the Soviet Union, and may have been proposed in order to enhance the prospects for East-West agreement on the non-proliferation of nuclear weapons. British spokesmen saw no necessary incompatibility between a non-proliferation treaty and NATO nuclear reform.[26] In fact, Britain appeared to attach at least as much importance as the United States to the conclusion of a treaty to halt the spread of nuclear capabilities and, like the United States, sought to reconcile an interest in the reform of the Atlantic Alliance with the conclusion of a non-proliferation treaty with the Soviet Union. The MLF-ANF controversy is illustrative of the difficulties in achieving consensus among even major Atlantic countries on the issue of nuclear weapons control.

Of all major U.S. allies, the German Federal Republic has been the most responsive to U.S. proposals such as the MLF and later the Special Committee of Defense Ministers. Like other major West European governments, the leaders of the Federal Republic have had as an objective to increase its own participation in NATO nuclear decisions, although they renounced the acquisition of a German national nuclear capability.[27] Because all German military forces are assigned to, and integrated into, the NATO structure, German security is dependent upon the ability of the Atlantic Alliance to meet Bonn's security requirements. As a result of German concern lest the concept of flexible response in Europe render the Federal Republic the major battlefield in a European conventional war, Bonn has supported the strategy of a forward defense. The German Government has argued that atomic demolition mines, nuclear air defense weapons, and possibly nuclear battlefield weapons must be available for early use in response to an attack upon Western Europe in order to deter an enemy from miscalculating the West's ability to oppose a ground strike. Minister of Defense Kai-Uwe von Hassel stated that:

> The concept of flexible response in Europe—both political and military—must be interpreted to mean that the so-called atomic threshold cannot be raised unduly high, without reference to political considerations. Apart from the fact that this would lead the potential aggressor to think that he could calculate his risk, it would create a situation in which he could seize pawns for future negotiations.[28]

After the shelving of the MLF late in 1964, the German government concentrated upon efforts to assure a greater place for Bonn in NATO nuclear planning. German spokesmen hinted that the Federal Republic's 12-division contribution to NATO defense, together with her considerable economic strength, did not receive adequate recognition under existing arrangements for the control of nuclear strategy. Thus, Bonn can be expected to seek rights similar to those enjoyed by other NATO partners in decisions about the use of U.S. nuclear weapons stationed on its territory. Should Britain and France decide eventually to coordinate or integrate their nuclear forces, Germany would expect at least a voice in planning for their use. Even if the British and French nuclear forces retain their separate status, France could grant the Federal Republic a role in planning for the potential use of the French *force de dissuasion.* The prospects for Bonn's gaining a voice in French nuclear planning depend, of course, upon the strengthening of links established between the two countries by the Franco-German Treaty of 1963.

Although the Germans have stressed their lack of interest in building a national nuclear force, the U.S. quest for a treaty to prevent the further dissemination of nuclear weapons aroused apprehension in Germany. Several arguments against such a treaty were raised in the Federal Republic: (1) there exists little possibility that the Soviet Union, in any case, would give physical control of nuclear weapons to its East European allies or to other countries; (2) the Federal Republic has already renounced the right, under the Western European Union, to produce atomic, biological, and chemical weapons; (3) in signing the Non-Proliferation Treaty without any comparable concession from the Soviet Union, Bonn would give up one of its most effective bargaining levers; (4) a non-proliferation treaty which included East Germany as a signatory would raise once again the problem of the recognition of two German states; (5) unless appropriate clauses were included, the Non-Proliferation Treaty would foreclose the possibility of creating a European nuclear force in which Germany could participate, while still renouncing national control over nuclear weapons; (6) unless appropriate safeguards were worked out, Germany and other European countries would be restricted in the development and exploitation of nuclear energy for peaceful purposes, thus contributing to the widening of the Atlantic technological imbalance. In fact, because of uncertainty about the future of NATO, the Bonn Government pressed the United States for a special nuclear guarantee, together with specific assurance about the provision of adequate supplies of nuclear fuel for the German peaceful nuclear program.[29] German misgivings about the Non-Proliferation Treaty were significant because for the first time since its founding, the Federal Republic was prepared to adopt on a major international issue a position different from that of the United States. Similarly, the unwillingness of the Bonn Government to accept U.S. formulae for the sharing of costs for the payment of troops stationed on German soil was indicative of German independence in foreign affairs unknown since World War II. If these cases are illustrative, the Federal Republic will show an increasing inclination to make further policy choices on the basis of criteria other than those of U.S. interest.

It is among the "core" members of the Atlantic Alliance—Britain, France, Germany, and the United States—that the discord on NATO military questions has been greatest. If these members of the Alliance had been able to reach agreement, the disintegration of NATO could have been reduced and perhaps even halted. Nevertheless, other members of the Alliance, with their own national perspectives, have developed policies on major NATO problems.

While never among the most enthusiastic supporters of the MLF, the Italian government was prepared to consider proposals for a multilateral force. In 1964 Italy agreed to contribute to a multinational crew for a U.S. destroyer designed to test the idea of mixed-manning.[30] Moreover, the Italian government expressed interest in the British ANF proposal.[31] Italian acceptance of the idea of a multilateral force derived in part from the presence of Soviet missiles targeted against Western Europe.[32]

For the most part, the smaller European NATO powers have not found fault with basic U.S. strategic concepts. Countries such as Belgium, Denmark, the Netherlands, Norway, Greece, and Turkey have held that the nuclear capabilities of the West should remain, to the greatest extent possible, under the control of the United States. Greece, however, on at least two occasions, in 1967 and 1968, urged that NATO place nuclear land mines along its frontier with Bulgaria. Such a defense system, it was argued, would provide protection against attack by Bulgaria alone or in concert with the Soviet Union.[33] Also, Turkey has sought greater national control of atomic land mines on her territory.[34] In 1968, Norway was engaged in a debate as to her future in the Alliance, with opponents of continued membership, including student organizations, arguing that outside NATO Norway "again free and independent, can work for disarmament, peace and international law and order."[35] The mounting of the so-called "Norway out of NATO Campaign" coincided with Soviet military maneuvers near the frontier which separates Norway from the Soviet Union. In particular, the Scandinavian members of NATO have expressed opposition to the building of a European nuclear force or to the development of national atomic capabilities in Western Europe. In October 1964 and February 1965, Norway took a position against the MLF and ANF respectively because of opposition to what she considered to be the proliferation of nuclear capabilities. Smaller NATO countries are generally convinced that in an age of nuclear weapons and technologically advanced delivery systems they cannot provide for their defense. The substitution of a nuclear guarantee by France or a European political unit which included Britain and the Six, would not have the credibility of the U.S. nuclear guarantee. In such a force, smaller NATO countries might have no greater influence than they have now. Hence they have little incentive to seek major changes in the existing Alliance structure.

Canada has long faced problems resulting from the great imbalance between her own capabilities and those of the United States. Canada never fully endorsed the building of MLF, partly because of the cost of the force. But Canadian reservations issued also from a belief that the MLF threatened to have a disruptive effect upon the Atlantic Alliance. In a speech at Windsor, Ontario, on November 23, 1964, External Affairs Secretary Martin maintained that Canada "could not conceive of an effective alliance in which France was not participating in a way . . . commensurate with her position in the world."[36] Faced with a possible split in the alliance, Canadian spokesman gave emphasis less to the need for "integration" than to the problems of assuring the preservation of even present levels of "unity" in the Atlantic Alliance. Canada, according to Mr. Martin:

> would be concerned . . . about any trend toward fragmentation of Atlantic defense. We would be particularly concerned if such a trend were to affect the preeminent part which the U.S. has played and is bound to continue to play in ensuring our collective security.[37]

Canada sought to assure the continued participation of France in NATO, while preserving U.S. predominance. Yet Canada has faced difficult problems, especially in defense, in her relations with the United States. After the formation of NATO, Canada's defense became ever more integrated with that of the United States. A military threat to Canada, it was recognized, was simultaneously a threat to the United States and vice versa. U.S. security was bound up with the defense of Canada.

With the advent of the missile age, the United States sought Canadian permission to deploy U.S. nuclear warheads in Canada. As the warning time for detecting an attack diminished, the possibility for consultation between the United States and Canada in situations of acute international crisis decreased. Especially under the Diefenbaker Government, Canada was reluctant to permit the United States to station nuclear weapons on its soil, and in 1962 even refused to accept nuclear missiles for deployment across the arctic frontier. The Pearson Government, less intransigent on the nuclear issue than the government headed by Prime Minister Diefenbaker which preceded it, accepted nuclear warheads for BOMARC missile sites and agreed to a nuclear role for the Canadian brigade and air unit assigned to NATO in Europe. There were indications that the Trudeau Government, which took office in 1968, would seek to reduce Canada's role in NATO.

In her defense policy, Canada clearly faces a dilemma. Only by contributing to the defense of North America and Western Europe can Canada expect to receive adequate consideration of the Canadian position on military issues of vital concern. Yet the cost of modern weapons systems, together with the reduced time for consultation since the advent of ICBM's, has made it increasingly difficult for Canada to gain an adequate hearing for her views. As a result, at best Canada can expect to achieve a higher level of participation and consultation only if institutions within the Alliance for contingency planning are strengthened and used effectively.

THE CONTROL OF NUCLEAR WEAPONS: A "NON-HARDWARE SOLUTION"

Unable to achieve European agreement upon the MLF, the United States abandoned this project late in 1964.[38] Subsequently, the United States pressed for a "non-hardware" solution to the control of NATO nuclear capabilities. Such a solution, like the MLF itself, was compatible with the U.S. objective of a non-proliferation treaty with the Soviet Union, and thus might enable the United States to reconcile its interest in East-West arms control with its interest in preserving the alliance. However, the United States failed to replace MLF with a proposal more responsive to the perceived needs of major Western European countries. Instead, in December 1966, two permanent groups for nuclear planning were established. The first, called the Nuclear Defense Affairs Committee, is open to the membership of all NATO countries, and is a general policy planning body.[39] Subordinate to this Committee, there is a Nuclear Planning Group.

Although its utility will be severely limited so long as France, the West European country least in accord with prevailing NATO strategy, is absent, the Nuclear Defense Affairs Committee represents one limited, but important, step in the broadening of European participation in Atlantic strategic decisions. The Committee provides an organizational framework not only for the continuing examination of strategic issues, but for the development of common policies on arms control and disarmament, including issues related to nuclear proliferation. A variety of kinds of planning for alternative contingencies, for the resolution of strategic differences, and for the development of weapons systems can be undertaken in the Committee.[40] In isolation from other measures to rebuild the shattered strategic consensus, however, the Special Committee cannot contribute greatly to the resolution of military problems facing the Alliance.

EUROPE AND THE ALLIANCE: PARTICIPATION AND INFLUENCE

Not a few Europeans have perceived a need for Western Europe to acquire the means for its own defense, to assume a greater part of the burden of European security than in the past, and to attain greater influence in Alliance decision-making. Yet Western Europe has not allocated to defense, or even to scientific and technological research and development, resources comparable to those devoted to such purposes in the United States.[41] The disparity between U.S. and European influence in NATO reflects in large part the disparity between their respective contributions to the defense of the West. It is unlikely that the United States will be prepared to agree to major changes in procedures for the control of nuclear weapons and strategy in NATO until Western Europe is willing, perhaps as the quid-pro-quo, to make a greater contribution to European defense. For their part, West European governments are reluctant to allocate greater resources to Western defense unless they can be certain of a greater voice in the control of nuclear weapons than they have enjoyed in the past.

In the final analysis, the institutional arrangements which are adopted for the North Atlantic area will reflect not only prevailing levels of consensus, but the respective contributions of member countries to defense. The United States, with practically all Western strategic power in its hands, cannot be expected to permit its weaker allies, even in a decision-making scheme with weighed majority voting, to determine whether or not the United States goes to war. Nor would a negative vote by European allies be necessarily sufficient to reverse the decision of the United States to take action deemed essential to safeguard vital U.S. national interests. Until Western Europe's impressive economic resurgence manifests itself in a major increase in defense capabilities, European allies will find it necessary to acquiesce in U.S. leadership so long as they remain members of an Atlantic alliance.

The defense expenditures of West European countries have not reflected increases in European economic growth, even though defense spending in Western Europe generally has risen since 1953. Economic prosperity has not increased the willingness of West European governments to devote greater funds to defense. Instead, the declining West European perception of threat from the Soviet Union may be measured by the decline in West European defense expenditures. With the exception of Germany and Portugal, the defense expenditures of all NATO countries, as a percentage of GNP, have fallen since 1953. (See Table I.) In some cases, as with the United States, for example, the decline registered after 1953 was a result of reductions in defense spending following the Korean Armistice in July of that year. Nevertheless, the United States, with a GNP far in excess of those of its allies, continues to devote to defense a percentage of GNP greater than any of its allies.

In 1964 U.S. expenditures for defense amounted to 8.8 percent of the GNP of the United States. Of NATO countries, Britain continued to bear the next greatest proportion of the Western defense burden, with expenditures totalling 6.9 percent of her GNP. Several NATO countries—Belgium, Canada, Greece, Italy, Luxembourg, Netherlands, Norway and Turkey—allocated less than 5 per cent of their GNP to defense. In the British White Papers on Defense issued in February 1966 and July 1967 it was announced that British military spending will decline considerably in the next decade both in absolute terms and as a percentage of GNP.[42] In July 1967, the German Federal Republic announced that, over the next two year period, it would make major reductions in defense spending and cut substantially the size of the Bundeswehr.[43] In the absence of a major new external threat, the general trend in Western Europe toward a reduction of defense expenditures as a percentage of GNP can be expected to continue in the years ahead.

Even France, with her ambitious nuclear program, devoted in 1964 a smaller percentage of GNP to defense in that year than in 1953, the year before the end of the Indo-China war. However, France's resources would be severely taxed if she attempted to make major technological breakthroughs in order to equip her military forces with an entirely new generation of weapons. So long as French technological efforts are confined, by and large, to the duplication of a limited sector of technology already developed in the United States and the Soviet Union, her economy may be able to bear the cost without undue strain. In fact, the French military establishment has been reduced in numbers of men under arms, thus releasing manpower for employment in France's growing economy; and the building of the *force de dissuasion* has stimulated industries based upon advanced technologies.

Together the Common Market Six and Britain possess resources comparable in some sectors to those of the United States or the Soviet Union. Together the seven nations, with a total population in excess of that of the United States, could raise an army of substantial proportions, thus relieving the United States of a considerable part of the burden of Europe's defense. Even with periods of enforced military service for the most part shorter than those of the United States, the combined military establishments of Britain and the Six exceeded 2 million men in 1966.[44]

A European community embracing Britain and the Six would have an industrial-technological base comparable to that of the United States and a GNP not greatly different from that of the Soviet Union. Such an industrial-technological base could give Western Europe a military capability far greater than the individual national units are able to provide. Even with such an industrial-technological base, however, Western Europe would be compelled, in order to narrow the Atlantic imbalance,[45] to devote a larger percentage of GNP to defense spending than in 1964. In contrast to U.S. defense spending of $52.3 billion, the combined military expenditures of Britain and the EEC Six in 1964 totalled $18.4 billion, and accounted for 4.8 percent of their combined GNP. (See Table I). Thus, to match U.S. levels as a percentage of GNP the defense spending of a European political community would have to be more than doubled, from 4.8 to 9.6 percent. Even with such an increase, Western Europe would still spend substantially less for defense than the United States, in absolute terms, so long as European GNP remained below that of the United States. Nevertheless, Western Europe would bear a greater portion of the burden of its own defense, and perhaps eventually even make an increased contribution to the defense of regions outside the North Atlantic area. At the very least, a greater European commitment to the defense of Western Europe would enable the United States, if necessary, to focus its efforts to a greater extent than in the last decade upon extra-Atlantic problems or to reduce its own defense budget. The burden borne by the United States might be reduced or, at the very least, might rise less rapidly than otherwise. Given the West European interest in major reductions in defense spending, however, the prospects for shifting the U.S. burden of European defense to Western Europe are not great.

The ability of Western Europe to assume a greater burden of European defense and to lessen the American military "hegemony" is related to the creation of collaborative arrangements in Europe itself. The strengthening of the integration movement in Western

TABLE I *Comparison of Defence Expenditures in NATO Countries*

Country	Defence Expenditure as % of Gross National Product						Defence Expenditures (million US $)		
	1953 (1)	1958 (2)	1962 (3)	1963 (4)	1964 (5)	1965* (6)	1963 (7)	1964 (8)	1965* (9)
Belgium	5.2	3.9	3.7	3.6	3.6	3.5	445	497	514
Canada	9.0	6.0	5.1	4.5	4.5	4.0	1,584	1,676	1,622
Denmark	3.7	3.3	3.4	3.5	3.3	3.2	239	255	277
France	11.0	7.9	7.3	6.8	6.7	6.6	4,628	4,918	5,125
Federal Republic of Germany	4.9	3.4	5.6	6.1	5.5	5.1	4,981	4,888	5,002
Greece	6.1	5.8	4.9	4.6	4.3	4.3	179	188	207
Italy	4.6	4.3	4.0	4.2	4.1	4.0	1,649	1,789	1,861
Luxembourg	3.2	2.1	1.5	1.4	1.6	1.5	7	9	9
Netherlands	6.2	5.0	5.0	4.9	4.8	4.3	637	735	734
Norway	5.6	4.0	4.1	4.1	3.9	4.3	205	220	260
Portugal	4.6	4.5	7.8	7.2	7.4	7.6	199	224	252
Turkey	5.4	4.5	5.9	5.6	5.7	5.5	351	382	402
United Kingdom	11.3	7.8	7.1	6.9	6.9	7.1	5,238	5,599	6,045
United States	14.7	10.9	10.1	9.6	8.8	8.4	52,295	51,213	51,935

Note: This table is based on a standard definition of defence expenditure which does not necessarily cover the same items as national defence budgets. For example, such items as military pensions, military research and development, and costs of establishing strategic stockpiles are included in the above figures, but may not be included in national defence budgets.

* Forecast.

Source: *The Military Balance 1966–67*, by permission of the publishers, The Institute for Strategic Studies, 1966, p. 45.

Europe would enhance the prospects for the eventual creation of a European deterrent. In the formation of a European nuclear force lies one avenue toward lessening but not eliminating Europe's military-technological dependence upon the United States. As they hinted during the discussion of MLF, U.S. policymakers might be prepared to assist a uniting Europe to develop such a force. However, the further deterioration in relations between France and the United States would reduce the political feasibility of this option for U.S. policymakers. Continued French opposition to U.S. policy in Southeast Asia or French denunciation of the North Atlantic Treaty would increase domestic opposition to U.S. military and technological assistance to Western Europe.

Especially in the British Conservative Party, interest in the formation of an Anglo-French nuclear force has increased in recent years.[46] On several occasions, British and French policymakers have hinted that if Britain joined the Common Market, an Anglo-French nuclear force could eventually be created. The utility of an Anglo-French force would lie primarily in the fact that it could become the nucleus for an eventual European force. Politically, the value of an Anglo-French force would lie in the greater influence which it would afford Western Europe in transatlantic relations. Unlike a European nuclear deterrent, such a force could be formed without prior European political integration. Initially, Britain and France could retain separate command structures, although the two countries might join in detailed planning as to the circumstances in which their forces would be used. If they reached agreement regarding strategic doctrine and the kinds of weapons systems to be developed in Western Europe over the next decade, they could extend technological collaboration to other projects designed to strengthen Europe's R & D base.

In recent years, the belief that a uniting Western Europe must have its own defense arrangements has attracted considerable support, especially in Britain. The reorientation of British thought on European defense has important implications for Anglo-American relations and for the future of Europe. If Britain is able to resolve major economic problems and thus prevent further large-scale defense reductions, she can strengthen British ground forces in Europe and naval forces in the Mediterranean and other waters adjacent to Europe,[47] after her withdrawal of military forces from posts east of Suez. Moreover, the reorientation of British thought on defense could give new impetus to the integration movement in Western Europe if, in the post-De Gaulle period, Britain were to regain a position of leadership in Western Europe. It is questionable, however, whether an Anglo-French nuclear force, in the absence of other steps to achieve a more integrated Europan defense establishment, would make it possible for Western Europe to narrow appreciably the disparity between its own military position and that of the United States.

The deployment of weapons systems such as the multiple warhead intercontinental re-entry vehicle (MIRV) by one or both superpowers will affect the credibility of European national nuclear forces. Given major advances in both Soviet and U.S. weapons technology, the French nuclear force may become credible only against another West European power, such as the Federal Republic. The ability of West European countries, singly or collectively, to reduce their military dependence upon the United States is closely related to their ability to achieve large-scale technological collaboration in defense. In the 1970's the rising cost of advanced weapons systems, the Soviet deployment of ABM defenses, and fear of growing dependence upon the United States could strengthen West European tendencies toward military interdependence.

The experience of the past decade in development of military technology by the superpowers has indicated that even a concerted West European effort to develop and produce the most advanced military capabilities may not succeed. On the one hand, Western Europe shows little if any inclination to contribute non-nuclear forces to its defense. On the other, in the development of advanced military capabilities, West European countries are likely to find themselves outpaced by the United States and the Soviet Union. In a situation of revived Soviet threat, Western Europe would undoubtedly be prepared once again to accept U.S. protection. But the ability, or the willingness, of the United States to provide a credible nuclear guarantee would be diminished as the Soviet Union attained strategic parity with the United States. Especially in the 1960's, the Soviet Union made strides in the development of intercontinental strategic capabilities. By the early 1970's, the Soviet Union can be expected to have approached parity with the United States in offensive forces even though parity will be difficult to define in the development and deployment of a new generation of offensive and defensive weapons systems.

Such a development in the U.S.-Soviet nuclear equation would increase the risk of destruction to the United States. In terms of potential destruction, the cost to the United States of a nuclear guarantee of Western Europe would rise, as it did after the Soviets acquired long-range nuclear capabilities in the 1950's. In the event that the Soviet Union and one or several West European countries became involved in limited war, the escalation of such conflict to the strategic nuclear level might prove attractive to the Soviet Union in the event that (a) Western Europe possessed little or no retaliatory capacity of its own and (b) the use of the U.S. nuclear force to protect Western Europe entailed risk of the destruction of at least a few U.S. cities. In such a situation, it has been argued, "An Anglo-French strategic force . . . would be called into full play as an almost automatic reaction to all the damage and suffering in their home territories that such an escalation would involve." [48] Herein lies an argument in favor of the development in the 1970's of an Anglo-French nuclear force as the nucleus of a more broadly based European deterrent.

In European strategic thought emphasis has been placed on the role of nuclear deterrence. In all likelihood, nuclear deterrence will continue to attract support for several reasons. (1) Nuclear programs may provide an avenue toward the development of some, but not all, advanced technologies. (2) A strategy based upon nuclear deterrence minimizes, in European minds at least, the need for substantial conventional forces. (3) West European perceptions of an overt Soviet military threat, barring an abrupt reversal in Soviet policy in Europe, will remain low. (4) Barring major technological breakthroughs by the superpowers, a contingency which can by no means be discounted, Western Europe, can achieve a measure of security at a cost which is not prohibitive.

Such European assumptions, together with a desire on the part of the United States to make reductions in U.S. forces stationed in Europe, do not augur well for any strategic doctrine which places great emphasis upon a conventional capability. If a greater West European conventional commitment is forthcoming at all, it is likely to result from a greater U.S. willingness than has been apparent in recent years to work out arrangements for the control of

Atlantic nuclear capabilities in a manner compatible with European strategic doctrine and security interests.

A U.S. initiative offering Western Europe greater participation in an alliance strategy which placed major emphasis upon nuclear deterrence would represent a concession to European interest in technologically advanced weapons systems. The development of such a strategic doctrine would increase the need for the modernization of West European military forces. Because of its technological preeminence in the Atlantic Alliance, the United States would play a major role in providing weapons systems or making available U.S.-developed technologies to Western Europe. In turn, the need for an Atlantic agency capable of developing criteria for the allocation of defense contracts would become urgent, if Western Europe were to be assured a major role in the modernization of its armies. Moreover, West European governments would find it necessary to develop new forms of European technological collaboration.[49] In either case, the United States, because of its technological position, would have considerable leverage in influencing the European level of participation as well as character of the political-military structure.

With the modernization of European military forces within a mutually acceptable framework, the United States could reduce its own military commitment in Western Europe, perhaps in return for the reduction of Soviet forces stationed in East Central Europe. For the United States such a change would represent a reduction in the U.S. defense burden. Western Europe, in turn, could achieve a greater voice in its own security and, with the reduction of Soviet forces in East Central Europe, a greater potential for effecting beneficial change there.

Although West European governments in the aftermath of empire have turned their attention primarily to European affairs, Europe retains interests not only in developing areas, but also in the Mediterranean area, where the Soviet presence has grown rapidly. Unless the United States is to bear the burden of defending European interests even in the Mediterranean, the need for a European military and naval capability which can be moved quickly will be great. Conceivably a European political-military community could provide for such a European force, or the individual European nation-states could contribute to a multi-national force to be used in instances where common European interests were threatened. This, however, would presuppose the existence of a common European outlook on extra-European affairs which does not yet obtain. However, if agreement is eventually reached about extra-European interests deemed vital, Western Europe could develop the capability needed for the defense of such interests and conceivably, in certain contingencies, for use under U.N. auspices in international police action. Although most discussions of European force posture have been focused upon the relationship between nuclear and conventional defense, there are also extra-European problems which concern European security. A European force posture should provide capabilties for dealing with these. Nevertheless, the growing West European preoccupation with European affairs does not augur well for the development of a European security force, much less for limited European participation in the resolution of problems in other parts of the world.

FUTURE PROSPECTS

Clearly, the restoration of Atlantic strategic consensus depends upon the willingness of both the United States and West European countries, notably France, to modify their prevailing strategic doctrines. For the United States the need for change is especially great, since neither U.S. nor West European conventional force levels are likely to remain adequate to support the strategy of flexible response. Thus the effect of the French withdrawal has been to increase the dependence of the Alliance upon nuclear forces, since the loss of the territory for defense-in-depth once provided by France renders difficult and perhaps impossible the deployment of large-scale non-nuclear forces in the Federal Republic. Thus the effect of French action has been to induce changes not only in the organization of the alliance, but in its posture and, perhaps ultimately, its strategic concepts. Pressures emanating from both sides of the Atlantic are pushing NATO toward a strategy which *de facto* gives greater emphasis to nuclear weapons than does the official strategy of the Alliance.

In NATO strategic affairs, the United States faces the need to bridge the gap between the prevailing European environment and a strategic doctrine which no longer conforms to that environment. For Western Europe the need exists to bridge the gap between force levels and the European aspiration for greater influence in decisions about European security. Even with more advanced weapons systems, together with a political framework beyond the nation-state, Western Europe is not likely, in military affairs as in other sectors, to reduce the U.S. "hegemony." At best, it may be possible only to lessen the growth of an Atlantic military imbalance which does not favor Western Europe. For both the United States and Western Europe the reconciliation of conflicting objectives presents a challenge of major proportions. Such is the task before the Atlantic countries if a strategic consensus is to be rebuilt and the deterioration in the military posture of the Alliance halted.

NOTES

1. For an examination of the impact of French withdrawal upon the Alliance, see Brigadier K. Hunt, *NATO without France: The Military Implications*. Adelphi Papers, No. 32 (December 1966). London: Institute for Strategic Studies.

2. For example, although Britain has placed great reliance on the U.S.-built polaris missile for her nuclear-powered submarine force, the United States has developed a more advanced missile, the Poseidon, which supposedly has the capability to penetrate ABM defenses. In all likelihood British submarines equipped with Polaris missiles will be inadequate as a nuclear deterrent against the Soviet Union. Yet Britain decided to purchase Polaris missiles from the United States after the Kennedy Administration in 1962 discontinued development of the Skybolt air-to-ground missile, which allegedly did not meet criteria of cost effectiveness. See *The Times* (London), February 17, 1968, p. 4.

3. In his first defense budget message to Congress in March 1961, President Kennedy declared: "Our arms must be subject to ultimate civilian control and command at all times, in war as well as peace. The basic decision on our participation in any conflict and our response to any threat—including all decisions relating to the use of nuclear weapons, or the escalation of a small war into a large one—will be made by the regularly constituted civilian authorities. I have not delegated to anyone else the responsibility for decisions which are imposed upon me by the Constitution. . . ."

—Recommendations Relating to Our Defense Budget. U.S. Congress, House Document No. 123. Washington: Government Printing Office, 1961, pp. 2-3.

4. In his speech at Ann Arbor, Michigan, in June, 1962, Secretary of Defense McNamara suggested: "In particular, relatively weak national nuclear forces with enemy cities as their targets are not likely to be sufficient to perform even the function of deterrence. If they are small, and perhaps vulnerable on the ground or in the air, or inaccurate, and a major antagonist came to believe there was a substantial likelihood of it being used independently, this force would be inviting a pre-emptive first strike against it. . . . In short, their nuclear capabili-

ties, operating independently, are dangerous, expensive, prone to obsolescence, and lacking in credibility as a deterrent." Robert S. McNamara, Commencement Speech, University of Michigan, Ann Arbor, Michigan, June 16, 1962. Department of Defense News Release No. 980-62.

5. However, the United States did provide certain kinds of assistance to France. For example, the United States made available to France tanker aircraft for the refueling of French strategic bombers.

6. ". . . The surprise use of the nuclear weapon permits the bringing of very great losses to the enemy, it depresses his troops morally, sharply lowering their combat ability, it quickly changes the relationship of forces and upsets command, thus creating conditions for completing his defeat. . . . The most important part of the principle is the constant struggle with means of nuclear attack with all available means and methods."

See V. D. Sokolovskii (ed.), *Soviet Military Strategy*. Englewood Cliffs, New Jersey: Prentice-Hall, Inc., for the Rand Corporation, 1963, especially Chapter IV.

Col. N. Miroshmichenko, "Change in the Content and Nature of Modern Combat." *Soviet Military Herald*. October 1, 1966. Translated by Harriet Scott. Emphasis added. See also XXX, "L'Adaptation des Forces Terrestres Sovietiques à une Guerre Nucleaire." *Revue de Défense Nationale* (France), February 1966, p. 223. "The Soviet armored and mechanized divisions are not organized and equipped to fight a battle of attrition, but rather to conduct a rapid exploitation after a massive strike of nuclear and chemical weapons. Thus, more and more the Soviet army assumes the shape of a force concerned for a single form of war, an organization that has been tailored to meet the requirements of a new doctrine."

7. One may speculate as to the potential implications of a "hardware" solution for NATO's nuclear problems. Conceivably, a "hardware" solution in NATO might lead to a tightening of the Soviet grip upon the Warsaw Pact. But other Warsaw Pact members, it may be postulated, might seek to revise the Pact in order to obtain greater participation in Soviet decisions as to the use of nuclear weapons.

8. Raymond L. Garthoff, "The Military Establishment," *East Europe* (September 1965), pp. 2-16; Thomas W. Wolfe, *The Evolving Nature of the Warsaw Pact*. Santa Monica: The Rand Corporation, 1965.

9. *The Military Balance, 1966-1967*. London: Institute for Strategic Studies, 1966, pp. 6-7. See also testimony by Richard Starr, United States Congress, House Subcommittee on Europe, Committee of Foreign Affairs, *The Crisis in NATO*. 89th Congress, Second Session, 1966. pp. 287-290.

10. See Harland Cleveland, "The Rejuvenation of NATO," *Atlantic Community Quarterly*, Vol. 5, No. 4 (Winter 1967-68), p. 513.

11. In a speech before the French National Assembly on April 13, 1966, Premier Pompidou offered the following criticism of U.S.

military strategy: "Within NATO itself, we have seen the replacement, gradual and without our agreement, of the initial strategy that was based on deterrence and, consequently, on the immediate use of atomic reprisals, by a strategy called "flexible" which, under the pretext of lessening the risk of total war, consists, in fact, in enabling the United States to limit the field of the initial operations by sparing the territory of the main potential aggressor."

"Such a formula cannot satisfy us, because it piles up the dangers for us French. The conventional forces of the alliance, alone integrated, and even equipped with tactical atomic weapons whose use remains under American command alone could not be sure of halting an attack from the East. Such a strategy seeks dooming us to atomic bombardment first, to invasion next."

—Ambassade de France, Service de Presse et d'Information. Speeches and Press Conferences, No. 243 (April 13, 1966).

12. See, for example, the writings of General Andre Beaufre. According to Beaufre: "The first objection comes somewhat naturally from those countries likely to be the scene of a 'limited' conflict. They do not find the idea of playing the role of battlefield—perhaps an atomic battlefield—very attractive. If the disaster was of world-wide proportions, the sacrifices they might be called upon to make would appear less unfair. Is not their security being sold off cheap, they say, for the benefit of the vital areas which could have been used to force the enemy to disperse his effort? I have already referred to the second objection; it is concerned with the deterrent. If it is accepted that a conflict must be kept limited, is not this tantamount to an invitation to start one and thereby to a reduction in the effect of the deterrent, and if a limited conflict should start, will not the risks of escalation be all the greater?"

—Andre Beaufre, *An Introduction to Strategy*. New York: Praeger, 1965, p. 89.

13. A similar rationale was used in justification of the British decision of 1957 to place major reliance for security upon nuclear weapons and to build a British nuclear deterrent. According to the United Kingdom White Paper on Defense, issued in April 1957:

"It must be frankly recognized that there is at present no means of providing adequate protection for the people of this country against the consequences of an attack with nuclear weapons. . . . This makes it more than ever clear that the overriding consideration in all military planning must be to prevent war rather than to prepare for it.

"While comprehensive disarmament remains among the foremost objectives of British foreign policy, it is unhappily true that, pending international agreement, the only existing safeguard against major aggression is the power to threaten retaliation with nuclear weapons."

—Great Britain, *United Kingdom White Paper on Defense*. London: Her Majesty's Stationery Office, 1957.

14 See, for example, L'Affaire de l'OTAN: Le Dialogue angoissant

de deux généraux français (General Pierre Gallois and General Paul Stehlin). *Paris Match,* No. 888, April 16, 1966, pp. 56-59.

15. See Charles De Gaulle, *The Army of the Future,* New York: J. B. Lippincott Company, 1941.

16. Charles Louis Ailleret, "Defense in all Directions," *Atlantic Community Quarterly,* Vol. 6, No. 1 (Spring 1968), pp. 17-25. Translated and reprinted from *Revue de Défense Nationale,* December 1967. General Ailleret was Chief of Staff, French Army, before his death in an airplane crash on March 9, 1968. In a speech at the Ecole Militaire on January 27, 1968, President de Gaulle endorsed this strategy. See *New York Times,* January 30, 1968, p. 12.

17. Ambassade de France, Service de Presse et d'Information, *Twelfth Press Conference Held by President de Gaulle.* Foreign Minister, Couve de Murville in a statement to the NATO Council in May 1964, declared that France wished to substitute for NATO an alliance without an integrated command structure. A restructured alliance, he suggested, would provide coordination of planning among its own national defense. *New York Times,* Section IV, May 10, 1964, p. 7.

18. See General Andre Beaufre, *L'OTAN et l'Europe.* Paris: Calmann-Levy, 1966; pp. 52-54.

19. *New York Times,* Dectmber 14, 1967, p. 16.

20. *New York Times,* November 21, 1967, p. 18.

21. For an examination of the spectrum of Western views on NATO strategy see Raymond Aron, *Le Grand Debate.* Paris: Calmann-Levy, 1963. See also *Le Grand Debate Nucleaire.* Bulletin S.E.D.E.I.S. Edited by Bertrand de Jouvenel, #10. Supplement, February 10, 1965.

22. Since the working group was not formally a part of the organizational structure of NATO, it was illegal under U.S. atomic energy legislation for the United States negotiating team to pass classified information to the group as such. But because access to certain classified materials was necessary in order to discuss the proposal, the Department of State resorted to the procedure of transmitting information under the terms of the bilateral treaties which established the "two-key" system of control for American IRBM's emplaced in Western Europe. From the point of view of U.S. atomic energy legislation the entire procedure was, at the very least, suspect and was so noted by the Joint Committee on Atomic Energy. See the testimony of Under Secretary of State George Ball in U.S. Congress, Subcommittee on Agreements for Cooperation of the Joint Committee on Atomic Energy, Hearings, *Agreement for Cooperation with NATO for Mutual Defense Purposes,* 88th Congress, 2nd. Session, 1964, p. 19.

23. In an address to the General Assembly of the Atlantic Treaty Organization in Copenhagen on September 27, 1962, McGeorge Bundy declared: "It would also be wrong to suppose that the reluctance which we feel with respect to individual, ineffective, and unintegrated (European) forces would be extended automatically to a European force, genuinely unified and multilateral, and effectively integrated

with our own necessarily predominant strength in the whole nuclear defense of the Alliance." Reprinted in Western European Union Assembly, Committee on Defense Questions and Armaments. *Nuclear Weapons.* Paris, November 30, 1964, pp. 60-61. See Address by George Ball to NATO Parliamentarians' Conference, November 16, 1962. "If Europe decides that it would be useful and appropriate for it to participate in a large way in nuclear defense, then the United States would be prepared to give very sympathetic attention to whatever proposals the European nations might together agree upon, with the understanding that what would be contemplated would be a (European) multilateral force with multinational manning, and that we would not attempt to prejudge this force or how it would be organized." Reprinted in *Ibid.,* pp. 62-63. See also Address by Vice President Johnson in Brussels, November 8, 1963: "Evolution of this missile fleet (MLF) toward European control as Europe marches toward unity is by no means excluded." Reprinted in *Ibid.,* p. 79.

24. See, for example, United States Information Agency, *Western European Press Cold to U.S. Proposal for a Multilateral NATO Nuclear Force.* Monograph No. R-60-63(AE), Washington, April 5, 1963. See also Thomas C. Wiegele. *The Multilateral Force: A Study in the Control of Nuclear Weapons.* Ph.D. Dissertation in International Relations, University of Pennsylvania, 1967, pp. 168-174.

25. In a statement about the MLF, Prime Minister Wilson declared: "We believe that a mixed-manned surface fleet adds nothing to Western strength, is likely to cause a dissipation of effort within the Alliance, and may add to the difficulties of East-West agreement. . . . In its present form and as long as the American veto remains absolute, it does not mean, in our view, additional fingers on the trigger. I suspect and always have suspected that the Soviet fear relates not so much to the present proposal, but more to the possibility, sometimes canvassed, that the American veto might be replaced by a system of majority voting capable of overriding American opposition to the bomb being used. To such a development we are irrevocably opposed. . . ." Great Britain, *Parliamentary Debates* (Commons), Vol. 702 (November 23, 1964), col. 943.

26. Discussing the relationship between the proposed ANF and a treaty to prevent the dissemination of nuclear capabilities, Prime Minister Wilson declared: "Our proposals, therefore, have two objectives: one, to secure greater cooperation and integration of nuclear weapons within the Alliance and thereby to make the Alliance more effective; and two, to provide built-in guarantees against the proliferation of nuclear weapons, by providing that existing nuclear powers renounce any measures of dissemination to non-nuclear powers and equally that non-nuclear powers renounce any attempt to achieve nuclear potentiality whether by manufacturing or acquisition." Text of the Speech by Prime Minister Wilson at the opening of the NATO Ministerial Meeting, London, May 11, 1965. British Information Services, New York. The Conservative Government of Prime Minister Home made

a similar declaration: "H.M. Government reaffirms that the principals of multilateral manning and membership will ensure that the Multilateral Force could be used only by decision of its governing body on which all members would be represented in accordance with control arrangements consistent with the principles of non-dissemination." Text of the U.K. Reply to the Soviet Note on July 11, delivered in Moscow, August 28, 1964. British Information Services, New York.

27. See, also, the statement of Chancellor Kiesinger to the Bundestag on December 13, 1966, in which the Chancellor set forth his Government's policy. Kiesinger declared: "The Federal Republic has given an undertaking to its partners in the alliance to renounce the production of atomic weapons, and has in that respect submitted to international controls. We seek neither national control nor national ownership of atomic weapons." *The Bulletin.* A weekly survey of German affairs issued by the Press and Information Office of the German Federal Government. Special supplement on the New Government's foreign policy. Bonn, December 20, 1966.

"The German Government believes that it is necessary for NATO to adjust itself to new political and military conditions. It is, in particular, necessary to solve such problems as result from the fact that some members of the Alliance now have nuclear weapons while others have not. All allies should, however, be given a share in the nuclear defense, which should be in keeping with the extent of the burdens they bear. We are thinking in terms of a joint nuclear organization. We have repeatedly made known that we do not desire national control of nuclear weapons. We should, however, not be kept out of any nuclear participation simply because we are a divided country."

News from the German Embassy, Vol. IX, No. 13, November 15, 1965. Mayor Willy Brandt, in a speech to the WEU Assembly on June 1 , 1965, stated his belief that the Federal Republic should not seek to build a national nuclear force. See *News from Germany,* June 1965.

28. Kai-Uwe von Hassel, "Organizing Western Defense," *Foreign Affairs,* (January 1965), p. 214.

29. *New York Times,* April 23, 1968, p. 10.

30. *New York Times,* January 12, 1964, p. 3.

31. *New York Times,* April 29, 1965, p. 3.

32. During a debate in the Italian National Assembly on December 4, 1964, President Saragat, then Foreign Minister, declared: "We are . . . convinced that in the present strategic situation, in which Soviet medium-range missiles are still pointed at Europe, a multilateral defense would constitute a reinforcement and not an upset of the existing military equilibrium." Translated from text supplied by Italian Embassy, Washington, D.C.

33. *New York Times,* April 26, 1968, p. 28.

34. The *Times* (London), April 20, 1968, p. 4.

35. See *New York Times,* March 22, 1968, p. 19; The *Times* (London), January 30, 1968, p. 3.

36. Text supplied by Canadian Embassy, Washington, D.C.

37. Text supplied by Canadian Embassy, Washington, D.C.

38. For a detailed account of the U.S. decision to abandon MLF, see Philip L. Geyelin, *Lyndon B. Johnson and the World*. New York: Praeger, 1966, pp. 159-180.

39. All NATO members except France, Iceland, Luxembourg, and Norway accepted membership in this Committee.

40. In testimony on June 21, 1966, before the U.S. Senate Subcommittee on National Security and International Operations, Secretary of Defense McNamara declared:

"We have entered a period which I believe to be a more mature period in our consideration of strategic and defense matters. In November of 1965 the North Atlantic Council formed a Special Committee composed of the Defense Ministers of 10 NATO nations to examine means of increasing allied participation in various aspects of nuclear planning and consultation. Since that time, my Defense colleagues and I, and our representatives in various specialized working groups, have held a number of meetings in which there has been frank and informal discussion of our respective views on these matters.

"A Working Group on Intelligence and Data Exchange has looked closely at the kinds and amounts of information and intelligence—what we call the "data base"—which would be necessary or useful to a member government in a consultation about the possible use of nuclear weapons. A Communications Working Group has considered a number of alternative communications schemes which could enhance materially the ability of alliance members to keep each other informed and to consult in an emergency. Finally, in a Nuclear Planning Working Group, we have examined and discussed the strategic nuclear resources of the alliance, the tactical nuclear weapons of the alliance, the potential circumstances of their use, and the way in which the alliance should organize to carry on future discussions of these subjects."

The Atlantic Alliance. Hearings before the Subcommittee on National Security and International Operations of the Committee on Government Operations, United States Senate. Eighty-Ninth Congress, Second Session (June 21, 1966) Part 6, p. 192.

41. See Chapter III.

42. See *The Defense Review*. Statement on Defense issued in London, February 22, 1966. Official text released by British Information Services, New York; *New York Times*, July 19, 1967, p. 1.

43. *New York Times*, July 12, 1967, p. 7.

44. See *The Military Balance, 1966-1967*. London: The Institute for Strategic Studies, 1966.

45. Figures for 1964 are used because, in the case of the United States, 1964 was the last year before the Vietnam build-up led to a major increase in U.S. defense spending. Since, one hopes, such spending is only a temporary feature of the U.S. military budget, U.S. fig-

ures for years which reflect the Vietnam conflict should not be used for purposes of comparison with West European military expenditures.

46. According to Edward Heath, leader of the Conservative Party: "There should eventually be defense arrangements on a European scale, including Germany, with an Anglo-French arrangement in the nuclear field. This European defense arrangement of course requires a political arrangement also, so that the European forces can work in a reconstructed North Atlantic Alliance." Edward Heath, "West European Integration and East-West Relations." *In Western and Eastern Europe: The Changing Relationships.* Adelphi Papers, No. 33 (March 1967) London: Institute for Strategic Studies, p. 34. Although Prime Minister Wilson had not specifically committed himself to an Anglo-French nuclear force, he declared, in his address to the Council of Europe Consultative Assembly, on January 23, 1967: Let no one here doubt Britain's loyalty to NATO and the Atlantic Alliance. But I have always said that loyalty must never mean subservience. Still less must it mean an industrial helotry under which we in Europe produce only the conventional apparatus of a modern economy, while becoming dependent on American business for the sophisticated apparatus which will call the industrial tune in the seventies and eighties." *New York Times,* January 24, 1967, p. 12.

47. Britain plans to strengthen her naval forces in the Mediterranean after the ending of commitments in Asia. The *Times* (London), January 22, 1968, p. 2.

48. Neville Brown, "British Arms and the Switch towards Europe," *International Affairs* (London), Vol. 43, No. 3 (July 1967), p. 477.

49. For a more detailed discussion of this problem, see Chapter III.

III. The Technology Gap

IN RECENT YEARS, THE SO-CALLED ATLANTIC TECHNOLOGICAL GAP has gained widespread attention both in Western Europe and the United States. In fact, on both sides of the Atlantic the question of the technological imbalance has rivaled the strategic and political problems of NATO for attention. European interest in the Atlantic technological gap is indicative of the shift of European concern from the alleged Soviet military threat to the industrial-technological-economic challenge supposedly posed by the United States. Whatever its actual dimensions, the Atlantic technological imbalance is important because it is symptomatic of a growing European apprehension about American hegemony in Atlantic relationships.

The natural sciences had their origin in Europe. Until World War II it was Europe, with its long tradtion of scientific achievement and creativity, not the United States, which provided by far the greatest proportion of scientific discoveries. Before World War II, although the United States lagged behind Europe in basic science, it developed great expertise in technology, or applied science, with its vast markets, advanced managerial concepts, and engineering skills. Even as early as 1835 Tocqueville noted the development of advanced manufacturing processes in the United States.[1] Since World War II, however, Western Europe has not matched either the United States or the Soviet Union in certain important fields of advanced technology. Both the Soviet Union and the United States have shown great ability, by dint of concentrated effort and managerial and engineering skills, to exploit the potential of modern science. Many of the major scientific and technological advances of the last generation have been registered in the United States rather than in Western Europe. In several fields in particular, electronics, computers, aircraft, space satellites, and launching systems, all of which are closely related to defense and space technology, the imbalance is greatest.[2] In comparison with the United States, West European countries have encountered formidable obstacles in their efforts to develop certain advanced technologies. European industries which led the world in the interwar period, such as aircraft, have been hard put to compete with their counterparts in either the United States or the Soviet Union.

Between Western Europe and the United States there is an uneven distribution of resources for the development and exploitation of advanced technology. This imbalance, of course, is not peculiar to U.S.-West European relations. Within nation-states there are technological imbalances. Between Eastern and Western Europe, there is a technological gap which has motivated East European interest in increased trade in order to gain access to advanced technologies of the West. Between the West and the less developed areas there is a technological imbalance of even greater magnitude than that within the North Atlantic area.

Perception of the Atlantic technological gap has led to proposals from both sides of the Atlantic for solutions. Early in October 1966 Italy's foreign minister, Amintore Fanfani, proposed a "technological Marshall Plan," designed to promote transatlantic technological collaboration in such fields as computers, aeronautics, space research, space satellites, atomic and general energy research, and research in desalting water and combating air and soil pollution.[3] In response, President Johnson declared that the United States and West European countries were "exploring how best to develop science and technology as a common resource." [4] In November 1966 Prime Minister Wilson proposed the creation of a European Technological Community.[5] A year later Wilson suggested the creation of a European Institute of Technology.[6] In contrast to Fanfani's essentially Atlantic orientation, Wilson favored primarily "European" solutions to the technological imbalance. The Atlantic technological gap has been considered in meetings of the NATO Council, Western European Union Assembly, the European Parliament, and the EEC Council of Ministers.

Undoubtedly, the relative decline of European technology has contributed to European dissatisfaction with the Atlantic Alliance, for the European ability to effect desired changes in the Alliance would have been greater had Western Europe been able to assume more responsibility for its own defense. Notwithstanding the British and French nuclear programs, Western Europe has not found it possible to develop advanced military technologies comparable to those of the United States or the Soviet Union. Hence the defense of Western Europe has fallen principally to the United States, which has relied upon strategic concepts not always to the liking of Europeans. In fact it is in those technologies which are closely related to U.S. government-sponsored R&D that the imbalance is greatest. The inability of West European countries to devote resources comparable to those of the United States to governmental R&D for military purposes and space exploration contributes to the Atlantic technological gap. Herein lies one of the important political implications of the technological imbalance. Those sectors where the gap is most pronounced are of great importance to Western Europe's military and economic future.

The United States has encountered European opposition to procedures for the allocation of defense contracts in the Alliance. In Western Europe, there has been resentment against what sometimes appear to be the over-zealous efforts of U.S. firms to persuade NATO allies to purchase U.S. weapons systems, even when European firms have developed what is believed to be a comparable or even a superior product.[7] Within NATO, calls for weapons standardization from the United States are often tantamount to a thinly veiled effort to obtain for U.S. firms major contracts for the arming of NATO forces. In Western Europe there is suspicion that a tacit agreement exists between U.S. governmental agencies and industry to assure that American firms obtain a major share of NATO defense contracts.

THE ATLANTIC TECHNOLOGICAL IMBALANCE: SOME CONTRIBUTING CAUSES

Several factors have contributed to the Atlantic technological imbalance. In contrast with Britain, France, and Germany, in the United States government-sponsored R&D, in the last decade has accounted for an increasing percentage of all R&D. Moreover, in the United States governmental R&D has risen, as a percentage of GNP, at a greater rate than R&D in the private sector. Total U.S. expenditures for R&D exceed by nearly five fold the total R&D expenditures of Britain and Germany, and are more than twice the combined R&D expenditures of France, Germany, Japan, and Britain.[8]

Over the past generation, the cost of R&D has risen greatly. For example, it costs many times more to design, build, and produce an aircraft today than twenty years ago. In comparison with the United States and the Soviet Union, Western Europe is deficient in the allocation of funds—governmental and private—for research and development. The disparity between U.S. and European expenditures in technology (see Table II) accounts in part for the inability of Western Europe to rival either the United States or the Soviet Union in certain important fields. In those sectors most often associated with the Atlantic technological imbalance, the United States government has made available funds for R&D far in excess of those in Western Europe.

From the above figures it is evident that U.S. government expenditures account for a major portion of total U.S. investment in R&D. The "spin-off" from expenditures for space and specifically military programs accrues to U.S. industry in a variety of forms. For example, aerospace research has produced new paints and medical sensoring devices. According to reports delivered at the meeting of the Amerian Institute of Aeronautics and Astronautics in December 1966, systems analysis highly perfected in defense and aerospace industries can be applied to problem-solving in civilian industries.[9] The technological spin-off from space and military programs is especially great in the development of physics, a science whose effects upon technology in the next generation are likely to be great. Research in such important fields as gravitation,

TABLE II

Estimated Gross Expenditures on Research and Development: Western Europe and the United States, 1962.

	Expenditures (US $)	% GNP at Market Price	R&D per capita (US $)	% of total supported by govt.	% of business supported gross R&D
U.S.A.	17,531	3.1	93.7	63	35
Belgium	133	1.0	14.8	37	63
France	1,108	1.5	23.6	70	30
Germany	1,105	1.3	20.1	40	60
Netherlands	239	1.8	20.3	35	65
U.K.	1,775	2.2	33.5	64	36

Source: C. Freeman and A. Young, *The Research and Development Effort in Western Europe, North America, and the Soviet Union.* Paris: OECD, 1965, pp. 71–72.

relativity, superconductors, cyrogenics, quantum theory, and elementary particle physics receives heavy subsidization from the U.S. government.[10] Clearly, new technolgies in such fields as nuclear energy, electronics, and aerospace would not have been developed and applied to non-military uses so soon without the impetus provided by defense R&D.[11] Hence European concern has risen that the United States, because of vast government-sponsored research efforts, will not only widen the technological imbalance, but gain a competitive advantage in industries which benefit from technological spin-off.

It is unlikely that any Western European country alone could equal U.S. expenditures for R&D. The total expenditures of Britain, Germany, and France are less than one-fourth those of the United States. Even though many research costs in Western Europe are lower than in the United States, the total European R&D effort is substantially less than one-third that of the United States. Considered either singly or as part of total West European expenditures for science and technology, the R&D programs of Western Europe lag far behind those of the United States.

To be sure, many American technologies have been made available to Western Europe through the transfer of patents, licensing of processes, and direct American investment. Yet this form of collaboration has contributed to concern in Western Europe about a deficit in Europe's "technological balance of payments," i.e., the difference between payments and receipts for patents, licenses, and technical know-how. According to OECD statistics, the combined payments of France, Belgium, Great Britain, the German Federal Republic, and Italy to the United States for advanced technologies totaled nearly $250 million in 1961, while receipts to the same European countries for the sale of technology to the United States in the same year were less than $50 million.[12] Since 1961, the "technological balance of payments has continued to favor the United States."[13]

Even in their own markets, European firms have found it difficult to compete successfully with U.S. corporations in certain fields of advanced electronics, especially computers. Europeans concerned about the future of European technology often illustrate their case by reference to the computer. Although British scientists contributed to the development of the computer, one U.S. firm, International Business Machines, supplies about 80 percent of the world market. The remainder is controlled largely by two other U.S. producers, Radio Corporation of America and General Electric.[14] American corporations supply more than 75 percent of the European computer market. U.S. firms have even secured a large measure of control over European companies which produce computers. Only one major European computer manufacturer remains beyond U.S. control: International Computer and Tabulator (ICT) of Great Britain, which has received substantial support from the British government. Nevertheless, ICT supplies less than one-half of the British market, while IBM alone accounts for about 40 percent of the sales of computers in Britain. President de Gaulle agreed reluctantly to permit General Electric to acquire a controlling interest in Machines Bull in order to enable France to benefit from the infusion of U.S. computer technology. Since computers will be of crucial importance to government, industry, and scientific-educational efforts during the next phase of the Industrial Revolution, without the most advanced computer technology, Western Europe will find itself even more disadvantaged in comparison with the United States. Even if Europe acquires computers on a scale comparable to the United States, the lack of a European computer industry will exclude Europeans from one of the most dynamic industries and fastest growing markets, and make them heavily dependent upon the United States.

In Western Europe there is apprehension that U.S. control of companies producing advanced technology will have adverse effects. Basic reasearch will be conducted in the United States, rather than Europe, thus contributing to the migration of some of the most talented European scientists and engineers. The United States will capture the markets for the products of the most technologically advanced industries. Decisions about the development and production of technologies vital to the future of European defense efforts will be taken in the United States, rather than Western Europe. In particular, two incidents have strengthened European apprehension about excessive dependence upon the United States in advanced technology; the U.S. refusal to sell to France an advanced computer deemed vital to the French nucelar military program, and U.S. pressure upon Britain to prevent the construction in France of a plant for the production of enriched nuclear materials. Thus outside influence, especially American, in key industries is deemed incompatible with France's effort to escape

U.S. "hegemony" in advanced technologies for both defense and civilian application.

Over the past generation the educational systems of the United States and, to an even greater extent, the Soviet Union have trained large numbers of scientists, engineers, technicians, and managers. In sheer numbers, if not necessarily in quality, Europe remains behind the United States and the Soviet Union in school enrollment. In 1963, for example, the United States granted approximately 465,000 undergraduate degrees in the natural sciences and engineering. Universities in Belgium, France, the German Federal Republic, Italy, the Netherlands, and the United Kingdom together awarded an estimated 100,000 degrees in the same year.[15] To be sure, because of important differences between European and American educational systems, statistical comparison is difficult. Yet West European countries award fewer degrees than the United States. Although European countries will probably narrow this gap in the 1970's, the number of persons enrolled in universities in Europe as candidates for degrees in science is likely to remain well below comparable enrollment in the United States.

In most countries the educational system offers an important avenue for social mobility. Especially in technologically advanced countries, institutions of higher learning provide the skilled personnel needed for the management of the economy. Compared with Western Europe, the larger sector of U.S. society which has received education at the college or university level contributes to the greater flexibility of labor as a factor of production. Because of higher educational levels, a broadly based segment of the U.S. population is prepared for a wide variety of employment. Such persons are more willing than the less educated to move from one part of the country to another in order to maximize their job potential. In all likelihood, they are more flexible than their European counterparts in other ways, including receptivity to change.

In comparison with that of Western Europe, the U.S. educational system is important for another reason. In the United States even more than Western Europe, career advancement is dependent upon merit, i.e., skills and expertise acquired in the educational process. Hence for the United States education is crucial to economic and social mobility. At the same time, the U.S. educational system is based upon the education of the masses of the population. Entry into the educational system is less restrictive in the U.S. than in many European countries. Because of the relative ease of entry, the U.S. educational system serves as a device for tapping the intellectual reserves of the U.S. population and assuring that persons with ability will receive the opportunity to contribute to the management of a technologically advanced society.

Nevertheless, European governments have made major efforts in recent years to improve training for careers in applied science. Since World War II, there has been a rising enrollment at all levels of education in Europe, especially in technical and professsional programs. Technical studies now occupy a place of greater importance, with more European students being trained as prospective engineers, draftsmen, scientists, and technicians. European governments are making great efforts to adapt their educational systems to an age of science and technology. The Netherlands government, for example, is creating new technical universities; France has built fourteen colleges of science; and in Britain new educational centers have been established, and greater emphasis has been placed on scientific training in older universities.

In certain European countries, notably Britain, occupations related to the applied sciences do not yet attract sufficient numbers of youths to fill the growing demand for engineers, technicians, and managers. British education in the applied sciences and business administration still lags behind the needs of the 1970's. According to the Robbins Report, studies leading to careers in pure science not only attract greater numbers of students, but also persons of "better quality" than does technology. The Robbins Report recommended the creation of five special Institutions for Scientific and Technological Education and Research. In other colleges, it was recommended that "a new system for degrees should be established, covering business studies, languages, and other subjects as well as science and technology." [16] Thus the Atlantic technological imbalance is undoubtedly related to differing value systems in Western Europe and the United States.

European countries have experienced yet another problem, namely, the exodus of scientists and engineers attracted to the United States by higher salaries, superior laboratory facilities, and greater opportunities for scientific achievement and personal advancement. According to one study, the United States has gained in recent years, as a result of immigration from other countries, scientists and engineers equal to the annual output of about 5 percent of the institutions of higher learning in the United States.[17] Statistics compiled by OECD reveal that the number of scientists and engineers who migrate from Western Europe to the United States is small—about 5 percent of the science and engineering students graduated each year in Western Europe.[18] However, for certain countries, as Grubel and Scott suggest, the "brain drain" represents the loss of a substantial proportion of their current output of first degrees (Bachelor's, or equivalent) in science and engineering. For example, between 1957 and 1961, Germany, the Netherlands, and the United Kingdom lost an average of 9.5, 19.1, and 16.5 percent of first degree scientific and engineering graduates to the United States.

Against the "brain drain," however, should be set the influx of trained personnel to Western Europe from other countries, including the return of Europeans from the United States. Thus the net outflow of technically trained people from Western Europe is probably lower than that suggested by the OECD statistics quoted above. Yet the so-called "brain drain" has caused considerable concern in several European countries, especially in Britain, whose economic future depends to a large extent upon her ability to utilize advanced technology to develop and sustain competitive export industries. In Western Europe, the exodus of scientific personnel is symptomatic of the existence of an Atlantic technological imbalance, for highly skilled Europeans leave their homelands because of the higher salaries and greater professional opportunities available in the United States. In fact, the so-called "brain drain" is indicative that Europe, far from not training adequate numbers of technical personnel, produces a surplus in certain fields.

COMPARATIVE MANAGERIAL AND MARKETING PRACTICES

In the development and utilization of managerial and marketing practices, the United States is substantially ahead of Western Europe. Education in business administration is far more advanced in the United States than in Western Europe. American mangement practices have enhanced the ability of U.S. corporations to plan, control, and evaluate their research programs. To a greater extent than their European counterparts, U.S. industrial managers have made use of market research in planning and guiding R&D programs. Moreover, the United States has led the world in the use of imaginative techniques for the marketing of products. The availability of such techniques and the familiarity of U.S. corporations with them have given the United States, in some cases, an advantage over European competitors.[20]

MARKET SIZE AND TECHNOLOGICAL IMBALANCE

Disparities between U.S. and West European national markets have contributed to the development of the Atlantic technological imbalance. In some, but not all, advanced technologies, European national markets are not large enough to permit the level of mass production needed to lower the unit cost of products. In Western Europe, however, governments are reluctant to purchase technologically advanced products, especially weapons systems, from other European countries unless the purchasing country has had some part in the development and production of the item in question.[21] The effect of such practices, of course, is to limit the market for European advanced technologies and to strengthen the argument for European technological collaboration.

The market problem has been particularly acute in aircraft, an industry in which an Atlantic technological imbalance is said to exist. An American manufacturer of aircraft can usually rely on a huge domestic market which may include the United States government as well as American commercial airlines. Because of this market, an aircraft manufacturer can extend production runs. The longer production runs of certain U.S. industries, such as aircraft, make it possible to produce products at lower unit cost than their European counterparts.[22] According to the report of the Committee of Inquiry into the British Aircraft Industry, the Plowden Commission:

> In spite of the scale of American (aircraft) exports, their home market is nine times larger than their export sales. The corresponding British ratio is 3½ to 1, and the French 2 to 1. With such a vast home market completely assured for Government purchases, and largely assured for civil aircraft, the Americans have a solid base for overseas operations.[23]

The size of the American market has had other implications for certain sectors of U.S. industry. The ability to exploit existing scientific data, although not necessarily to produce new ideas, lies with those countries able to support large corporate enterprise either through government subsidization or vast markets or both. Although it is difficult to assess the relationship between the size of a firm and its ability to develop new technologies, large firms enjoy certain advantages, including the funds necessary to employ large numbers of scientific and technical personnel and to build well-equipped laboratories. Much of the R&D effort of corporate enterprise is undertaken by large firms: of all firms in the United States undertaking R&D, only 16 percent of medium-sized firms (1,000-5,000 employees) conducted any basic research; for firms employing more than, 5,000 people the figure was 47 percent.[24]

Even in the "New Europe," industrial units remain smaller and for the most part spend less on R&D than their competitors in the United States. For example, General Motors produces at least 4 times as many vehicles as Volkswagon and 6 times more than Fiat. General Motors boasts an annual volume of business equal to that of the 17 largest West European firms. In fact, the sales of General Motors in 1964 were greater than the GNP of several European countries—Austria, Belgium, Denmark, or the Netherlands. Chrysler, the 3rd largest U.S. manufacturer of vehicles, builds more automobiles than all French competitors together. At peak production the output of the United States Steel, the leading U.S. producer, is about equal to that of all its German competitors combined. If U.S. and Common Market firms were ranked by annual volume of business for 1963, the largest German corporation would be in 27th place, while the largest Italian and French Companies would be 33rd and 57th respectively.[25] European realization of such disparities contributed to mergers within industries, especially in aircraft and computers. For the most part such mergers have taken place among firms within the same nation-state, rather than across national frontiers. There are disparities in the allocation of research which favor the United States. In addition to higher expenditures on R&D as a percentage of total industrial spending, a larger part of U.S. spending, as compared with Western Europe, is concentrated in the so-called research-intensive industries such as electronics and pharmaceuticals.[26] Although smaller U.S. firms have often registered major technological breakthroughs, the fact remains that most industrial research in the United States is conducted by large firms, i.e., those employing more than 5,000 persons. Seventy-one percent of the funds which such firms allocated to R&D were spent for programs of more than $100 million.[27]

Standardization and concentration among firms have gone further in the United States than in Europe. For example, in the field of avionics the United States has 2 firms which develop and build interceptor fire control radars; there are 4 such companies in Western Europe. Four U.S. firms build ground surveillance radar for air defense and traffic control; Western Europe has 8 suppliers of this product.[28] Such a division of effort reduces the opportunities for specialization in R&D and limits the capabilities of European firms for large scale production.

In short, disparities in research funds, governmental expenditures, laboratory facilities, educational systems, value systems, flexibility of factors of production, market size, firm size, communications, and mobility among government, industry, and university, have contributed to the Atlantic technological imbalance. Without further research it is not possible to rank these factors in order to specify the relative importance of each; but the interaction among these factors, it is feared in Europe, will increase the imbalance unless Western Europe somehow finds the means to counter them.[29] Such factors are said to have contributed to an Atlantic technological imbalance which has the following dimensions:

1. A social-economic imbalance related to disparities in the economic and social structures of Western Europe and North America;
2. A management imbalance as a result of differing management and business practices;
3. A foreign investment imbalance with large-scale U.S. direct investment in Western Europe and consequent European perceptions of U.S. dominance in the technologically advanced industries in Western Europe;
4. An education imbalance—with greater emphasis in the United States on mass education and training in applied science and business administration;
5. A "brain drain"—with the immigration of European scientific personnel to the United States as a result of higher salaries, superior laboratory facilities, and greater opportunity for advancement;
6. A research and development imbalance—with greater funds allocated to R&D in the United States, especially in the development of space and defense technologies.[30]

EUROPEAN TECHNOLOGICAL EFFORTS

European countries remain wedded essentially to a "national" approach to R&D. A comparison between European and U.S. national technological efforts is illustrative of the problems confronting individual European countries in their efforts to sustain programs of defense and of research and development more nearly comparable to those of the United States and the Soviet Union. Britain, for example, has encountered seemingly insurmountable difficulties in her attempt to maintain a modern aircraft industry and to develop delivery systems, such as the Blue Streak rocket, for her nuclear force. France, however, has set for herself the ambitious goal of narrowing the gap which separates her militarily and technologically from the superpowers. In an apparent effort to avoid excessive dependence upon the United States in a new field, the French space program includes the development of a rocket for the launching of telecommunication satellites. France launched her first satellite in the autumn of 1965.[31] Beyond the desire to reduce dependence upon the United States, the French hope to derive important technological advances from programs such as those necessary to place satellites into orbit and to build a nuclear capability. Although they remain dependent upon the United States for much of the advanced technology needed to complete their space and military programs, the French have increased substantially the number of modern facilities for research and development.[32]

European national programs in space research, including that of France, are miniscule by comparison with their U.S. counterparts. The French Government, for example, allocated only $57 million for space programs in 1965, an increase from a meagre $8 million in 1961.[33] The German Federal Republic has provided even fewer funds for space research. Government funds available for the Federal Republic's Boelkow program through 1968 were about $8 million, excluding booster and launcher costs, a sum scarcely sufficient to make possible a duplication of some of the simplest achievements of the United States and the Soviet Union, much less the development of a technology comparable to that of the United States.

As a result of her expenditures France is expected to have in the 1970's a military establishment which includes some of the most advanced aircraft, land-based ballistic missiles, a small naval force with at least one nuclear submarine equipped with intermediate-range missiles, and two aircraft carriers.[35] The existence of such a French nuclear force, its proponents suggest, would reduce the likelihood of a Soviet first strike. Yet the prospects for the French developing a force which would seriously cripple the Soviet Union will be diminished as a result of the Soviet deployment of anti-missile defense capabilities and the development of advanced offensive capabilities, including multimegaton warheads. Hence, in the 1970's the existence of an independent French nuclear force will not have a great effect upon the East-West strategic equation if France is unable to develop advanced technologies comparable to those which the United States will have acquired.

Especially in non-military fields, the formidable obstacles to purely national efforts have led European governments to place increasing emphasis upon technological collaboration within Europe. For example, Prime Minister Wilson announced in the House of Commons on February 2, 1965, that because of the heavy costs of research and development for modern aircraft "joint production rather than separate costly ventures must be the aim of the future." He also informed the Parliament that the Government was exploring "a number of possibilities of joint research and development with the United States and with the French and other continental partners." [36]

European firms can be expected to engage in greater collaboration in R&D, as well as in the production and marketing of the products of advanced technology. European governments perform the function of bringing together firms which are prospective collaborators in international projects. However, in its day-to-day aspects, collaboration takes place between companies, rather than governments. Over the next decade, detailed operational agreements between firms can be expected to increase, as European governments and industry attempt to enhance their competitive position vis-a-vis the United States.

Several European countries have established joint programs for the development of advanced aircraft. Among the most publicized is the Anglo-French supersonic airliner, the Concorde. If Western

Europe is to maintain an aircraft industry which is competitive with that of the United States and independent of U.S. control, projects which include two or more aircraft corporations in two or more countries must become the rule rather than the exception. Already several other collaborative ventures have been discussed or initiated: the building of a strike-trainer aircraft, an airbus, and helicopters. For the most part, major European transnational collaborative ventures in aircraft development have been confined to Britain and France. Nevertheless, even the combined industries of Britain and France, together with the markets and financial resources available to these two countries, will be inadequate. Great disparities will remain between the size of a combined Anglo-French aircraft industry and the U.S. aircraft industry. Only an industry based upon the resources of Britain and the Common Market Six would make it possible for Western Europe to retain a position of importance in the development and production of advanced aircraft.

The creation of a European aircraft industry presupposes the development of common procurement policies among European airlines, which would form one of the principal purchasers of aircraft in Europe's enlarged "domestic" market. Such a common policy presupposes as well the acceptance in Western Europe of the idea of interdependence in defense industries. European governments, and the United States, continue to view defense procurement primarily as a national undertaking. Weapons systems are developed to meet the military needs of the country in which they are built rather than for an export market. Such procurement policies are understandable, since the strategic doctrine of major Atlantic countries, especially France and the United States, provides for situations in which unilateral national military action would be taken. Nevertheless, the persistence of such policies increases the difficulty of achieving a "European" armaments industry.[37] Moreover, a decision by West European countries to develop and produce weapons systems such as military aircraft would make necessary a high level of agreement as to the strategic circumstances in which such weapons would be used, since Western Europe would provide, as in the case of commercial aircraft, the principal "domestic" market. In reaching accord upon the potential uses of such aircraft, the Europeans, in turn, would find it necessary to agree upon a range of foreign policy issues.

If European governments extend technological collaboration on the pattern of Concorde, it will become necessary to develop criteria based upon efficiency for the allocation of contracts to firms in participating countries. In the Concorde Project an effort was made to give each country 50 percent of the development and production work. There was duplication in assembly lines in Britain and France. Such factors, as well as the expense of administering a bilateral project, contributed to the increase in the cost of Concorde well beyond the original estimate.[38]

Over the past decade, other forms of technological collaboration, beyond agreements between corporate enterprises, have taken shape.[39] Programs in space research are illustrative of the new kinds of technological collaboration developed in Western Europe in recent years. The European Space Research Organization (ESRO) was formed, according to its Charter, "to establish European collaboration, exclusively for peaceful purposes, in the fields of space research."[40] In particular ESRO was to provide the framework for a European effort to design, develop, and construct rocket nose cones, satellites and space probes; a space data center for the analysis of the problems of estimating and analyzing orbits; telemetry and tele-command stations, and launching sites.

In 1962, the year of ESRO's formation, the European Space Vehicle Launcher Development Organization (ELDO) was established in London.[41] Its purpose, according to its Convention, was to enable member governments to "cooperate in the development of space vehicle launchers and to study their scientific and commercial application." The negotiations for ELDO resulted from a British proposal, in the Council of Europe in September 1960, for European collaboration in the development of the "Blue Streak" rocket (originally designed as a British strategic missile) as the launching vehicle for a joint European satellite. At that time, Britain sought to find an application for the Blue Streak rocket and to give evidence, on the occasion of her first Common Market application, of her commitment to European collaboration. Britain was to contribute the first stage of the rocket, France the second, and Germany the third. Italy was given the task of building the first of a series of experimental satellite test vehicles. Belgium was to provide down-range ground guidance stations. The Netherlands agreed to furnish long-range telemetry links, and

Australia was to make available its Woomera launching site for firings.

Even though ELDO possesses a Council in which decisions are taken by weighted majority voting and thus is more advanced institutionally than most other programs for European technological collaboration, it has experienced difficulties in achieving the necessary coordination of effort among participant nations, especially in meeting production deadlines. Moreover, the cost of launching a European satellite will be substantially in excess of original budgetary allocations. The cost of launching ELDO's first rocket rose at least $100 million above the original allocation of $200 million.[42] ELDO received from its member governments a budget of $196 million for its initial five-year program. This multinational scientific project came up for critical review and faced a major crisis in 1966 when it was recognized that costs would exceed original estimates, even though ELDO expenditures are small in comparison to those of the United States. The British Government, whose percentage contribution to ELDO was the highest of any member nation, was reluctant to bear the major cost of producing a launching vehicle, which would be obsolescent by the time it was completed.[43] In April 1968, the British government announced that Britain would not participate in any further development of an ELDO rocket after the fulfillment of her existing commitment in 1971. Nor was Britain willing to participate in a proposed experimental television relay satellite project under the auspices of the European Conference on Satellite Communications.[44] Britain was not prepared to help finance European space projects which appeared unlikely to offer a return commensurate with the British investment. Yet the abandonment of the ELDO project, it was acknowledged, would leave the United States as the only Western nation capable of developing a global tele-communications satellite system.[45]

In a European collaborative effort in technology, it would be necessary to attain levels of political, military, and economic integration which thus far have eluded Western Europe. Western Europe has no centralized institution comparable to the National Aeronautics and Space Administration, with its own budget and authority to modify projects and place contracts. Only a central authority would be capable of adopting a common European policy toward U.S. investment in Europe and allocating efficiently the expenditures needed for research and the development and production of advanced systems. In the absence of a "European" government, the organization directing a centralized effort for research and development would have to be endowed with some power of taxation. It would be necessary to plan and sustain expenditures over a period of several years and to develop joint European procurement programs in technologies in which a national market is clearly inadequate. The creation of an integrated European technological effort would be dependent upon European willingness to take the political decision to build institutions possessing considerably greater decision-making authority than is now found in the European Community.

The problems of ELDO and ESRO stem in large part from the lack of a broad research strategy for Western Europe. If the Europeans could reach agreement on the sectors of advanced technology upon which emphasis would be placed, the level of expenditure, and the allocation of research responsibilities, they could make more effective use of their resources. The problems of achieving agreement among separate national governments in Western Europe have led to delays in the completion of multinational projects such as ELDO. In the absence of a European research strategy, Western Europe faces the prospect of falling even further behind the United States in those areas of advanced technology where an Atlantic technological imbalance now exists. Last but not least, the shortcomings of ELDO and ESRO can be traced to the unwillingness of member governments to make available the the best of their R&D effort to a European organization. Instead, emphasis continues to be placed upon national or bilateral R&D, while European organizations often become the recipients of R&D which governments no longer deem it possible or important to conduct at the national level. France, for example, spends twice as much on her national space program as on ELDO and ESRO together. The persistence of nationalism, together with continuing inability to agree upon the level and the form of political integration, poses formidable obstacles to European collaborative programs for the development of advanced technologies. As a result, Western Europe finds itself unable to mount at either the national or the European level an effort sufficient to narrow the Atlantic technological imbalance.

MAJOR OBSTACLES TO ATLANTIC TECHNOLOGICAL COLLABORATION

If Western Europe represents a reservoir of scientific and technological potential, it is appropriate to inquire whether the United States should adopt policies which, if agreeable to its allies, might enable the West as a whole to develop more effectively its resources in science and technology. Could the United States make available to European allies certain forms of scientific knowledge which would enable them to avoid duplication in their research efforts? Would this policy allow even greater specialization in research undertaken in the North Atlantic area, conceivably producing even more spectacular advances in man's exploitation of science than would otherwise be possible?

The transfer of technologies from the United States to Western Europe by the sale of data and processes as an alternative to their development in Europe would produce, at least in the short run, an even greater dependence on U.S. technology—unless Europeans themselves made a greater effort to develop advanced technology.

In the absence of greater European R&D efforts, even the transfer of U.S. technology would not reduce substantially existing disparities, for the technological revolution is dynamic in nature. After the passage of a few years, technologies today become obsolescent. Thus the future position of Western Europe in those important fields of advanced technology where a gap exists will depend even more upon the efforts of Europeans themselves than upon the infusion of advanced technology from the United States.

In undertaking a program of technological collaboration with Western Europe, the United States would face problems of patents, licensing, and differing styles of business behavior. Many advanced technologies are the product of collaboration between the U.S. government and private industry. Other technologies have been produced largely by the efforts of U.S. corporations without large-scale governmental assistance. Holders of patents would not always be willing, even in view of a very favorable consideration, to transfer advanced technology to European firms which might become major competitors. For European industrialists, the fear would exist that U.S. firms would not be prepared to make available the most advanced technologies to potential, or actual, European competitors.

AVENUES TO TECHNOLOGICAL COLLABORATION

Advanced technologies developed in the United States have been, and can be, made available to Western Europe in a variety of ways. U.S. direct investment overseas represents an important avenue for technological transfer. Through professional contacts, the various national scientific communities have access to a common body of information. The essential question is whether and to what extent the United States should undertake to share advanced technologies with NATO allies. To answer these questions the United States and the potential recipients of its technology must determine whether it is best for each to go it alone as well as how a given U.S. technology might be transferred. The United States should regard its technological capabilities as a national asset acquired in large part through taxes levied upon the American people and through the investments which Americans have made in U.S. industry and education. Consequently, any proposal for sharing U.S. technology must be designed to advance U.S. and, more broadly, Western security and the general well-being of those nations and peoples who wish to associate themselves with us.

The question before the United States is the extent to which the economic and social conditions which have enabled this country to achieve such impressive technological advances are relevant to a larger geographic area such as the Atlantic Community. If Western Europe remains, as it is, a region possessed of scientific potential, the major problem confronting Europeans as well as the United States is the place of European science in a world paced by East-West competition in major fields of scientific endeavor. Even a political unit of the size of the United States may one day find it difficult to conduct the many kinds of research needed to exploit most effectively the potential of modern science. One day the United States may face problems not dissimilar from those which have plagued West European efforts to achieve scientific and technological breakthroughs. The manner in which the United States and Western Europe resolve the problems of advanced technology depends in no small measure upon the U.S. conception of Europe—as a partner of the United States or a subordinate member of the Atlantic Alliance—as well as upon European efforts to transcend the limitations imposed by the legacies of the past.

The solution chosen depends on the definition and analysis of the Atlantic technological imbalance. If the gap is considered a manifestation of general backwardness in European industry and education as well as of value systems which place less emphasis on acquisitiveness than U.S. value systems, then a set of solutions designed to overcome such deficiencies should be formulated. Although the United States has shown greater inclination to train large numbers of scientific manpower, has chosen to emphasize R&D and product innovation, and has proven able to develop huge corporate structures in a vast continental market, the fact remains that the Atlantic technological imbalance—according to the voluminous literature which it has brought forth—is most pronounced in space and other defense-related industries. Hence solutions to the imbalance should be directed to the strengthening of European R&D capabilities in these fields.

NOTES

1. Alexis de Tocqueville, *Democracy in America.* New York: Vintage Books, 1955, Vol. II, pp. 165-166. "The United States of America has only been emancipated for half a century from the state of colonial dependence in which it stood to Great Britain; the number of large fortunes there is small and capital is still scarce. Yet no people in the world have made such rapid progress in trade and manufactures as the Americans." See also H. J. Habakkuk, *American and British Technology in the Nineteenth Century.* New York: Cambridge University Press, 1962; Richard R. Nelson, *Big Technology, the Technology Gap, and a Dangerous Policy Pitfall.* RAND Corporation (March 1968), pp. 6-10.

2. In certain fields, however, Western Europe either leads the United States or has registered technological advances comparable to those of the United States. See Robert A. Charpie and Charles S. Shoup, Jr., *Comparative U.S. and European Achievements: Nuclear Energy, Metallurgy, Chemicals.* Paper prepared for Conference on Transatlantic Technological Imbalance and Collaboration, Deauville, France, May 25-28, 1967. According to the authors, there is no Atlantic technological imbalance in these three fields. "To be sure, there are variations in emphasis from field to field, but on the whole, the technological assets and competences of Western Europe are comparable to those of the United States in the nuclear, metallurgical, and chemical areas." p. 12.

3. *New York Times,* October 8, 1966, p. 12. This plan was first set forth at the NATO Council meeting in Brussels in June 1966.

4. *Ibid.*

5. *The Observer* (London), November 20, 1966.

6. Speech by Prime Minister Wilson at Lord Mayor's Banquet,

Guildhall, London, November 13, 1967. Text supplied by British Information Services, New York. A Conference on Atlantic Technological Imbalance, co-sponsored by the Foreign Policy Research Institute and the North Atlantic Assembly produced a similar proposal. The Conference, held in May 1967, in Deauville, France, brought together 40 European and 30 U.S.-Canadian participants from government, industry, scientific, and academic backgrounds.

7. See, for example, *The Observer* (London), July 18, 1965, p. 6.

8. Robert L. Pfaltzgraff, Jr., Chander T. Rajaratnam, and Thomas W. White, *Research and Development Expenditures: A Comparative Analysis.* Paper prepared for the Conference on Transatlantic Technological Imbalance and Collaboration, Deauville, France, May 25-28, 1967. See also OECD, *Reviews of National Science Policy: United States, Paris,* 1968, pp. 29-40.

9. *New York Times,* December 2, 1966, p. 22.

10. Antonie Knoppers, *American Investments in Europe: The Role of Science and Technology.* Paper prepared for Conference on Transatlantic Technological Imbalance and Collaboration, Deauville, France, May 25–28, 1967. Moreover, Knoppers contends: "Research in applied physics is even more U.S.-Government supported (85 percent). Here one begins to see the shape of things to come in the exciting newer developments in communications, satellites, integrated electronics circuitry (30 million electronic functions per cubic decimeter), optical systems (lasers, holography), utilization of solar energy, and in the field of signal detection and sensing so important for the seeing, hearing, feeling and counting of the future (important for all exact sciences)." p. 9.

11. See Richard B. Foster and Francis P. Hoeber, *The Technological Feedback from Defense R&D: The U.S. Institutional Framework.* Paper prepared for Conference on Atlantic Technological Imbalance and Collaboration, Deauville, France, May 25–28, 1967.

See also OECD, *Reviews of National Science Policy: United States,* Paris, 1968, pp. 257–262.

12. C. Freeman and A. Young, *The Research and Development Effort in Western Europe, North America, and the Soviet Union.* Paris: OECD, 1965, p. 53.

13. See OECD, *Reviews of National Science Policy: United States,* Paris, 1968, p. 327.

14. See the *Economist,* September 26, 1964, pp. 1251–1253.

15. Organization for Economic Cooperation and Development, *Resources of Scientific and Technical Personnel in the OECD Area.* Paris: OECD, 1963, pp. 214–215.

16. *Higher Education.* Report of the Committee appointed by the Prime Minister under the chairmanship of Lord Robbins, 1961–63, Cmnd. 2154. London: HMSO, 1965, pp. 126–146.

17. H. G. Grubel and A. D. Scott, "The Immigration of Scientists and Engineers to the United States, 1949–61." *Journal of Political Economy,* Vol. LXXIV, No. 4 (August 1966), p. 377.

18. Freeman and Young, *op. cit.*, pp. 57–59; 76.

19. Grubel and Scott, *op. cit.*, pp. 374, 377.

20. See Knoppers, *op. cit.*, pp. 4–6; Jean-Jacques Servan-Schreiber, *The American Challenge.* New York: Atheneum, 1968.

21. Calmann, *op. cit.*, p. 17.

22. *Report of the Committee of Inquiry into the aircraft industry appointed by the Minister of Aviation under the Chairmanship of Lord Plowden,* 1964–65. London: Her Majesty's Stationary Office, 1965. Cmnd. 2853, pp. 8–10. "In summary we can see that the United States is able, mainly because of the volume of her production, to overcome the disadvantage of high cost levels and produce aircraft on average for significantly less, excluding research and development costs, than they cost in the United Kingdom. She can secure a further cost advantage by having a greater volume of production over which to spread research and development expenditure. For the largest and most complex aircraft her advantage will tend to be higher still." Nevertheless, in 1968 Rolls Royce won a $240 million contract to produce engines for the American Lockheed Airbus. One of the biggest export orders ever won by British industry, the contract is expected to provide exports of British aircraft engines exceeding $2 billion by 1980. *Manchester Guardian Weekly,* April 4, 1968, p. 11.

23. *Ibid.*

24. OECD, *Ministers Talk Science* (Paris: 1965), p. 103. According to the General Manager, Defense Electronics Division, General Electric Company, one of the largest U.S. corporations:

"For large companies like General Electric, a broad technological base is essential. Tomorrow's products and services will be coming from research carried out today, and any major industrial organization, to compete effectively, must be willing to devote a healthy effort to new technology and reasonable risk-taking. An example of this situation is the fact that half of General Electric's $5 billion worth of business today is estimated to come from new products introduced since World War II." Gerald A. Hoyt, "Industrial Strength and National Security: The Management of Change." *The General Electric Forum,* July-September 1965, p. 23.

25. See OECD *Reviews of National Science Policy: United States.* Paris, 1968, p. 324. "Out of the 460 international companies surveyed by the review *Fortune* for 1965 with a turnover of more than $250 million, 60 percent are American."

26. See OECD, Committee for Science Policy, *General Report on Technological Gaps between Member Countries.* Paris, 1968.

27. OECD, *Reviews of National Science Policy: United States,* pp. 268–269. "In 1964, 3 percent of firms doing R&D spent 87 percent of total R&D expenditure. Within this group, consisting of 419 firms, 111 had research programmes of more than $10 million each, the total of which represented 80 percent of industrial research and development expenditure."

28. See Philip J. Klass, "European Defense Efforts Mold Future of

Avionics." *Aviation Week and Space Technology*. June 25, 1965, p. 109.

29. See *Report of the Conference on Transatlantic Technological Imbalance,* Deauville, France, May 25–28, 1967, p. 7.

30. For an analysis of literature on the Atlantic technological imbalance, see Theodore Suranyi-Unger, Jr., "What Is the Technology Gap?" *Interplay,* Vol. 2, No. 1 (June-July 1968), pp. 22–25.

31. For a review of the French national space program, see *The French Space Program: Past, Present and Future Projects*. New York: Ambassade de France, 1966.

32. Roy Battersby. "French Eyes on the Future." *Listener,* July 1, 1965, pp. 5–7. Reprinted in *Survival,* September 1965, pp. 219–223. For an examination of the French scientific and technological program, see also *L'Industrie Aéronautique et Spatial* (Paris: Union Syndicale des Industries Aéronautiques et Spatiales: 1965); Ambassade de France Service de Presse et d'Information, *The French Space Program: Past, Present and Future Projects*. April 1966.

33. *The French Space Program. Op. cit.,* p. 3.

34. "R&D, Missile Efforts are Keys to Boelkow's Major German Space Role," *Aviation Week,* September 30, 1963, p. 58.

35. Pierre Messmer, "The French Military Establishment of Tomorrow." ORBIS (Summer 1962), pp. 205–216. Judith H. Young, "The French Strategic Missile Program." *Adelphi Papers,* No. 38 (July 1967).

36. See British Information Services, *British Record,* February 18, 1965, No. 4, pp. 3–4.

37. Calmann, *op. cit.,* p. 7.

38. *Ibid.,* pp. 7–8. According to Calmann: "Little attempt has been made to encourage those firms in either country which can put forward the lowest tenders, or to regard the two countries as one market. Instead, contracts have been largely awarded on the basis of filling up each country's quota. Cost control has proved exceptionally difficult; it is conducted by an intergovernmental management committee which leaves each government to deal directly with the firms in its own country. This means that there is no single agency to manage the project from the government point of view and, according to the severest critics, that firms are running the project just as they please."

39. The European organizations for technological collaboration created in Europe include the European Organization for Nuclear Research (CERN), Euratom, The European Nuclear Energy Agency (ENEA), the European Space Research Organization (ESRO), and the collateral European Launcher Development Organization (ELDO).

40. ESRO's members include Belgium, Denmark, France, Germany, Italy, the Netherlands, Spain, Sweden, Switzerland, and the United Kingdom.

41. The members of the ELDO include Australia, Belgium, France, the German Federal Republic, Italy, the Netherlands, and the United Kingdom.

42. See *Christian Science Monitor,* June 1, 1965, February 21, 1965.

43. See Great Britain, *The European Space Vehicle Launcher Development Organization (ELDO).* Second Report from the Estimates Committee, Session 1966–67. Ordered by the House of Commons to be printed 8th August 1966. London: Her Majesty's Stationary Office, 1966. See also, *CECLES-ELDO, 1960–1965: Report to the Council of Europe 1965.* Paris: CECLES-ELDO, 1965.

44. *Manchester Guardian Weekly,* April 18, 1968.

45. See Assembly of Western European Union Twelfth Ordinary Session (First Part), *State of European Space Activities: The ELDO Crisis.* Document 371. 23 May 1966.

IV. Atlantic Economic Relationships

THE ECONOMIC POLICIES WHICH ATLANTIC COUNTRIES ADOPTED IN the post-war period contributed decisively to European recovery and to the building of the "new Europe." During the past decade, however, Atlantic countries, especially the United States and Britain, and more recently, France, have faced formidable domestic economic problems. Moreover, a series of intra-Atlantic problems have arisen. They include the lowering of barriers to trade among Atlantic countries, the flow of investment across national frontiers, especially U.S. investment in Western Europe, and the achievement of balance of payments equilibrium. Such problems result from growing economic interdependence among industrial countries, which makes more difficult the pursuit of specifically national economic objectives.[1] Other economic problems facing Atlantic countries affect even more directly the international economic system: the expansion of trade, the flow of aid to less developed areas, and the reform of the international monetary system. Problems related to trade, balance of payments, investments, and international liquidity have contributed to U.S.-West European tensions. Despite the emergence of an economically strengthened "new Europe," a series of imbalances in the economic sector favoring the United States contribute to West European apprehension about U.S. hegemony. But in economics, Western Europe has achieved a high level of economic integration and enjoys a position of strength not present in military or technological affairs. This fact, together with European misgivings about U.S. economic policies, has deepened the Atlantic cleavage in the economic sector.

ATLANTIC TRADING RELATIONSHIPS

About one-fifth of U.S. exports find markets in the EEC.[2] The Common Market conducts about 12 percent of its trade with the United States. Together, the United States, Britain, and the EEC constitute the major suppliers of goods to less developed countries, as well as the principal markets for their exports. Hence the future of trading relationships throughout the Free World depends to a considerable extent upon the freeing of trade within the North Atlantic area.

In May 1967, the representatives of 53 nations, accounting for about 80 percent of world trade, reached agreement in Geneva on tariff reductions. In the so-called Kennedy Round, the product of tariff-cutting authority granted to the President by the U.S. Congress in the Trade Expansion Act of 1962, the major parties were the United States and the Common Market Six, together with 2 other important industrial and trading nations, Britain and Japan. The negotiators overcame formidable problems, which included the lowering of EEC restrictions on imports of agricultural products, the reduction of U.S. tariffs on certain industrial products, especially chemicals, the liberalization of British tariffs on steel, and the achievement of agreement among industrialized countries for a food aid program for less developed coutnries, many of which face the prospect of severe agricultural shortages. In each of these broad categories of issues, the Kennedy Round registered a measure of success.

The outcome of the Geneva Trade Negotiations is important for several reasons. Failure of the negotiations would have represented a setback of considerable proportions to the movement toward the liberalization of international trade. Moreover, failure would have strengthened doubts both in Europe and the United States about the existence of a community of interest in the North Atlantic area, for the Trade Expansion Act represented the first major step of the Kennedy Administration toward the creation of an Atlantic partnership. In addition to having a potentially beneficial effect psychologically upon U.S.-European relations, the successful outcome of the negotiations will result in important tariff cuts totaling at least $40 billion dollars on at least 60,000 products. In the United States alone, tariffs will be lowered on some 6,300 products, accounting for more than $15 billion in trade.

Between the United States and the Common Market Six, the future of agricultural trade, as well as of trade in certain industrial products, including chemicals, provided formidable problems for the negotiators in Geneva. The Common Market Six have seen their interest as lying in the reduction of imports which compete with EEC farm production. Since together the Common Market Six have had a trade deficit with the United States, a reduction in agricultural imports, other factors remaining constant, would result in a narrowing of this imbalance since the EEC is a large importer of U.S. farm products. For the United States, however, there is an interest in retaining stable and even expanding outlets for U.S. agriculture not only because of the importance of European markets to U.S. farmers, but because of the need to narrow the U.S. balance of payments deficit. Although the formation of the Common Market is estimated to have resulted in the annual loss of about $200 million in U.S. export sales of farm products,[3] U.S. agricultural exports annually to the EEC in recent years have exceeded one billion dollars, more than 20 percent of total U.S. sales of farm products overseas. In agriculture, which accounts for about one-third of total U.S. exports to the Common Market,[4] the United States and the EEC do not share common interests. The formation of the Common Market has led to the creation of a European agricultural policy which, in most respects, does not accord with U.S. interests. In the agricultural sector, Western Europe has narrowed whatever imbalance it once had with the United States. The EEC provides a framework for the expansion of European agriculture, especially French agriculture, and the substitution of high-cost European farm products for lower-cost U.S. farm products.

The existence of the Common Market has helped to accelerate trends already under way in West European agriculture. As a result of population growth and rising incomes, food consumption in Western Europe has risen steadily in recent years. Since 1950 the net imports of agricultural commodities into the EEC have increased, but on a lower scale than the growth of consumption. European farmers, spurred by modernization, are increasing output rapidly. By 1962, the Common Market had become about 96 percent self-sufficient in agricultural production.[5]

The EEC has already become, or is expected to become, largely self-sufficient in certain agricultural products, including bread grains, potatoes, butter, sugar, eggs, and cheese. Rising per capita income has led to a decline in demand for bread grains, since persons with higher incomes tend to substitute other foods. This trend, together with increasing wheat production, made it possible for the EEC to achieve self-sufficiency in wheat in 1963-64 and even a surplus in 1964-65.[6] Although two other important U.S. farm exports to Western Europe, coarse grains (animal feed) and high quality meats, will continue to enjoy substantial and perhaps even expanding markets as a result of rising income levels, the markets for certain U.S. farm exports can be expected to decline as a result of increasing production in Western Europe as well as the farm policy of EEC. Although the United States scored greater gains during the Kennedy Round in the lowering of tariffs on industrial products, the agreement on agriculture represented a major breakthrough in international trade accords. For the first time, agriculture, one of the most highly protected industries, was the object of an international trade agreement. Accord was reached on world price levels for wheat as the result of a compromise between wheat-importing countries such as Britain and Japan and exporters such as Australia and Canada. The price upon which agreement was reached is about 20 percent higher than that at which the wheat in question is shipped from the United States. The extent to which U.S. producers of grain will derive gains from this agreement will depend upon the success of European efforts to increase EEC feed grain production. Given the interest of the Common Market in boosting agricultural output, especially grain, the agreement on agriculture may have greater symbolic than monetary value for the United States. Viewed from the standpoint of world food needs, however, the increase in West European agricultural output, together with the continuing U.S. need for overseas markets in farm goods, may present the North Atlantic countries with a new opportunity for collaborative action.

While the United States sought during the Kennedy Round to reduce the protectionist features of the EEC agricultural policy, the Common Market Six had as a major objective to achieve a lowering of U.S. tariff levels in industrial products, especially chemicals. Of particular concern to European negotiators was the valuation of certain chemical products for the purpose of calculating tariffs upon the basis of what is known as the American Selling Price.[7] Instead of basing the tariff upon the price of a product in the country where it is produced, the tariff is calculated upon the substantially higher price of a competing product in the United States. The Six sought to induce the United States to abandon this procedure for tariff valuation. U.S. trade negotiators had no authority to negotiate to remove the American Selling Price, since this procedure for valuation was established by the U.S. Congress. Nevertheless, subject to Congressional approval, the United States agreed to reduce tariffs on chemicals by 50 percent in return for a reduction of 20 percent in similar products by the Common Market. The EEC agreed to lower chemical tariffs by an additional 30 percent, thus matching U.S. reductions, in return for U.S. repeal of the American Selling Price valuation procedure. This agreement, together with the accords on agriculture, contributed considerably to the successful outcome of the Kennedy Round. In fact, it is unlikely that the Six would have been prepared to make concessions in agricultural trade had the United States not been willing to lower tariff restrictions on imports of chemicals.

When the Kennedy Round reductions are put into effect, the levels of tariffs will be such as to render the tariff considerably less important than it once was as a means of restricting the flow of trade on a wide range of products of major importance in international commerce. Provided governments do not enact other restrictive measures such as quotas,[8] the chief remaining obstacles to increased trade in many industrial goods will be such non-tariff barriers as border taxes, import licensing requirements, quotas, exchange control, sanitary and health regulations, and road taxes imposed by certain countries upon imports of vehicles. There were European objections, for example, to the U.S. refusal to sign the Brussels Convention of 1950, which defined customs value and outlined uniform methods and principles for duty assessment. Trade with the United States was said to be restricted by the existence of a series of complicated headings ascribed to products by varying rates of duty and by differences in the assessment of customs values. U.S. anti-dumping legislation, despite liberalization, was alleged to hamper trade by placing an additional duty on goods (based on the difference between the original price and the import price) at a time when the U.S. Treasury Department declares that "dumping" exists. Moreover, it was claimed that U.S. customs law is in violation of GATT provisions in allowing duties to be charged on products subsidized by private organizations in exporting nations and on products which constitute no "serious" damage to U.S. industry.

Objections were raised against the "buy American" policy of the U.S. Government, which gives American firms preference over foreign competition for government purchases if the cost is no more than 6 to 12 percent higher than for the same product made by a foreign company. The only condition U.S. firms must meet is the use of American raw materials equivalent to at least 50 percent of the total cost. This policy, hitherto covering only materials bought in the United States, was extended to governmental purchases abroad when President Kennedy ordered the purchase of U.S. goods for U.S. installations so long as they were available, as a means of reducing the balance of payments deficit. The EEC suggested that such a policy is equivalent, in some cases, to a duty on imported goods.[9]

For its part, the United States called attention to certain European practices which restrict trade. U.S. exporters of numerous commodities (e.g., agricultural products, oil, coal, radio and telephone sets, electric lights) have sometimes found themselves faced with quota restrictions. Criticism was raised against the general secrecy which shrouds the conclusion of many contracts—public and private—in Europe. European tax systems, particularly the turnover, value added, and automobile taxes, provide another issue of contention. For example, European taxes based upon cylinder capacity rather than price have restricted the market in Europe for U.S. exports of automobiles. Health regulations in some European countries provide formidable barriers to trade in agricultural products, such as chickens and citrus fruits.[10] Cumbersome customs procedures and restrictive practices in the granting of import licenses constitute other non-tariff impediments to the flow of international trade.

The greatest part of U.S. industrial exports to the EEC consists of machinery, vehicles, and chemicals. The growth of these categories of exports has been rapid; they more than doubled between 1958 and 1963. Because the United States is in the forefront of the development of advanced technologies, markets in Western Europe are assured for U.S. producers of a variety of new products, even though European interest may increase in erecting barriers to protect European producers of certain advanced technologies such as computers and aircraft from U.S. competition. European efforts to acquire advanced technologies through the purchase of U.S. equipment will lead to a further expansion in overseas markets for the United States. Thus U.S. trade with Western Europe is likely to consist increasingly of the sophisticated products of advanced technology. While the United States is naturally anxious to preserve European markets for its exports of agriculture, the prospects for the expansion of trade in industrial goods give the United States, over the long run, an even greater interest in achieving a substantial lowering of remaining barriers to trade in industrial goods than in pressing for the preservation of markets in agriculture, however difficult may be the process of adjustment for certain segments of the U.S. farming community. Although Western Europe has freed itself from large-scale dependence upon the United States in agriculture, its dependence in advanced technologies is likely to remain substantial even in the event that a European technological community is formed.

The United States faces another obstacle in its efforts to achieve agreement with the EEC on the future of trade in the North Atlantic area. For many years the United States has enjoyed a trade surplus with the Common Market. In the period between 1958 and 1965, U.S. exports to the EEC nearly doubled, rising from an annual average of $2.4 billion to $4.6 billion. During the same period U.S. imports from the EEC rose from $2.1 billion to $3.1 billion, an increase of about one-third.[11] U.S. exports to the Common Market have risen more rapidly than EEC exports to the United States. If the United States continued to increase its markets in Western Europe, all other factors remaining constant, its balance of payments deficit would be reduced. Given the European reaction to increasing dependence upon the United States, however, new U.S. inroads into European markets, especially in the products of advanced technologies in electronics, aircraft, and communications systems, will arouse concern.

With the completion of the Kennedy Round negotiations, attention turned to possible future steps toward trade liberalization. It is widely recognized that international trade is hampered by nontariff barriers including certain health regulations on food imports, the valuation of imports on the basis of the American selling price rather than the price in the country of origin, "buy American" or "French" policies, and taxes based on criteria such as weight in the case of U.S. automobile exports which discriminate against foreign products. Such trade impediments are likely to be the object of negotiations among the governments which negotiated the Kennedy Round.

Even before the end of the Kennedy Round, the idea of an Atlantic free trade area attracted attention in the United States, Canada, and Britain. In 1965 Senator Javits proposed that the United

States consider formation of a free trade area initially with Britain, to be extended to include Canada and other EFTA countries. Later, a private British group, called Maxwell Stamp Associates, proposed a North Atlantic Free Trade Area (NAFTA).[12] In addition to the United States, Canada, Britain, and other EFTA countries, NAFTA would be open to other industrially advanced nations. Less developed countries would be given freedom of entry into the markets of industrially advanced members without equivalent concessions.

The NAFTA proposal provided an alternative to British membership in the Common Market. In fact, the idea of Atlantic free trade was attractive to not a few opponents of British EEC entry. But given the opposition manifested in Europe to U.S. hegemony, the prospects for British entry into the Common Market would have been dimmed by British membership in NAFTA. Although the proponents of NAFTA saw Britain as benefiting from a new infusion of U.S. technology and British industry gaining access to a vast new market, Britain would have foregone the option of adding her weight to that of the EEC as a counterpoise to the United States in an Atlantic partnership. Many of the fears expressed in recent years about U.S. technological, financial, and economic hegemony might have been reinforced as a result of an Atlantic free trade area.

In all likelihood NAFTA would have contributed to a deepening of the cleavage with France and to the accentuation of disparities between continental Europe and the "Anglo-Saxon" powers. Nevertheless, the free trade area idea, which attracted support in the 1950's, continues to hold salience as a device for increasing the flow of international commerce.

RELATIONS WITH THE LESS DEVELOPED COUNTRIES

Over the past generation, trade among Atlantic countries has increased at a more rapid rate than has trade between the more advanced and less developed areas of the world. The future development of many countries outside the North Atlantic area is related to their ability to achieve higher levels of trade. Unless developing nations can increase exports to industrialized countries, they will be unable to acquire the foreign exchange to finance imports for economic programs. Hence the policies which the countries of the North Atlantic area adopt, separately or in collaboration, toward them will affect their capacity to undertake successfully the formidable tasks of economic modernization and political development. Efforts of industrialized countries to reduce trade barriers are of considerable importance to the economic future of less developed nations.

The United Nations Conferences on Trade and Development (UNCTAD), held in Geneva in 1964 and in New Delhi in 1968, addressed themselves in detail to the question of trade between the industrialized and less developed countries. At the 1964 conference, there was general agreement that "no new tariff barriers should be created (or existing barriers increased) by developed countries against imports of primary products of particular interest to developing countries." Moreover, it was suggested, the industrialized countries should "substantially reduce, and where possible eliminate, customs charges on primary products." The 1968 UNCTAD Conference produced agreement on the stabilization of world market prices in rubber and hard fibers, cocoa and sugar. There was unanimous agreement in favor of the early achievement of generalized, non-reciprocal tariff preferences for less developed countries. Western industrialized nations endorsed a recommendation that economically advanced countries should allocate at least one percent of their GNP for aid to less developed countries.

In all likelihood, future trade negotiations will be focused upon the increase of commerce between the industrialized nations and the less developed countries. Yet it is doubtful that even the granting of tariff preferences by industrialized countries for imports from less developed countries, as has been proposed, can reverse the trend.[13] Nevertheless, the establishment of such preferences would at least reduce the decline in trade between developed and less developed countries and provide additional foreign exchange for economic modernization.

One of the most remarkable developments of the postwar period was the growing recognition by industrialized nations of a responsibility for assisting other countries in their economic advancement. It is difficult to measure the impact of foreign aid programs. Undoubtedly, their effectiveness varies as a result of many factors, including the sectors of the economy emphasized, the capabilities of recipients to utilize aid, and the quality of the donor country's administrative facilities. The aid programs of North Atlantic countries have remained but a small percentage of their GNP. As Table III illustrates, the flow of official and private capital from France to overseas countries, although it declined from 1.6 in 1963 to

TABLE III

Total Aid Official and Private Capital Flow to Less Developed Countries and Multilateral Agencies, and GNP during 1963 and 1965—Selected Atlantic Countries

Country	Aid In Millions of Dollars		GNP in Millions of Dollars		Aid as a percent of GNP	
	1963	1965	1963	1965	1963	1965
1. Belgium	184.0	238.7	13,610	16,860	1.35	1.41
2. Canada	130.5	153.0	39,781	48,180	0.32	0.31
3. Denmark	10.5	31.8	7,864	9,990	0.13	0.31
4. France	1,264.6	1,318.6	78,572	94,150	1.6	1.4
5. Germany	589.0	705.3	94,200	112,380	0.62	0.62
6. Italy	343.2	277.2	44,791	56,760	0.76	0.48
7. Netherlands	147.2	224.3	14,257	19,070	1.03	1.17
8. Norway	28.7	38.2	5,525	7,000	0.51	0.54
9. Portugal	51.1	30.7	2,905	3,860	1.75	0.79
10. U.K.	694.6	923.1	83,200	99,040	0.83	0.93
11. U.S.A.	4,635.0	5,478.2	586,445	692,300	0.79	0.79

Sources:
1. Development Assistance Efforts and Policies, 1964 Review, OECD, Statistical Annex, Table 1, p. 147.
2. Bernard Mueller, *A Statistical Handbook of the North Atlantic Area,* New York: Twentieth Century Fund, 1965, pp. 70-71.
3. *OECD Observer,* February 1967.

1.4 percent of France's GNP in 1965, was the highest of any North Atlantic country, with the exception of Portugal. In the case of six countries (Belgium, Denmark, the Netherlands, Norway, Portugal, and the United Kingdom), the percentage of GNP devoted to governmental and private capital flow to less developed countries increased between 1963 and 1965. The remaining countries, which include, except for Britain, all major North Atlantic nations, registered either constant or declining governmental and private capital flow to less developed areas, measured as a percentage of GNP.

It is unlikely that many North Atlantic countries will be prepared to continue to bear even their existing share of assistance to less developed areas. The reduction of European political influence outside the North Atlantic area may produce a diminution in European interest in maintaining aid programs. Pressures for increased emphasis on domestic anti-poverty programs in the United States and demands upon the French government for the allocation of greater financial resources to economic advancement in France can be expected to reduce still further the funds available for foreign aid. Dissatisfaction with aid programs has already risen in Western Europe, especially in France and Germany, and in the United States. Some European governments have drawn up plans for economic modernization in backward regions of their own countries which may compete with less developed nations outside Europe for aid funds. In the years ahead, foreign aid programs may be displaced by domestic economic programs, especially if countries in Western Europe continue to become preoccupied with exclusively European concerns.

In the examination of problems of trade and development, the OECD has provided a forum of considerable importance. Under OECD auspices, studies of trade, aid, and development have been undertaken. The Development Assistance Committee (DAC) of OECD has furnished a device for the joint examination of the national aid policies of its members and for the study of long-term assistance needs of developing areas.

As a result of DAC, member countries have gained a better understanding of each other's national aid programs. The DAC has had the task of increasing the flow of financial and technical assistance to developing areas and achieving agreement among donor countries on terms less burdensome to recipients. There is need for the DAC to play a more active role in the coordination of respective Western aid programs within individual recipient countries, especially in cases where the political and economic objectives of Western donor nations are not in harmony.[14]

In the resolution of food problems facing less developed countries, the need for collaborative action among Atlantic nations is likely to become urgent. Many developing countries face food shortages—a so-called "food gap"—which can be expected to increase over the next decade. Although less developed countries generally have registered increases in total food production, population growth has proceeded at an even more rapid rate. For example, both Latin America and Western Europe, over the past decade, have expanded food production at rates between 2.5 and 3.0 percent annually. In Western Europe, however, population has increased at the rate of about one percent a year. In contrast, in Latin America population has risen at the rate of nearly 3 percent per year. While in Western Europe the ratio of population growth to farm output has led to agricultural surpluses, in Latin America per capita agricultural output as a whole has not increased. The Latin American experience is illustrative of the food gap which faces other less developed regions.[15]

During the 1960's world food production has only kept pace with increases in population. As a result of rising incomes in developed countries, the demand for and the price of many basic agricultural commodities, such as wheat and rice, have increased. Countries with greater purchasing power have raised their per capita consumption of foodstuffs. In contrast, less developed countries with rising populations in many cases have been hard pressed even to maintain existing levels of consumption, let alone increase their caloric intake. This general trend, together with such natural calamities as drought in India in 1966 and 1967, have contributed to food shortages.

Over the next decade the food gap is likely to increase to such proportions that many less developed countries may face famine. Even if it increases substantially its acreage devoted to farming, the United States is not likely to have food surpluses adequate to eliminate the food gap.[16] Hence among those countries with agricultural surpluses the need for collaboration in the development of food aid programs will become urgent.

In recognition of this prospect, the Kennedy Round negotiators in Geneva reached agreement on a food aid program to less developed countries which would make available from the commercial market about five million tons of wheat. The financial burden of the program, whose value is estimated to total $350 million, is to be shared by major industrialized countries, including the United States, the Common Market Six, and Japan. Although this program will hardly prove adequate to close the food gap, it may provide at least the framework for greater collaboration among industrialized and food-surplus countries.

In addition to a major effort to make agricultural products available to countries experiencing food shortages, the long range solution to the food gap lies in the adoption of measures to increase agricultural output in less developed areas. Both Western Europe and the United States, together with other major world food producing countries, have a fund of expertise in advanced farming technology which could be made available to less advantaged countries. Clearly, there exists the basis for collaboration among advanced agricultural countries, many of which are North Atlantic countries, in a two-pronged effort to eliminate the food gap through making available agricultural surplus and increasing farm production in less developed areas.

U.S. INVESTMENT PATTERNS

In the last generation Western Europe has become increasingly important to U.S. investors, and, as a result, the United States has developed important new links with Western Europe. The formation of the Common Market, together with the high levels of economic growth attained by European countries, attracted the interest of U.S. industry and, in many cases, afforded impressive new opportunities for expansion overseas.[17] However, U.S investment patterns have contributed to European apprehension that economic and even political decisions of great importance to Western Europe will be taken by Americans, rather than Europeans.

The factors that contribute to the decision of a U.S. firm to establish itself in Western Europe in one form or another are numerous. One consideration is the level of protection—tariff and non-tariff—which a country or a customs union affords its own industry. Hence the ability of the United States and the Six to reach accord on the freeing of transatlantic trade will influence U.S. businessmen in deciding whether to make a direct investment in Western Europe or to focus upon an expansion of exports to European markets from the United States. However, U.S. businessmen for other reasons as well have stepped up their investment in Western Europe.

Possibilities for high profit margins and European demands for capital, especially in the 1950's, provided considerable incentive to U.S. investors. In the 1960's, moreover, investment in many sectors of European industry remained profitable. U.S. companies, in many cases, saw in Western Europe the opportunity to invest profits accumulated from the long period of economic expansion which the United States has experienced over the last generation. For U.S. industry the formation of the EEC provided an additional stimulus to investment. An American exporter who before the formation of the Common Market was able to compete with a French product exported to Germany may be faced with a higher EEC tariff. This fact, in turn, may contribute to a decision to establish a plant in Germany. But the creation of the EEC furnishes yet another incentive: by establishing a factory in Germany, an American industrialist has access to the larger market of the EEC. Within this market, he may achieve lower unit costs of production and economies which were not previously available in Western Europe. In the five-year period before the formation of the EEC, U.S. investment in the Six increased at an annual rate of 16 percent, but rose to an annual rate of 18.5 percent in the seven subsequent years.[18]

As a result, U.S. companies, to an extent unparalleled in their history, have taken an interest in overseas markets, especially in Western Europe. American corporations are without counterpart in establishing "European" production facilities; whereas German and French firms have generally lagged behind their U.S. competitors in recognizing the need for and the benefits which may accrue from the establishment of corporate activities across national frontiers within the Common Market. American firms, accustomed to production in the United States, with its differing state corporate regulations and sales within the huge domestic American market, have often had a built-in advantage vis-à-vis their more tradition-bound European competitors, oriented as they are toward sales and operation within a smaller domestic market.

There is a remarkable balance between U.S. investment in Western Europe and West European investment in the United States. At the end of 1964, European investment totalled $17.7 billion compared with U.S. long-term private investments of $17.5 billion in Western Europe.[19] However, U.S. and European investments differ in composition. For the most part Europeans have purchased American securities and bonds ($10.8 billion), rather than made direct investments ($5.8 billion). But Americans have more sizable direct investment in European industry ($12.1). It is in direct investment that an Atlantic imbalance which favors the United States has developed.

The growth of U.S. direct investment in Western Europe has given rise to charges of American economic "hegemony" as a result of the influence which U.S. affiliates are sometimes alleged to have upon the economies of European countries. Although U.S. investment accounts for only 6 percent of total investment in the EEC, it is by far the largest single component of foreign investment in Western Europe. U.S. capital is established in key fields such as petroleum, chemicals, electronics, and automobiles.[20] It is heavily concentrated in many of the newest and most rapidly growing industries. Through direct investment in new enterprise in Western Europe or the purchase of older European firms, U.S. corporations have gained a dominant position in several fields. As in the case of the technological imbalance, the rapid influx of U.S. investment appears menacing to Europeans who wish to retain European control over major sectors of their economies. U.S. investment in Western Europe provides one means for the transfer of advanced technology, but at the cost of subordinating some of the most important growth and "glamor" industries to U.S. domination.

The financial strength of U.S. corporations, in comparison with their European competitors, produces concern in Western Europe. Not only do American corporations often possess superior financial resources. In many cases, they are able to borrow on terms more advantageous than those granted to European firms. Banks in Western Europe, it has been alleged, lend to U.S. corporations operating in Europe more readily than to European enterprise because of the greater strength of the American firms, and hence the lower risk. Because of its program to reduce its payments deficit, the United States encouraged U.S. corporations operating in Europe to borrow abroad rather than in the United States. This reduced the amount of capital available to European corporations and increased the cost of borrowing money for expansion and modernization. In 1966 alone, U.S. corporations borrowed $600 million in Europe to finance U.S. direct investment there. U.S. corporations have greater access to the U.S. capital market, with its generally lower interest rates than are available in Western Europe. By contrast, European corporations, if they are able to borrow in the United States, are subject to an interest equalization tax. Moreover, the influx of U.S. managerial practices, marketing techniques, advertising methods, and new products has sometimes had an unsettling effect upon European industries accustomed to older ways of conducting business. Not unexpectedly, therefore, U.S. investors have become the object of European criticism. Restrictions on U.S. overseas investment, such as those announced by the U.S. government in January 1968, will have the effect of increasing the efforts of U.S. corporations to borrow capital in Europe.[21] Rising European interest rates, together with the need for European corporations to compete for capital, may increase resentment in Western Europe against U.S. corporate investors.

U.S. investment has made a major contribution to European economic modernization. The presence of U.S. industry in Western Europe has provided an important source of technological innovation. Through direct investment as well as licensing agreements, industrial processes pioneered or perfected in the United States have been made available to Western Europe. U.S. firms have introduced new technologies as well as products and marketing previously confined to the United States. In short, industry provides an important avenue for transatlantic technological collaboration.

In many cases U.S. direct investment in Western Europe has led to marked increases in productivity, in growth of mass markets, in jettisoning of restrictive practices in trade unions, and in the creation of new, increasing income levels in some of the industrially backward regions of Western Europe, such as the northeast of Britain, the lower Rhone Valley in France, southern Italy, and the coal region in Belgium. U.S. industry has been less bound by geography than European firms, since it has lacked a corporate base in any one European country. Such factors have enabled U.S. industry to move from one part of Europe to another in response to profit potential and to establish itself in several countries. In fact, the most "European" firms in Europe are for the most part those controlled by U.S. investors, for Americans have been more accustomed than Europeans to operating in a market of larger dimensions than that provided by any single nation-state of Western Europe. Moreover, in establishing manufacturing facilities in Western Europe, U.S. corporations, in contrast to European competitors, have not been bound by an industrial structure or business practices designed specifically for a European national market.

U.S. capital has contributed to the development and growth of some of the most dynamic sectors of industry in Western Europe. In Britain's vital export industries, for example, sales abroad of companies which are affiliated with U.S. firms rose by an estimated 65 percent in 1964, while British exports as a whole increased by a modest 4 percent.[22] To a considerable extent this startling contrast reflects the fact that U.S. investors in recent years have invested heavily not only in growth sectors, but in industries which have registered rising exports. Even without the influx of U.S. capital, such industries would have contributed to a rise in British exports, although the increase would have been less without the advanced technology and managerial concepts which often accompany U.S. investment. In short, some, but by no means all, of the stimulus to export industries in Europe can be credited to U.S. investment.

Although the impact of investment overseas upon the U.S. balance of payments is not easily determined, the United States has been the object of European criticism for having permitted large-scale U.S. investment in Western Europe at the cost of balance of payments deficits.[23] Ultimately, the return flow of capital to the United States generated by foreign investment may be expected to exceed the outflow. In the short term, U.S. investment abroad may contribute to a payments deficit, while in the long run it may lead to a payments surplus.[24] Moreover, the flow of funds from the United States to other countries has contributed to an increase in U.S. exports. Almost one-fourth of U.S. exports in 1963 were shipped to U.S. subsidiaries in other countries.[25] Undoubtedly, overseas investment contributes to foreign demand for exports from U.S. industries which themselves have not placed capital abroad. In many cases, U.S. companies have received substantial licensing fees from foreign firms for products and processes produced abroad. Finally, profits generated from large-scale U.S. investment in Western Europe may be returned to the United States, if they are not re-invested overseas. U.S. tax policy, however, has encouraged corporations to reinvest earnings abroad, since earnings are not taxed in the United States until they are returned to this country.

TRENDS IN THE U.S. BALANCE OF PAYMENTS

Despite the impressive growth of U.S. foreign trade, the United States has incurred deficits in its balance of payments for every year since 1950, except for 1957, when the Suez crisis created shortages, especially of petroleum, in Western Europe and led to increased imports from the United States. With the ending of the Suez crisis, the U.S. payments deficit increased sharply in 1958 and became the object of official concern. The increased payments deficit was accompanied by the flow of gold from the United States to central banks overseas.

The U.S. payments imbalance occurred at a time when U.S. exports were rising. For each year between 1958 and 1967 U.S. exports increased. Exports rose from $16.3 billion in 1958 to $31.5 billion in 1967. However, this rapid increase in exports was offset by the expansion in imports, which rose from $13 billion in 1958 to $26.8 billion in 1967.[26] Clearly, if the United States could increase substantially its exports or reduce imports, U.S. payments could be balanced while still maintaining vast overseas military commitments. Given the dynamism of the U.S. economy and the excess of U.S. exports over imports, the payments deficit is related more to such factors as the responsibilities which the United States has continued to bear in international affairs and to the flow of U.S. investment abroad than to a lagging economy. In fiscal year 1965, $1.4 billion of U.S. defense expenditures in Europe entered the U.S. balance of payments.[27] This figure represented a slight reduction from comparable figures in previous years, the result perhaps of the efforts made by the U.S. government to achieve greater economies in overseas spending. Although the United States should not permit payments problems to govern strategic decisions,[28] the fact remains that the United States bears the major burden not only of European defense, but of security elsewhere in the non-communist world. If it is to continue to honor major overseas commitments and permit large-scale capital outflow, the United States must increase substantially its export surplus.

The unilateral, bilateral, and multilateral measures which the United States has adopted have not been sufficient to end the deficit. Unilateral measures include the use of monetary and fiscal policy, changes in the Federal budget, reductions in defense spending abroad, restrictions on duty-free purchases by U.S. tourists travelling abroad, and voluntary restrictions on investment by U.S. corporations. In the bilateral category, the most prominent examples are agreements between the United States and Germany for the assumption by Bonn of certain costs for the maintenance of U.S. forces in the Federal Republic. In fact, the periodic U.S. efforts to obtain from the German Government a greater financial commitment to NATO defense have contributed to friction between the two countries. Moreover, the Bonn Government has taken exception to U.S. efforts to increase sales of U.S. armaments which, in certain cases, either were not deemed vital to the defense of the Federal Republic or Western Europe in general, or did not accord with European strategic concepts. The erosion of alliance cohesion will increase the reluctance of Germany to bear the burden of military forces which appear at best marginal to its security. Under such circumstances, the U.S. government will find it increasingly difficult to justify to the U.S. taxpayer the cost of military forces based in Western Europe.

None of these efforts—unilateral, bilateral, or multilateral—has been adequate to eliminate the U.S. payments imbalance. To be sure, the United States has increased the sale of U.S. military equipment abroad ($300 million in 1961 vs. $1.3 billion in 1965). In improving its position in this sector, however, the United States has contributed to European dissatisfaction because of over-zealous efforts to sell U.S.-built weapons systems to other members of the Alliance. The effect of such programs is to reduce the scope for European sales of armaments and thus to make Western Europe more dependent upon the United States for military technologies. This, in turn, has contributed to the Atlantic technological imbalance. Thus, the measures adopted by the United States to reduce its payments imbalance are fraught with political implications for U.S.-European relations.

Not only have U.S. attempts to enlist European support to resolve its payments problem, as in the case of troop off-set costs in Germany, contributed to tensions between the United States and Western Europe. They have reinforced European doubts about the ability of the U.S. government to adopt adequate domestic economic policies. Inflationary pressures within the United States, together with increases rather than cuts in governmental spending, unaccompanied by increases in taxes, have not conveyed the image of a government capable of resolving basic economic problems. The waning of international confidence in the U.S. economy has been reflected in large-scale pressure against the U.S. currency in the conversion of dollars into gold.

The large-scale commitment of the United States to regions outside Europe, together with the U.S. payments problem, reduces the likelihood that the United States will increase its share of the burden of providing for the defense of Western Europe in the absence of intensified Soviet political-military pressure against

Western European countries. In fact, so far as non-nuclear capabilities are concerned, the United States is likely to reduce its contribution despite the existence of a NATO strategy of "flexible response." Similarly, Western European expenditures for non-nuclear defense, it can be expected, will continue to exhibit similar trends downward at a time when Western Europe as a whole possesses economic resources of unprecedented dimensions. At the same time European commitments outside Europe have been reduced, while the United States has assumed many of the burdens of assisting newly independent peoples to build viable political and economic structures. The imbalance between U.S. and European efforts has increased, rather than diminished, despite high levels of economic growth in Western Europe. In fact, the burdens borne by the United States outside the North Atlantic area have contributed to the strengthening of Western Europe economically. As a result of its transactions especially with countries other than the United States, since 1961 Western Europe has increased its gold and dollar holdings. Having trade surpluses with less developed countries, West European countries have received a major addition to their reserves from the Third World.[29] Large-scale U.S. expenditures in Vietnam have contributed to French holdings of dollars as a result of its economic links with France. Thus, in addition to domestic economic reforms, the solution to the U.S. balance of payments problem is related to political decisions about U.S.-European relationships and the allocation of defense burdens between the United States and Western Europe.

THE BRITISH ECONOMIC CRISIS

Alone among major West European countries, Britain has international military and economic commitments which strain her national capabilities. She has striven to maintain a military presence in Asia, the Middle East, and until recently, Africa, in addition to her contribution to NATO. With meagre gold and currency reserves, Britain has attempted to retain for the pound sterling a position as a major reserve currency. As a result of its burdensome international economic commitments, Britain has found it necessary to adopt domestic policies designed to curb industrial growth in order to defend the exchange rate of the pound. The devaluation of sterling in November 1967 reflected the failure of the British government to reconcile its domestic and international economic policies.

Beyond the considerable international responsibilities which Britain has borne since the Second World War, the weakness of the British economy lies at the root of Britain's recurrent balance of payments problem. Although heavily dependent upon imports and exports for her national livelihood, Britain experienced a decline in her share of international trade from 32 percent in 1914 to 15 percent in 1963.[30] Over the last generation Britain's economic difficulties have forced her to rely heavily upon borrowings from other nations and financial assistance from the International Monetary Fund in order not only to bolster her economic position, but also to retain for pound sterling a role as a reserve currency. Britain's future, as banker for the sterling area or as a member of the Atlantic Alliance, and potentially the EEC, is intimately related to her ability to find solutions to pressing economic problems. Given the experience of the past decade, however, Britain is not likely to achieve greater economic modernization and industrial expansion without major reductions in her international economic role.

Britain's economic crisis has been used as an argument both for and against British entry into the Common Market. Among proponents of EEC entry, the idea has currency that the British economy, exposed to the rigors of competition in the Common Market, would be strengthened. British industrialists would receive a new stimulus to modernize facilities and expand production in anticipation of gaining new markets. In opposing Britain's entry into the Common Market, however, French officials stressed the weakness of the pound sterling as a reserve currency and the adverse impact in the short-run of EEC entry upon the British balance of payments.[31] France was not prepared to provide economic assistance to enable Britain to make necessary adaptations in her economy after joining the Common Market. Thus the British faced a dilemma. Although EEC membership was deemed vital to the strengthening of the British economy, there was opposition to Britain's Common Market membership stemming from her economic weakness.

The inability of Britain to solve her major economic problems outside the Common Market can but have adverse repercussions upon the economies of the Six. A reduction in British imports from devaluation can be expected to affect exports from the EEC countries, whose trade with Britain has increased substantially since the formation of the Common Market. At the same time continental countries, given the objective of devaluation, will face greater competition in their own markets from British exports. Since growth rate in the EEC itself amounted only to 2.5 percent in 1967, British entry into the Common Market would have provided a powerful stimulus not only to Britain, but to the continental countries as well, for they would gain greater access to the large British domestic market. Even if Britain faced major problems of adjustment, the gains both to Britain and the Six would far outweigh the potential effects upon Western Europe and the international monetary system of repeated British failure to find a purely national solution to major economic problems.

The inability of Britain to retain for the pound sterling a role as reserve currency, at least until new means of assuring an adequate or growing supply of international liquidity were found, would undermine the world monetary system. Both President de Gaulle and the EEC Commission concluded that Britain must abandon the reserve currency function of sterling if she joined the Common Market.[32] According to this view, no EEC member could retain an economic and financial policy in which outside interests and commitments were in potential conflict with Community interests and commitments. Even without prevailing doubts about the future of sterling as a reserve currency, the need to assure adequate levels of liquidity for the international monetary system would remain urgent.

REFORMING THE INTERNATIONAL MONETARY SYSTEM

The spectre of an international monetary crisis precipitated by a shortage of international liquidity has been raised at the highest policy-making levels in the North Atlantic area.[33] Although the major Atlantic governments have been in agreement as to the need for changes in the international monetary system, there has been discord as to the appropriate measures to be adopted. Although visions of an impending collapse of the international monetary system are usually dismissed as fanciful, many thoughtful economic analysts have addressed themselves to the problems of international monetary reform. These efforts, together with the work of the

Group of Ten and the studies of the International Monetary Fund (IMF), provide an indication of the importance attached to this problem.[34]

The British devaluation of November 1967 pointed up major deficiencies not only in the British economy, but also in the international monetary system. As one of the world's two reserve currencies, sterling no longer enjoyed the full confidence of the international trading community. So great was the rush to convert sterling that Britain was unable to obtain international support sufficient to preserve the value of the pound at $2.80. In the aftermath of the devaluation of sterling, there was a rush to convert dollars to gold, the effect of which was to undermine the strength of the dollar as the other major international reserve currency. Although there are basic differences in the U.S. and British economic positions, successive waves of pressure against the dollar similar to those which periodically have been mounted against sterling would diminish the position of the dollar as a reserve currency. Moreover, massive efforts to convert dollars to gold have the effect of reducing the amount of international liquidity. But such conversions have far greater implications since they reflect a lack of international confidence in the currency of the most important member of the international monetary system.

With the 1967 British devaluation, the threat both to the dollar as a reserve currency and the international monetary system had by no means passed. The inability of Britain to resolve her domestic economic problems, together with another devaluation, would further weaken the international monetary system, and perhaps lead to its destruction. Clearly, the British economic crisis of 1967 is indicative of the need for measures to strengthen the international monetary system.

For the second time in less than a year, in March 1968 the international monetary system faced a crisis which threatened to undermine both the dollar and sterling as reserve currencies. Despite the devaluation of sterling several months earlier and steps taken by the United States in January 1968, including restrictions on the flow of U.S. investment capital abroad, the world's two leading reserve currencies came under attack again. During the first two weeks of March 1968, holders of dollars and sterling, in panic proportions, converted these currencies into gold. So great was the demand that between March 1 and 14, some 750 tons of gold were purchased. On March 14 alone, just before the London Gold Exchange was temporarily closed, 225 tons of gold changed hands. At the official price of $35 per ounce, a ton of gold is valued at $1.1 million.

On March 4 demand for gold rose rapidly in the gold markets of London and Paris and during the next few days reached the level of $45 per ounce—five dollars above the high point of October 1967 and ten dollars above the official world price supported by the United States and other leading countries who are members of the so-called Gold Pool, a 1960 agreement by the United States, Germany, Britain, France, Italy, Switzerland, Belgium, and the Netherlands to make available a portion of their national reserves in support of the world gold price in an effort to bring private speculation under control.

Although the Gold Pool was patently inadequate as a deterrent to gold speculation, it contributed, nevertheless, to its control during the crises of October 1967 and March 1968. At the time of the March crisis period members of the Gold Pool, with the exception of France, which withdrew in 1967, sold gold at the price of $35 per ounce in an effort to lower the price in the London and Paris markets to that level. The result of panic purchasing of gold was to reduce officially held reserves, especially those of the United States and Britain, as officially held gold was sold to stabilize the price of gold at $35 per ounce. The increase in gold held privately represented a reduction in international liquidity as gold passed from reserves of countries into the hands of hoarders fearful of the future of paper currencies and speculators who saw an opportunity for financial gain.

During the early days of March, the stampede to purchase gold received impetus from rumors that several members, including Belgium and Switzerland, would leave the Gold Pool, thus reducing the stock of gold available to support the official price. Whatever the implications of such rumors, the governors of central banks of gold pool members held consultations in Washington during the weekend of March 16-17. At the end of their deliberations, they issued a communique calling for a two-level gold price. The official price of $35 per ounce would remain in effect for transactions between governments. A freely fluctuating price for other buyers and sellers of gold was established, thus reducing the value of paper currencies in terms of gold.

In November 1968 the third crisis in a year to threaten the international monetary system was precipitated, this time by France. The loss of production during the strikes which accompanied the civil unrest of May-June 1968, the large-scale wage and price increases which followed the strike, and the consequent increase in the price of French exports all led to the November 1968 crisis. In the period from May to November, France is said to have lost about half of her gold reserves. In meetings of central bank authorities and finance ministers held in Bonn, the United States, Britain and France argued against devaluation of the franc, and instead, pressed for an upward revaluation of the West German mark. The old World War II coalition, all countries with payments deficits, sought to bring pressure upon the Federal Republic to increase the value of its currency, and thus to bear the principal burden for restoring equilibrium to the international monetary system. The unwillingness of the Bonn government to yield on this issue, like the Federal Republic's reluctance to sign the Non Proliferation Treaty, is indicative of the growing German independence in international affairs. For their part, the French government, refusing to devalue the franc, made cuts both in defense and domestic public services, took steps to administer more vigorously France's tax legislation, and imposed foreign exchange controls. The immediate effect of President de Gaulle's action was to stem the speculative tide against the franc. The devaluation of the franc at this time as a result of speculation against it would undoubtedly have led to further speculative action against the pound and dollar.

Within the international monetary system as its exists several sources of liquidity are available. They include gold, dollars, and pound sterling, which are widely used in international trade and are held as reserve currencies by many countries. Moreover, international liquidity derives from the rights of nations experiencing payments imbalances to draw upon the IMF.[35] Another form of liquidity consists of claims upon the IMF by creditor nations, the so-called Super Gold Tranche, which may be drawn subject to the approval of Fund authorities. Finally, there are bilateral or multilateral arrangements, including the General Arrangements to Borrow of the Group of Ten, currency swaps,[36] reciprocal credit agreements, and Roosa Bonds,[37] which have contributed to the international liquidity in recent years.

Especially since 1958, the operation of the international monetary system has given rise to concern for the future. Between 1958 and 1964 the U.S. payments deficit resulted in an increase of officially held foreign reserves totaling nearly $13 billion. In the aftermath of the British devaluation of November 1967 there was a rush to convert dollars into gold. The U.S. and British payments deficits, whatever their contribution to the increase in international liquidity, have led to an acceleration in the conversion of reserve currencies, namely, holdings of dollars and pound sterling, into gold. Between 1958 and 1966, the reserves of the United States fell from $22.5 billion ($20.6 billion in gold) to $14.6 billion ($13.8 billion in gold).[38] Stated differently, in 1952 the United States had reserves equivalent to 211 percent of its imports for that year; by 1965 U.S. reserves would have paid for only 67 percent of its imports. During the same period France, in contrast, experienced a reverse trend. In 1952, French reserves totalled only 16 percent of imports; in 1965 they were sufficient for the purchase of 67 percent of France's imports in that year. Germany and Italy experienced trends similar to those of France.[39]

In several respects the economic position of the United States differs fundamentally from that of Britain. In contrast to Britain, the United States is not heavily dependent upon foreign trade. Moreover, as a result of the vast increase in U.S. investment abroad, the United States, to a far greater extent than Britain, possesses assets which, sold, would produce a major increase in foreign currencies, dollars, and gold. Nevertheless, the U.S. and British balance of payments deficits have diminished confidence in Western Europe and elsewhere in both the dollar and pound as reserve currencies. Since the adequacy of liquidity is dependent in large part upon the supply of the dollar and pound as reserve currencies, the less willing foreign monetary authorities are to hold dollars as reserves, the more urgent becomes both the problem of international monetary reform and the adoption of measures by the United States to resolve domestic economic problems. Hence the strengthening of the dollar and pound sterling, by the correction of U.S. and British payments deficits, is necessary to assure a level of liquidity adequate for the conduct of world trade until another reserve unit can be created to ease the international burden borne by the U.S. and British currencies.

Paradoxically, the efforts of Britain and the United States to restore confidence in their currencies by eliminating payments imbalances, if successful, will result in the reduction in the major source of new liquidity over the last generation. The British and U.S. payments deficits, by placing large amounts of these key reserve currencies in the hands of foreigners, have been major factors contributing to increases in international liquidity, since new gold production has not been adequate to provide major increases in reserves. In recent years new gold has added only about $700 million per year to reserves, and in 1966 there was even a decrease in monetary gold. In the period between 1950 and 1966 the supply of monetary gold rose at an average annual rate of 1.4 percent. In the same period, world trade increased at an average annual rate of 7.5 percent. It is unlikely that other countries will be willing to make major increases in their holdings of dollars and pound sterling as reserve currencies. In fact, there has already been a decline in holdings of dollars as reserve currency by other countries. In the case of pound sterling, reserves of this currency held by monetary authorities in the sterling area were no higher in 1966 than they had been in 1951. In 1966 there was a decline in holdings of both dollars and pound sterling.[40] This development, together with the reduction in monetary gold, produced a decline in total world reserves in 1966. Moreover, the United States cannot allow its own gold reserves to be depleted. Therefore, there is little scope for the redistribution of gold held by the United States to other countries in order to increase their liquidity as was the case in the postwar period when the United States held most of the world's gold reserves. Finally, the IMF does not provide an adequate source of future reserves, since the purpose of the Fund is to provide assistance in specific instances to countries in payments disequilibrium. Such operations, in themselves, do not necessarily produce major additions to world monetary reserves. Sooner or later, more reserves will be needed. As the Group of Ten statement, known as the Ossola Report after the Group's Chairman, Signor Rinaldo Ossola of Italy, has suggested:

> The problem arises from the considered expectation that the future flow of gold into reserves cannot be prudently relied upon to meet all needs for an expansion of reserves associated with a growing volume of world trade and payments and that the contribution of dollar holdings to the growth of reserves seems unlikely to continue as in the past.[41]

An evaluation of the present adequacy of liquidity is a difficult undertaking.[42] Different national experiences give rise to different perspectives on the question of the adequacy of international liquidity. A surplus country may view with apprehension the expansionary effect of its balance of payments and conclude that liquidity is ample. A deficit country may regard the same amount of liquidity present in the system as inadequate because of the restrictionist stabilization policies required to restore its payments equilibrium. Nevertheless, it is possible to suggest guidelines for assessing the adequacy of international liquidity: (1) Liquidity should be sufficient to finance temporary payments imbalance while a country with a balance of payments crisis takes steps to eliminate its deficit; (2) Additional liquidity in the form of credit should be readily available so that a country in deficit can restore payments equilibrium.[43]

Between 1954 and 1963, the eight major non-reserve countries of the Group of Ten and Switzerland acquired the equivalent of $18.5 billion in reserve assets. In fact, Western Europe has accounted largely for U.S. gold losses and dollar liabilities. Although the EEC has a deficit on current account with the United States, dollars have flowed to Western Europe as a result of U.S. direct investment and military expenditures for the maintenance of U.S. forces. Moreover, Western Europe has received dollars as a result of trade surpluses with other countries. Dollars are often used in the settlement of such trade surpluses. In some European countries the growth in reserves is considered to have been a contributing factor to inflationary pressures on the European continent. Dr. Blessing of Germany expressed this view at the 1965 meeting of the IMF. He declared that "if the world were really in for a crisis, it would be because of persistent inflation." Thus his perspective on the liquidity problem followed: "If all leading countries were to aim at balance of payments equilibrium, the need for reserves would be small." [44] Liquidity may be regarded as excessive if U.S. balance of payments deficits extend over protracted periods without effective corrective measures. M. Valery Giscard d'Estaing, speaking for France at the same meeting, believed this to be the case since the reserve currency countries "are in a position to obtain implicit credit facilities over long periods of time through the holding of their own currencies by partner countries." [45] This practice is held to be a "dangerous usage, as these countries are tempted to misuse such facilities by postponing as long as they can the implementation of appropriate adjustment policies." In response to this French critique, however, there is little evidence that the United States and, least of all, Britain, as countries with reserve currencies, possess the means to obtain unlimited credit as a result of foreign reserve holdings of their currencies. In fact, there are bounds, which may already have been reached, especially as a result of the British payments crisis and currency devaluation of November 1967, to the willingness of other countries to hold dollars and pound sterling. To the extent that foreigners are not prepared to increase their dollar holdings, it is not possible for the United States to maintain a payments deficit without an equivalent reduction in reserves of gold.

The American response to the French critique is that the United States has not misused its privileged position. U.S. authorities, it is maintained, have been diligent, if not fully successful, in their efforts to restore payments equilibrium. Despite inflationary tendencies in the U.S. economy, the purchasing power of the dollar is said to have been better preserved than that of any other major currency.[46] However, inflationary pressures in the United States, to the extent that they have increased the prices of U.S. exports and led to a greater domestic demand for imports, have contributed to the U.S. payments deficit. Monetary and fiscal policies designed to prevent domestic demand from exceeding the supply of goods and services would dampen the increase in U.S. imports and help to direct U.S. production into exports. This, in turn, would contribute to a reduction in the payments imbalance and the strengthening of the dollar as a reserve currency.

It is not the adequacy of present reserves but the question of the future growth of liquidity which is of central concern to monetary authorities. Forecasts of the probable need for liquidity are fraught with uncertainty. It is difficult to anticipate tendencies toward inflation or contraction in the world economy and to predict the patterns of distribution of reserves and surpluses among countries at any given time. Yet there is a consensus among most monetary authorities that the need for international liquidity is likely to increase in the decade ahead.

To be sure, as French and German authorities have pointed out, the development of uniformly sound national economies not subject to short-term or chronic payments disequilibrium would diminish the need for increased international liquidity. Such an ideal state of equilibrium is not likely to be obtained in the real world of the foreseeable future. Persistent balance of payments problems, together with increasing levels of international trade, will make necessary a growth in the media of international exchange and their more efficient utilization.

For certain countries, the expansion of the world economy may lead to payments disequilibrium. For example, developing countries with large import needs relative to their export incomes and reserves will have a rising need for financial resources. Yet in the period between 1958 and 1964 their reserves fell by about 10 percent.[47] For the most part, developing countries can ill afford to accumulate currency reserves at a time when they face a shortage of capital for an even more urgent task, namely, modernization.

The amount of liquidity that will be available at a particular time is as difficult to predict as the demand for liquidity. The IMF has concluded that the growth rate of all forms of international liquidity averaged 3.3 percent annually between 1954 and 1964. In the same period gold increased at the annual rate of 1.6 percent; foreign exchange, 4.3 percent; and gold tranche, 7.6 per annum.[48] The rapid expansion of foreign currency reserves was attributable to the fact that countries with payments surpluses vis-a-vis the United States obtained much of their surplus in dollars. In an effort to ensure sufficient international liquidity, the IMF has expanded the resources available to member countries in payments difficulties. In 1958–1959 Fund quotas were increased by 50 percent across the board, with additional selective increases. In 1964 a general 25 percent increase, together with additional amounts for certain individual countries, was authorized. This increase has not fully alleviated the problem of the adequacy of funds that faces the IMF. Although the IMF in theory has ample funds from member countries' subscriptions, it faces a shortage of widely accepted currencies to make available to members experiencing payments difficulties.

There is growing sentiment that measures beyond the bolstering of existing reserve currencies must be taken in order to provide adequate liquidity. Except by France, it is generally conceded that gold, at a fixed price, should be retained as the basic monetary reserve commodity and ultimate medium for the settlement of international accounts. Agreement exists upon the need to maintain the arrangements that have been developed since World War II to aid countries in balance-of-payments difficulties.[49] There is even greater consensus that Britain and the United States must reduce their balance of payments deficits markedly if confidence in the pound and dollar as reserve currencies is to be strengthened.

Despite the agreement of most governments that ways must be found to ensure adequate liquidity, there are fundamental differences of opinion about the appropriate solutions. The United States proposed a new monetary unit, to be backed by the currencies of the leading industrial nations, a so-called composite reserve unit (CRU). In addition to the new unit, the United States has favored the enlargement of automatic borrowing rights in the IMF for nations experiencing balance of payments difficulties,[50] and the development of contingency plans for reserve creation.[51] Unable to redeem sterling liabilities to foreigners in gold or dollars, Britain has attempted to strengthen its monetary position by obtaining long-term credits to repay short-term loans for the defense of the pound sterling. The British government, therefore, will support proposals such as these favored by the United States to increase monetary reserves. They will ease the task of defending the pound sterling as reserve currency, in any future financial emergency.

In contrast, continental West European countries favor different approaches to the international liquidity problem. France has put forward a proposal to replace the existing system of reserve currencies with one more closely tied to gold. Jacques Rueff, financial adviser to President de Gaulle, suggested that the value of officially held gold be increased by one-third and that CRU's, be issued[52] in quantities based upon a national currency in proporation to gold reserves. De Gaulle himself called for the establishment of the international monetary system "on the basis of immutability, impartiality and universality, which are the privileges of gold."[53] The French proposals would favor countries such as France, which have accumulated substantial reserves of gold, and would undermine the position of the United States and Britain, countries with reserve currencies. In part because of its potential impact upon existing reserve currencies, there is no evidence that under this French proposal levels of liquidity could be increased or even maintained. Other European countries, including Germany and

Italy, see less need than the United States for haste in effecting reform. German and French financial authorities have maintained that if all leading countries could achieve balance of payments equilibrium, the need for liquidity would be less than it is today. Temporary deficits could be financed either from nationally held reserves or from the IMF or other financial institutions. Therefore, the strengthening of national economies would ease chronic payments deficits and lessen the need for great increases in international liquidity.[54]

There is general agreement, however, that in themselves specifically national solutions to international monetary problems will not be fully satisfactory to meet the liquidity needs of the future. At their September 1967 meeting in Rio de Janeiro, IMF members reached agreement on the creation of special drawing rights (SDR's). The so-called SDR's would be distributed in annual amounts to all IMF members in proportion to their respective financial contribution to the Fund. Countries could accumulate SDR's in much the same way as they save currency reserves. Unlike existing claims on the IMF, the SDR's would not be borrowings. A country experiencing payments problems could draw upon its accumulated SDR's for the purchase of currencies needed to settle its international accounts. For example, if Britain needed U.S. dollars, it would exchange SDR's for an equivalent amount of the needed currency. Although the United States would gain SDR's as a result of this transaction, Britain's reserves would not decrease until she had spent the dollars obtained by the exchange of SDR's. As in the case of gold, the real value of SDR's would lie in their convertibility into currencies.

Although the SDR plan contains considerable potential, it must be reconciled with differing U.S. and European perspectives as to the nature of and appropriate solutions for international monetary problems. For example, to what extent are countries such as France which emphasize the importance of gold likely to accord the same value to the SDR's? Differing perspectives about international monetary problems contribute to differing national policies on the rules for the operation of the IMF. France sought for the Common Market a veto power over the activation of SDR's as well as over other Fund activities in the field of international liquidity. Thus the French, with support from Germany, have attempted to link agreement on SDR's with changes in IMF voting procedures.[55]

The EEC has provided a framework for the gradual development of a European position on international monetary reform. The finance ministers of the Six are in accord that any new reserves created in response to a shortage in international liquidity should take the form of credit rather than of a new monetary unit not linked to gold, as originally proposed by the United States. The EEC holds, too, that supplementary credits to be drawn from the IMF should be repayed within a fixed period. In contrast, the United States and Britain have proposed that the reimbursement period be left to the administrators of the IMF. Thus the EEC position on international monetary affairs, as on trade, differs from that of the United States. In order to achieve a common position, the Common Market Six have had to make major concessions to France, whose interests have differed from those of the United States and Britain. A test of Britain's "Europeanization" will be the extent to which her policies on international monetary problems evolve toward those of her continental neighbors.

Whatever the solution chosen, the leading industrial states of the North Atlantic area will have a major voice in decisions about the future of the international monetary system. Proposals for monetary reform should be designed to permit continental European countries to make a greater contribution to the international monetary system in return for a greater voice in its operation, even though the United States and perhaps Britain will retain an inordinate share of the burden of ensuring its smooth operation. At the end of 1965, the total gold and foreign exchange holdings of members of the EEC ($19.7 billion) exceeded those of the United States ($14.6). As Table IV reveals, in 1965 the gold holdings of each of the three major EEC countries were greater than those of Britain. The continental countries of Western Europe have the resources to make a major contribution to an augmented IMF, a new reserve unit, or other schemes for assuring sufficient international liquidity. In return for a greater contribution to the IMF, voting procedures in the Fund could be altered in order to give major West European contributors a greater voice. In fact, the EEC has already reached accord upon the need for reform in the Fund's statutes to give the Common Market Six voting equal to that of the United States. The international monetary system, like the defense of the West, has been dominated by the "Anglo-Saxon" powers, despite changes in the capabilities of continental

TABLE IV

Gold and Foreign Exchange Holdings of EEC and U.K.—1965 and 1966

Countries	I		II		III		IV		I(1966)	
	Gold	Foreign Exchange	Gold	Foreign Exchange	Gold	Foreign Exchange	Gold	Foreign Exchange	Gold	Foreign Exchange
EEC Members	13,740	5,990	14,514	4,848	14,646	4,734	14,834	4,897	14,889	4,396
1. France	4,197	1,119	4,433	917	4,556	825	4,706	753	4,806	765
2. Germany	4,243	2,617	4,378	2,015	4,390	1,913	4,410	1,943	4,402	1,719
3. Belgium	1,484	519	1,563	437	1,554	464	1,558	437	1,556	400
4. Italy	2,093	1,389	2,384	1,225	2,390	1,223	2,404	1,462	2,369	1,271
5. Netherlands	1,723	346	1,756	254	1,756	309	1,756	302	1,756	241
United Kingdom	2,111	219	2,226	566	2,139	616	2,265	739	2,036	1,537

Note: Data refer to holdings at the end of each period.

Source: *International Financial Statistics;* International Monetary Fund.

West European states during the last generation and the severe economic crises through which Britain has passed. If Britain were to join the Common Market, the enlarged Community could eventually create a European currency to replace sterling as a reserve currency, although the Six have shown little interest either in providing support to the pound sterling as a reserve currency if Britain became an EEC member or in giving such a function to one of their own currencies. The Europeans are far from agreement upon even the need for a new reserve currency, not to speak of the form it would take or the role it would play in the international monetary system.

The problem of international monetary reform is complicated by the presence of many more countries concerned than at the time of the Bretton Woods discussions in 1944. Then the two major countries whose interests had to be satisfied were Britain and the United States. By 1968, however, the IMF included 106 members. The very size of the IMF contributed to the difficulty of achieving agreement. At the very least, agreement among the Group of Ten, all of whose members except Japan are Atlantic countries, is vital to the reform of the international monetary system. If such accord could be reached, it might then be possible, because of the weighted voting procedures in the IMF, to make changes deemed necessary to assure adequate levels of liquidity. However, the level of consensus among Atlantic countries is not now such as to enable them to present a unified front in the IMF.

CONCLUSION

In sum, in recent years intra-Atlantic economic problems have assumed growing importance. In contrast to the early post-war period, when economic problems had a unifying effect, they have contributed more recently to friction between the United States and Western Europe and to tension within Europe. In the early postwar period, the need for common solutions to pressing economic problems led to the strengthening of the European integration movement, as well as to collaboration between the United States and Western Europe. In the past decade, however, economic problems, especially those associated with Britain's domestic economic weakness and balance of payments deficits and with the future of sterling as a reserve currency, have deepened the cleavage between Britain and the Common Market Six. Differing perspectives on the solution of the U.S. balance of payments problem, the future of international reserve currencies, U.S. investment in Europe, and trade policy have contributed to transatlantic frictions. Action both at the national and international levels is vital to the solution of major economic problems. The finding of solutions to such problems, in turn, is vital to the development of an Atlantic consensus in the 1970's.

NOTES

1. See Richard N. Cooper, *The Economics of Interdependence: Economic Policy in the Atlantic Community*. New York: McGraw-Hill, 1968, esp. Chapters 3–6.
2. Canada provides markets for another fifth of U.S. exports.
3. Lawrence B. Krause, *The Meaning of European Economic Integration for the United States*. Washington: Brookings Institution, 1967. (Mimeographed). Pp. 4–42.
4. See Paul H. Douglas, *America in the Market Place: Trade, Tariffs and the Balance of Payments*. New York: Holt, Rinehart and Winston, 1966, p. 144.
5. John O. Coppock. *Atlantic Agricultural Unity: Is It Possible?* New York: McGraw-Hill, for the Council on Foreign Relations, 1966.
6. See Krause, *op. cit.*, p. 37.
7. For an examination of the American selling price problem, see Jules Backman, *Foreign Competition in Chemicals and Allied Products*, published by Manufacturing Chemists' Association. Washington, D.C., 1965, pp. 21–23.
8. After the conclusion of the Kennedy Round, there was discussion in Congress of quotas to restrict imports of a wide variety of goods, including electronic components, dairy products, shoes, and furs. See *New York Times*, May 26, 1968, p. 14.
9. "Europeans Weigh Non-Tariff Obstacles to Trade," *European Community*, No. 82, June 1965, pp. 8–10.
10. "European Non-Tariff Obstacles to Trade Criticized," *European Community*, No. 84, August 1965, pp. 7–9.
11. See Randall Hinshaw, *The European Community and American Trade: A Study In Atlantic Economics and Policy*. New York: Praeger, 1964, especially pp. 143–145; and *United Nations Statistical Papers*, Series D, Vol. XV, No. 1–3, especially pp. 299, 350.
12. Maxwell Stamp Associates, *The Free Trade Area Option: Opportunity for Britain*. London, 1967. See also Paul H. Douglas, *America in the Market Place*. New York: Holt, Rinehart and Winston, 1966; Ralph I. Straus, "A Proposal for New Initiatives in U.S. Foreign Trade Policy." ORBIS, Spring 1967.
13. For an analysis of the question of trade preferences, see Sidney Weintraub, *Trade Preferences for Less Developed Countries: An Analysis of United States Policy*. New York: Praeger, 1967.

14. For an examination of the work of the DAC, see Seymour J. Rubin, *The Conscience of the Rich Nations: The Development Assistance Committee and the Common Aid Effort.* New York: Harper and Row, for the Council on Foreign Relations, 1966; Milton J. Esman and Daniel S. Cheever, *The Common Aid Effort: The Development Assistance Activities of the Organization for Economic Co-operation and Development.* Columbus: Ohio State University Press, 1967.

15. See Orville L. Freeman, "Malthus, Marx and the North American Breadbasket," *Foreign Affairs,* Vol. 45, No. 4 (July 1967), pp. 579–593.

16. According to the U.S. Secretary of Agriculture, "Five years ago, we in the United States had the world's two major reserves in the race between food needs and food production: some fifty million tons of excess grain in storage, and a large area of fertile cropland made idle under our farm programs. During the early 1960's, idle cropland increased and in 1966 exceeded fifty million acres. Decisions within the past year to increase acreages of wheat, feedgrains, rice and soybeans will bring nearly one-half of this cropland back into production. Once this ready reserve is exhausted, it will become much more difficult for the world to achieve any abrupt increases in production to meet additional demand." *Ibid.,* p. 591.

17. For a comprehensive examination of U.S. investment trends in Western Europe, see Christopher Layton, *Trans-Atlantic Investments.* Paris: Atlantic Institute, 1966; Anthony Edwards, *Investment in the European Economic Community.* New York: Frederick A. Praeger, 1964; Jean-Jacques Servan-Schreiber, *The American Challenge* New York: Atheneum, 1968.

18. Krause, *op. cit.,* V. 8–9.

19. Layton, *op. cit.,* p. 3.

20. According to a business survey published in April 1965 by the Union des Industries de la Communauté Européene, of the 500 largest companies in the world (classified by 1963 sales figures) 306 were American, 53 British, 33 German, 25 French, 7 Italian, 6 Swedish, 6 Swiss, 4 Dutch, 3 Belgian, 1 Luxembourgian. In this list the EEC accounted for only 74 companies, while EFTA provided 66. The report suggested the need for greater concentration in those industries in Western Europe where large-scale investment is necessary for technological advance. See *European Community,* No. 81 (May 1965), pp. 12–13.

21. On January 1, 1968, President Johnson issued an Executive Order prohibiting new direct investment outflows to continental Western Europe and "other developed nations not heavily dependent on our capital" in 1968. The Federal Reserve Board was authorized to tighten its program restraining foreign lending by banks and other financial institutions. The Secretary of State was instructed to enter negotiations with NATO allies to minimize the foreign exchange cost of U.S. forces in Europe. Finally, an attempt was made to curb U.S. tourism in Europe by voluntary action to defer trips outside the West-

tern Hemisphere and by legislation limiting tourist expenditures abroad.

22. *Wall Street Journal,* (New York), January 25, 1966.

23. According to De Gaulle, "It is true that we find ourselves faced with an American hold on certain of our businesses, but we know that this is due, to a great extent, not so much to the organic superiority of the United States as to the dollar inflation that it is exporting to others under the cover of the gold exchange standard. It is rather remarkable that the total of annual deficits in the American balance of payments over the past eight years is exactly the total of American investments in the countries of Western Europe. There is in this, obviously, a unilateral and artificial external element that is weighing on our national patrimony, and it is known that France wishes that an end be put to this abuse to the interest of the entire world, and even to the interest of the United States, for whom the payments deficit and inflation are as lamentable as they are for everybody." *Speeches and Press Conferences.* November 27, 1967. Text released by Ambassade de France, Service de Presse et d'Information, New York.

24. For a detailed discussion of the implications of overseas investment for a country's balance of payments, see Lawrence B. Krause and Kenneth W. Dan in *Federal Tax Treatment of Foreign Income.* Washington: The Brookings Institution, 1964.

25. Layton, *op. cit.,* p. 46.

26. Committee for Economic Development, *The Dollar and the World Monetary System.* New York: CED, 1966, p. 40. U.S. Department of Commerce, Office of Business Economics: Survey of Current Business, January 1969, Vol. 49, No. 1, pp. S-21 and S-22.

27. Figures furnished by the Office of Assistant Secretary of Defense.

28. Taking one component of the payments account and making that the marginal outlay to which the deficit is attributable may well lead to irrational treatment of that component. Moreover, such a procedure is not technically legitimate. The net balance of payments will, presumably, never change by the amount precisely equal to a reduction in a given outlay. Expenditures abroad generate return flows. The estimation of the ratios of these return flows during given time periods is complex and subject to great uncertainties. The singling out of a given sector, like overseas military expenditures or foreign investment, said to be "about equal to the deficit" and therefore to account for the deficit, may create the risk that appropriate policies toward other components of the payments balance will be overlooked.

29. See Layton, *op. cit.*

30. *British Record,* Political and Economic Notes by British Information Services, No. 2, January 27, 1965, and February 3, 1965.

31. See President de Gaulle's Press Conference of May 16, 1967. Ambassade de France. *Speeches and Press Conferences,* No. 260A, May 16, 1967.

32. See President de Gaulle, *Speeches and Press Conferences*

(November 27, 1967). Text released by Ambassade de France, Service de Presse et d'Information, New York; see also Commission of the European Communities, *Opinion on the Applications for Membership Received from the United Kingdom, Ireland, Denmark and Norway.* Brussels, 29 September 1967.

33. The international liquidity of a nation consists of all the resources that are available, directly or indirectly, to its monetary authorities to support its rate of exchange when its external payments are in deficit. The present international payments system calls for the free convertibility of currencies at specified exchange rates which can be adjusted only if a "fundamental disequilibrium" exists. Monetary authorities of a country experiencing "transitory disequilibrium" in its payments may stabilize its currency within the agreed limits by using reserve currencies to purchase needed currencies. If inadequate resources are available to support the currency within the IMF limits, a crisis of confidence may occur. A country with adequate resources or reserves can, in effect, purchase the time to restore payments equilibrium.

34. Ministers and Governors of the Group of Ten Countries participating in the General Arrangements to Borrow with the International Monetary Fund, Report of the Study Group on the Creation of Reserve Assets. Government Printing Office, Washington, May 1965, p. 13. Hereafter cited as Group of Ten, *Report of the Study Group on the Creation of Reserve Assets.* Also, International Monetary Fund, *Annual Report,* Washington, D.C., 1964 and 1965. The Group of Ten includes the major industrial and trading nations of the Free World—Belgium, Britain, Canada, France, the German Federal Republic, Italy, Japan, the Netherlands, Sweden, and the United States, with Switzerland as an observer. The Group agreed to supplement the holdings of the IMF by making available the currencies of its members on a short-term basis. The IMF is then able to extend such currencies to countries experiencing balance of payments crises. In 1965, the Group made available reserves totaling $1.4 billion to Britain in order to support the pound.

35. In the IMF, each member country has a borrowing quota based upon payments of gold and national currency which it has made to the Fund. One quarter of its drawing rights are based on its contribution of gold. Access to this quarter of its quota, the gold tranche, is virtually automatic. The so-called "super gold tranche" represents claims totaling about $5 billion. Moreover in the negotiations carried on during 1961 which produced agreement on the General Arrangements to Borrow, the leading industrial countries comprising the Group of Ten agreed to provide loans to the Fund under specified conditions in amounts up to $6 billion in order to increase the reserves available to countries in need of greater liquidity. Swiss authorities set up a parallel arrangement to furnish up to $200 million in Swiss francs directly to the Fund.

36. Currency swaps are bilateral arrangements under which a coun-

try with balance of payments problems temporarily receives the currency of an economically stronger country in exchange for its own currency. A currency swap is designed to strengthen the weak currency in foreign exchange markets.

37. Roosa Bonds, named after the former Under Secretary of the Treasury, are intermediate-term U.S. government securities which can be sold to foreign official banks holding U.S. dollars. The sale of Roosa Bonds is designed to reduce the likelihood that foreign-held dollars will be used to buy U.S. gold.

38. *General Statistics 1966,* Statistical Office, European Community (Brussels).

39. International Monetary Fund, *Annual Report: 1966.* IMF: Washington, 1966, p. 13.

40. *New York Times,* July 5, 1967, p. 53.

41. Group of Ten, *Report of the Study Group on the Creation of Reserve Assets,* p. 17.

42. *Ibid.* As the Senior Financial Adviser of the *Neue Zürcher Zeitung* has suggested: "Regarding international liquidity one might, on the one hand, lay down the same rule as is prescribed in the Bretton Woods statute for credit facilities: the rule that these ought to enable countries to make an adequate adaptation without imposing restrictions harmful both to their own and their partners' economies. On the other hand, however, liquidity should not be so considerable as to tempt the countries to relax their monetary discipline and slow down their adaptation." F. E. Aschlinger, "Problems of an International Currency Reform." *Swiss Review of World Affairs,* Vol. XV, No. 12, Special Supplement, March 1966, p. 6.

43. See Walter S. Salant, *et al., The U.S. Balance of Payments in 1968.* Washington: The Brookings Institution, 1963, pp. 248–250.

44. International Monetary Fund, *Summary Proceedings of the Twentieth Annual Meeting of the Board of Governors,* Washington, D.C., 1965, p. 117. The Germans appear to have a phobia about inflation, resulting from a confusion in their minds between the traumatic experiences of hyper-inflation after two world wars and the phenomenon of gradual inflation persistent throughout most of history and related to periods of prosperity. The second type of inflation differs, in both its causes and effects, from the first. In the case of French official criticisms of the international monetary system, however, the question arises whether the French concern with the U.S. payments deficit and the French devotion to gold is related to Gaullist dissatisfaction with the U.S. position in the Atlantic Alliance, as well as French apprehension about U.S. hegemony in technology and investments.

45. *Ibid.*

46. Gottfried Haberler, "The International Payments System" in *International Payments Problems,* Symposium sponsored by the American Enterprise Institute, Washington, D.C., September 23–24, 1965, pp. 4–7.

47. The underdeveloped nations are defined for this purpose to include all of Latin America, all of Africa except the Union of South Africa, and all of Asia except Japan.

48. International Monetary Fund, *Annual Report,* Washington, D.C., 1964, p. 30.

49. *International Payments Problems, op. cit.,* pp. 71–75.

50. *New York Times,* January 28, 1966, p. 1. For an elaboration of similar proposals, see Robert V. Roosa, *Monetary Reform for the World Economy.* New York: Harper and Row, for the Council on Foreign Relations, 1965, pp. 73–129.

51. Henry H. Fowler, "A World Monetary System." *Atlantic Community Quarterly,* Vol. 5, No. 2 (Summer 1967), pp. 234–240.

52. See U.S. Congress, Joint Economic Committee, "Guidelines for International Monetary Reform" *Hearings,* Subcommittee on International Exchange and Payments, Part 2, supplement, 89th Congress, First Session. Washington: U.S. Government Printing Office, 1965, pp. 226–227.

53. *Speeches and Press Conferences.* November 27, 1967. Text issued by Ambassade de France, Service de Presse et d'Information, New York.

54. See, for example, the statement by the Governor of the IMF for the Federal Republic of Germany, Karl Blessing. International Monetary Fund, *Summary Proceedings, Annual Meeting 1965.* Washington, D.C., 1965, pp. 115–119.

55. See the *Economist,* September 2, 1967, pp. 799–800; September 30, 1967, pp. 1208–1209.

V. Eastern Europe and the West

OVER THE LAST DECADE, IN BOTH EASTERN AND WESTERN EUROPE, interest in the expansion of East-West contacts has risen.[1] European governments have embarked upon efforts to increase trade, travel, and many other kinds of transactions between communist and non-communist Europe. All of the major powers of the West and most of the lesser ones as well have altered their policies toward Eastern Europe. In Britain, the expansion of contacts and trade with Eastern Europe has been seen as a means of lessening the communist grip and at the same time providing new markets for British exports. In the German Federal Republic, the development of contacts with countries to the East is designed to calm East European fears of German revisionism and thus to enhance the prospects for eventual German reunification. In the French official view, a rising volume of transactions with commuinst states in Europe may strengthen French influence in Eastern Europe and contribute to the eventual creation of a Europe "from the Atlantic to the Urals," or at least from the Atlantic to the Carpathians. The United States has called for the building of "bridges" between Eastern Europe and the West and has adopted a policy of "peaceful engagement" with the countries of Eastern Europe. Present U.S. policies designed to speed desired changes in Eastern Europe have their antecedents in the programs of the early post-war period between the United States and Yugoslavia after that country's dispute with Moscow in 1948. In the 1960's the U.S. interest in the development of new relationships with East European countries accords with U.S. conceptions of the prospects for East-West detente. West European interest in the expansion of contacts with East European countries is consistent with the increasing European, rather than global, orientation of the foreign policies of West European governments. Conceivably, in the 1970's, a major foreign policy preoccupation of West European countries will be Eastern Europe.

Western perceptions of change in Eastern Europe hold important implications for the Atlantic alliance to the extent that they portend basic changes in the East-West relationships that have obtained since World War II. The growth of interest in East-West detente to tensions between the two halves of Europe, has led NATO members to consider a new role for the Alliance. According to the Harmel Report,

> The Alliance affords an effective forum and clearing house for the exchange of information and views: thus, each of the Allies can decide his policy in the light of close knowledge of each other's problems and objectives. To this end the practice of frank and timely consultations needs to be deepened and improved. Each Ally should play its full part in promoting an improvement in relations with the Soviet Union and the countries of Eastern Europe, bearing in mind that the pursuit of detente must not be allowed to split the alliance. The chances of success will clearly be greatest if the allies remain on parallel course, especially in matters of close concern to them all: their actions will thus be all the more effective.[2]

Western perceptions of change in Eastern Europe have contributed to the growth of the belief that Atlantic security arrangements are no longer of such great importance as they once were. Unless the changes in Eastern Europe are fundamental and permanent in nature, representing a basic transformation in the ideological commitment of the communist leadership, the political systems of East European countries, and the relationship between East European countries and the Soviet Union, it would be hazardous to conclude that these changes have fully benign implications for the West. In the absence of basic changes in Eastern Europe, the West would be the loser if, as a result of Western misconceptions of change in Eastern Europe, Western security arrangements were weakened or dismantled and West European integration efforts sidetracked. Thus the problem confronting Western policymakers is to assess the nature of change in Eastern Europe in order to design Western policies which will reconcile the security of the North Atlantic area with the taking of steps to hasten the process of change in Eastern Europe, including the reduction of Soviet influence in that region. Thus, no examination of U.S.-West European relationships is complete without an assessment of the nature of change in Eastern Europe and of the policies of Atlantic countries toward this region.

CHANGE IN EASTERN EUROPE

Many students of East European affairs have noted the "erosion" of communism in Eastern Europe which, it is argued, has occurred over the past decade. The "true believers" of communist ideology, it is pointed out, are declining in numbers. Communist regimes are undergoing what is variously described as "internal liberalization." In foreign policy a quest for independence from the Soviet Union is noted, at least on certain categories of issues. Yet it is difficult to make broad generalizations about the nature of change in Eastern Europe. Some regimes more than others have introduced "reforms" in their economic systems. But, generally, increased emphasis upon consumer goods, recognition of the profit motive, and modifications in central planning have marked economic policy in East European countries. Political change as well has occurred. Some regimes have placed restrictions upon police powers and increased the flow of East-West travel, including cultural and educational exchanges with the West. In general, East European communist regimes have sought to expand trade with the West and to improve intergovernmental relationships. Yet the pattern of change varies.

In Poland, the period of greatest change since the death of Stalin occurred in the time span between the beginning of 1956 and the end of 1958. The revolutionary events of 1956 were climaxed with the accession to power of the Gomulka Group, supported by moderate and liberal elements within the Polish Communist Party. Simultaneously, many of the hardline Stalinists were swept out. The Gomulka regime encouraged the process of internal liberalization, which by then was well underway, but at the same time sought to place restraints on the unlimited development of this process.

The changes that transpired during this period may be summarized as follows. Police powers were curbed. Agricultural collectivization largely disappeared. The parliament acquired a limited role in the making of national policy. Other groups in addition to the Communist Party were allowed to participate in the legislature. Freedom of expression was tolerated to a significant extent. Partial decentralization in the national economic structure took place. The workers gained a foothold in the management of the various government enterprises. Private enterprise was encouraged to play a more important part in Poland's economic life. Church-state relations improved considerably. In foreign policy, however, the Polish leaders did not depart greatly from the Soviet line, perhaps because of the German question, Poland's geographical proximity to the Soviet Union, and the Polish leadership's evaluation of the events that accompanied Hungary's October Revolution. On such issues as the Sino-Soviet dispute, disarmament, East European defense, the Atlantic Alliance, and the Vietnam conflict, Poland's policy has not differed greatly from that of the Soviet Union.

During 1958, the Gomulka regime adopted and continued to pursue thereafter a policy aimed at restoring many of the former Stalinist hardliners to leadership positions of importance and at easing out of such positions members of the "liberal" faction of the Party. This move was followed by a halt in the trend toward liberalization. In some areas retrogression occurred. Centralized control of the economy was reestablished. Obstacles were again placed in the way of private enterprise. Freedom of expression was curtailed. A campaign of harassment of the church was begun. Finding themselves incapable of coping with the serious problems that continued to plague the economy, the centralists began in 1964 to make some concessions to those elements within the Party who advocated decentralization and the utilization of a number of the more pragmatic practices of a free market economy. However, there has yet to be an all-out effort to place such practices into operation.

In March 1968 Poland experienced the greatest outburst of rioting since 1956. Students demonstrated against Polish cultural policy, in particular, the banning of a play with anti-Russian overtones. They expressed opposition to the stalemate in Polish liberalization policy, which was a pacesetter in 1956, but had become by 1968 a laggard in Eastern Europe both in the movement toward intellectual freedom and economic reform. The response of the Gomulka regime was to mount an anti-Jewish propaganda campaign against so-called Zionist influence in Poland's intellectual life. Jews were accused of having fomented student disorder, and several Jewish members of the Polish Communist Party and holders of government posts were dismissed. Undoubtedly, such action reflected the determination of the Gomulka government to deflect from itself criticism of its restraints on Polish intellectual life, as well as of its continuing inability to resolve major economic problems.

Of all communist states in Eastern Europe, East Germany is most clearly aligned with the Soviet Union in foreign policy. The East German Communist regime remains heavily dependent for its survival upon Soviet support. Over the last decade, there has been but a slight diminution in Soviet domination of its foreign and domestic policies. Since 1956 East Germany has experienced a considerable rise in living standards and a major increase in industrial productivity. Since the construction of the Berlin Wall in 1961, the East German economy has benefited from the presence of skilled workers and professional people who otherwise might have escaped to the West. Moreover, the building of the Wall has served to develop a greater sense of identification with the East German state among the population. The presence in increasing numbers of trade missions from the West as well as the growth of trade with other nations appears to have given the East German regime a position of greater respectability among its population in that it gives evidence of a form of de facto recognition.

Especially since 1963, East German economic planners have given greater discretion to factory managers in the planning of investment and the determination of bonuses to workers. Now the world's tenth-greatest industrial power, East Germany has increased its trade with the Federal Republic. Since 1957, East German trade with developing countries has grown rapidly. Despite the expansion of economic contacts outside the communist world, however, East Germany remains the most important trading partner of the Soviet Union because of her industrial capabilities. Thc Soviets obtain much of their imports, including chemicals, optics, and certain kinds of capital goods, from East Germany. More than that of any other East European country, the East German economy is geared to the needs of the Soviet Union. Of all communist states, East Germany politically is the most stalinist. Over the last decade, cultural policy has fluctuated between freeze and thaw. The authority of internal security forces under rigid central control has not been altered substantially over the last decade. In sum, East Germany has neither experienced great internal liberalization nor exercised substantial freedom from the Soviet Union in foreign policy.

Until 1968, Czechoslovakia, of all the countries of Eastern Europe, appeared to be the laggard regarding change in both foreign and domestic policy. Almost intuitively, Prague followed the Soviet lead on the German question and other aspects of international affairs, and few domestic reforms were instituted. Although greater freedom had been granted to writers and intellectuals, they ran the risk of official disapproval and faced the possible loss of party membership and of professional status. The disenchantment of the intelligentsia with the regime dates from 1962, when the Slovak Writers Union petitioned the regime to rehabilitate both dead and living victims of the purges of the early 1950's. The government of President Antonin Novotny responded favorably but reluctantly, and the rehabilitation of the living victims was limited to professional but not political activity.

The limited nature of gains in intellectual freedom in Czechoslovakia was consistent with the vicissitudes of economic reform. In 1958 and 1960 minor adjustments were made in the organization of the Czechoslovak economy, but these changes were not adequate to prevent an economic crisis in 1961 and 1962, when additional minor economic reforms were instituted. Prepared primarily by the economist Professor Ota Sik, Director of the Prague Institute of Economics and a member of the Central Committee of the Czechoslovak Communist Party, the New Economic Model was adopted by the Central Committee in January 1965. The initial plan included reform of wholesale prices based on production costs, consumer demand, and the world market. Wage egalitarianism was to be replaced by merit incentives, and management at the factory level was to be made less dependent upon central control. Although he was a member of the Party's Central Committee, it seems that Professor Sik did not have sufficient political support to defend his plan against the traditionalists in the Party apparatus. The plan ran afoul of conventional Marxian economic thought, but also it gave rise to fears that its adoption might bring undesired political change. Moreover, the plan threatened the position of the central planning organization and local party apparatus, and potentially of those factory managers who could not adapt to the new system and of workers who had become accustomed to low work norms and lax work discipline. The success of the opposition to the plan is illustrated by the successive delays in putting various portions of the plan into operation and by the continued debate over various aspects of the plan, particularly whether it should be put into operation immediately or over an extended period of time.

The intellectual ferment, mounting economic problems, and ethnic cleavage between Slovaks and Czechs led to the resignation of Novotny as First Secretary of the Czechoslovak Communist Party in January 1968 and President of Czechoslovakia in March

1968. Novotny's successor as Party leader was Alexander Dubcek, a Slovak, regarded as a reformist. He was forced to deal with demands by writers, students, journalists, farmers, and even trade unions. Liberal groups within the Communist Party have pressed for changes in the role of the party in government and society, for abolition of censorship, for an independent judiciary, and for government responsibility to the National Assembly. There have been demands for a reevaluation of the pre-communist past and of the rehabilitation by the communists. The ferment has contributed to major reductions in press censorship and an investigation of the role of Soviet and Czech communists in the death of Jan Masaryk in 1948 and in the purge trials of 1952. At a hastily convened meeting of Warsaw Pact members in Dresden on March 23, 1968, Dubcek found it necessary to explain his government's domestic policies and to assure other communist leaders of his regime's continuing solidarity with the Warsaw Pact.

During the summer months of 1968, Soviet apprehension about liberalization within Czechoslovakia increased. In an apparent effort to appease the Soviets, the Dubcek regime in early August 1968 took several steps to slow the momentum toward liberalization. These included restrictions on public criticism of the Soviet Union and assurances to the Soviets, in a meeting of Soviet and Czechoslovak leaders at Bratislava between July 27 and August 3, that the Communist Party would retain the "leading role" in Czechoslovakia.

Nevertheless, on August 21, Soviet troops, with token forces from Poland and East Germany, crossed the Czech frontier and within a few hours occupied all of Czechoslovakia. The Soviets appear to have intervened after having concluded that the Dubcek regime might not be able to halt the movement toward change. In the period before the Soviet invasion, public debate had begun to center on guarantees for a free press and the restoration of a multiparty system. Liberalizing tendencies, the Soviets may have concluded, threatened not only the existence of the Communist system in Czechoslovakia, but the stability of Communist regimes elsewhere in Eastern Europe. Similar demands for liberalization might have spread to other Communist states, including the Soviet Union itself. Geographically, Czechoslovakia, sharing a western frontier with the German Federal Republic and an eastern boundary with the Soviet Union, separates the northern and southern parts of the Communist bloc. Czechoslovakia provides a "corridor" from the West to the Soviet Union. Undoubtedly, the Soviets saw potential strategic consequences from the liberalizing tendencies in Czechoslovakia. But for the longer run the question remains as to whether the presence of Soviet armies can prevent the re-emergence of forces making for change in Czechoslovakia, as well as elsewhere in Eastern Europe.

In Hungary some changes have been registered. The crushing of the Hungarian Revolution of 1956 largely wiped out gains in internal liberalization that had been attained following the death of Stalin; however, in the two years following the Revolution, the Soviet installed Kadar regime sought to eliminate the last pockets of resistance to its rule. The Kadar Government showed itself to be thoroughly committed to the goals of communism, completing the collectivization of agriculture between 1959-1962. However, it abandoned methods of the former Rakosi regime employing terror.

The Kadar Government remains committed to the achievement of the communist state, but since 1961 the regime has followed an overall policy characterized in many ways by pragmatic considerations. The changes which have occurred during this period may be summarized as follows. Many government jobs have come to be filled on the basis primarily of relevant skills, rather than Party membership. As early as 1958, a profit-sharing system of a limited sort was established in industry. Partial decentralization of the powers of the central ministries has occurred. Farmers now receive a certain portion of the collective's land to cultivate, and they are guaranteed a percentage of the total harvest—regardless of whether the production plan is fulfilled. The government has come to cater more to the interests of the consumer. In the cultural sphere, it has tolerated to a significant degree the free expression of criticism concerning both past and present conditions in the country.[3] In foreign policy, however, the Hungarian government has been critical of Romania's apparent anti-Soviet policies. In general, Hungary's foreign policy has not departed greatly from that of the Soviet Union.

In Bulgaria, the communist regime has introduced several changes. In 1963, the Bulgarian government began to experiment cautiously with the use of the profitability concept as a criterion for assessing the success of an enterprise. As in the Soviet Union, one of the compelling reasons for the experiment was the consistently low quality of many industrial products. By the end of 1964, some 50 enterprises had switched over to the new system. At the end of 1965, "non-state financed" factories accounted for about 44 percent of Bulgaria's industrial production. By 1966 the system had proved itself beyond the highest expectations of the ruling group, and plans were under discussion to adopt it for the entire industrial sector of the economy. Although the price structure was modified to make the profitability principle a realistic indicator of industrial performance, it is not envisaged that the government will abandon price controls. Nor did Sofia give up its prerogatives with respect to central planning; however, the reform program did call for greater cooperation between the central and local levels in the formulation of short and long run economic plans. As an indirect control device, the state can levy taxes upon income and assets at will. On the whole, economic change in Bulgaria is characterized by caution rather than boldness. Politically, Bulgaria has experienced little, if any, liberalization. In foreign policy, Bulgaria has sought to expand contacts with the West at both the official and the unofficial levels without, however, deviating from the Soviet position on foreign policy issues.

Yugoslavia is at least a decade ahead of the other countries in Eastern Europe in adjusting its economic structures to industrialization. After expulsion from the Cominform in 1948, Yugoslavia began to decentralize her economy. In the early fifties workers' councils became the primary administrative units of Yugoslavia's economy. Subsequently, agriculture was largely decollectivized in recognition of the fact that collectivization did not provide an adequate remedy to Yugoslavia's food problems. Large scale grants and loans by the United States and other Western nations helped Yugoslavia overcome the handicap of her political and economic isolation from the Soviet bloc, and made for Western orientation of her trade. The Yugoslav leadership has continued to profess adherence to communist doctrine, application of which to the Yugoslav economic system has been both creative and pragmatic. There is now greater freedom of speech and movement in Yugoslavia than in any other country of Eastern Europe. The courts exercise a measure of independence which is unknown elsewhere in the communist world. In foreign policy Yugoslavia has sought to develop a position of leadership among non-aligned countries.

While receiving large-scale Western assistance, the Belgrade government has expressed basic agreement with the Soviet Union on major foreign policy issues, including the Atlantic Alliance, the Vietnam conflict, and U.S. foreign policy generally. In foreign economic questions Yugoslavia attempted to retain links with other communist states, while developing commercial ties with the West. For example, the Yugoslavs accepted associate membership in COMECON while joining GATT and exploring the prospects for the development of some form of association with the Common Market.

It is Romania, however, which has attracted greater attention in the West than other East European communist countries, with the exception of Czechoslovakia. After embracing for more than a decade a policy of apparent subservience to the Soviet Union, Romania has gone further than all other East European communist countries in successfully defying the Soviet Union. Nicolae Ceaucescu, head of the Romanian Communist Party, linked a cultivation of Romanian nationalism to an anti-Soviet policy. The Romanian Communist Party has been among the least securely based parties of Eastern Europe. To an even greater extent than elsewhere, the Party came to power as a result of Soviet support. Especially in the past decade, Romania's communist leaders have striven to broaden the base of domestic support for the party. Statements by Romanian officials, including, for example, Ceaucescu's speech on May 7, 1966, marking the 45th anniversary of the Romanian Communist Party, contain passages stating that the present-day communist regime has roots deeply embedded in Romania's past. Communism, it is anticipated, may be strengthened by an appeal to Romanian nationalism.

Romania balked at Soviet efforts to reassert Moscow's control over the other communist states in both economic and political affairs. The Soviets attempted to use first COMECON and later the Warsaw Pact to strengthen their position. Yet the Romanian communist leadership, undoubtedly concerned foremost with the strengthening of its domestic position, was not prepared to sacrifice Romania's program of industrialization to acquiesce in Soviet designs for international specialization in COMECON.

Romania appears also to have differed with the Soviet Union on the question of strengthening the Warsaw Pact. After 1956 the Romanian leadership became less and less convinced of the need for an integrated military organization in Eastern Europe. From the Hungarian Revolution the Romanian communist leadership may have drawn the conclusion that, contrary to Soviet propaganda, they need not fear a Western policy of "liberation." Since the West was not prepared to take action to unseat unstable communist regimes in Eastern Europe, Romania no longer needed Soviet troops on her territory, nor was the Warsaw Pact as vital as once it appeared to Romania's security. Therefore, the Romanians sought, wherever possible, to lessen the Soviet military presence in Romania.

In response to a Soviet memorandum calling for changes in the structure of the Warsaw Pact, circulated among member-governments in the autumn of 1965, Romania prepared her own memorandum. The Romanians called for greater consultation with the Soviets on nuclear matters, pointing out that they did not wish to become the object of a nuclear attack. In recent years, Romania has not participated in military maneuvers of the Warsaw Pact. A difference in outlook concerning the West separates Romania from communist governments to the north, i.e., Poland, East Germany, and Czechoslovakia. Not only does the Romanian regime fail to perceive a major threat from the West; she does not see Germany as a potential danger to her existence. Unlike the Poles, for example, Romania has no outstanding frontier differences with the Germans, whose wartime ally Romania was. Instead, in 1967 Bucharest established diplomatic relations with the Bonn Government.

Although the Romanian government has voiced objection to certain foreign policy positions, including the Non-Proliferation Treaty[4] and the Arab-Israeli confrontation, in which Romania expressed support for Israel, the extent to which Romanian foreign policy has diverged from that of the Soviet Union is open to question. Ceaucescau's statements concerning "military blocs," including NATO, do not differ fundamentally from those of the Soviet Union. Since the founding of the Warsaw Pact, the Soviet Union, either singly or in combination with other communist governments, has called for the signing of a non-aggression treaty with NATO or for an all-European collective security pact.[5] Especially since 1963, the Soviet Union has suggested that the dismantling of NATO would obviate the need for the Warsaw Pact.

In his speech of May 7, 1966, Ceaucescau too called for the

dismantling of alliance systems.[6] Shortly after a visit by Brezhnev to Bucharest in May 1966, Romanian officials declared that the dissolution of NATO must precede the dismantling of the Warsaw Pact.[7] The publication of the Ceaucescau speech in *Pravda* on June 12, 1966, just before President de Gaulle's state visit which began on June 20, may have been designed to encourage further French action against NATO.

In a meeting of Warsaw Pact members in Moscow in June and in Bucharest in July 1966, agreement was reached concerning a declaration on peace and security in Europe. The so-called Declaration of Bucharest, which Romania signed, contained a denunciation of the German Federal Republic although, perhaps in deference to Romania, it was agreed to forego "strengthening" the Warsaw Pact.[8] The Declaration contained proposals which did not depart from previous Soviet statements regarding European peace and security: Germany must never be given access to nuclear weapons; existing German frontiers must be recognized as irrevocable; all foreign bases must be liquidated; NATO and the Warsaw Pact should be dissolved; flights by foreign aircraft carrying nuclear weapons over the territory of European states must be banned; bases for nuclear-armed submarines of foreign powers in Europe must be abolished; economic relations among all European states should be developed without discrimination; East Germany and West Germany should reduce the numerical strength of their armed forces by mutual agreement; an all-European conference, excluding the United States, of course, should be convened for the discussion of European peace and security. This final point was repeated in the joint statement issued by Premier Kosygin and President de Gaulle at the end of Kosygin's visit to France in December 1966.

Whether real or contrived, Romania's independence in foreign policy provides the Soviet Union with a new opportunity to achieve a long held goal, namely, the weakening of NATO. The Bucharest Declaration attracted considerable interest in the West. For example, in a speech before the Belgian-American Society on January 24, 1967, Belgium's foreign minister, Pierre Harmel, called for the development of a European security system similar in many ways to that set forth in the Bucharest Declaration.[9] Whatever the reason for Bucharest's independence from the Soviet Union, in the West the perception of Romania as the France of the Warsaw Pact has grown.

Internal liberalization has made less progress in Romania than in most other East European communist countries. While emphasizing in foreign policy its independence on some issues from the Soviet Union, the Bucharest regime has remained a repressive dictatorship. The domestic policies followed by the government have been designed to strengthen the position of the Communist Party. In fact, Romania's foreign policies are in keeping with a domestic policy whose objective is to strengthen the hold of the communist regime.

As this brief review suggests, the pattern of change has varied from country to country in Eastern Europe. There is no correlation between internal liberalization and the quest for greater autonomy in foreign policy. Poland, for example, which has experienced considerable internal liberalization, adheres to a foreign policy more akin to that of the Soviet Union than does Romania. In contrast, Romania has departed on certain foreign policy issues from the Soviet policy, but internal liberalization has not progressed so far as it has in Poland. Although Yugoslavia has gone further than any other East European country in internal liberalization, Belgrade's foreign policy bears many similarities to that of the Soviet Union.

In East European political systems the role of the Communist Party in decision-making remains paramount. All decisions of national importance continue to be made within the respective politburos. Yet it is worthy of note that within Eastern Europe there is pressure from within the Party itself for the confinement of the Party's role to ideological, political, and educational functions, granting to managers and technicians a greater voice in the taking of decisions about the implementation of Party programs. In all countries there has been an effort in the taking and execution of policy decisions to replace wasteful methods with more efficient ones.

On balance, writers in Eastern Europe enjoyed greater freedom of expression in the 1960's than they had in the previous decade. Nevertheless, by and large they have not created works which incurred the wrath of the communist leadership. In fact, in the 1960's, the state has exerted a control more subtle than before. Now government-imposed changes in the editorial boards of journals rather than imprisonment of writers provide the means of preserving government censorship. However, the Party, no longer enjoying a monopoly in the market place of ideas, faces a dilemma: Communist ideas, when expressed by orthodox writers, are often presented with such drabness that they no longer arouse the interest of the masses. On the other hand, writers with the ability to communicate ideas effectively are not prepared to communicate communist ideas.

It would be surprising indeed if the countries of Eastern Europe had not experienced change, especially in the past decade. It has proven ever more difficult to isolate peoples in one country from developments elsewhere in the world. The scientific-technological revolution has affected the lives of peoples in both communist and non-communist political systems. Changes within Western Europe —the attainment of sustained high levels of economic growth, rising living standards, and the emergence of the European Community—have had an impact upon Eastern Europe. Moreover, Western perceptions of change in the political, social, and economic systems of Eastern Europe have affected Western foreign policies, especially the Western outlook toward the security arrangements appropriate to the defense of the West. Eastern Europe, Western Europe, and the United States have been engaged in an interactive process.

As Eastern European communist regimes have shown signs of having gained some degree of autonomy in foreign policy or of having relaxed internal pressures upon their populations, not a few leaders in NATO countries have concluded that the East-West confrontation has either ended or altered substantially. For example, President de Gaulle, on the occasion of his visit to the Soviet Union in June 1966, declared his interest in "the start of the implementation of new relations with the so-called Eastern European states, toward detente, entente and cooperation."[10] The changed French perception of the Soviet threat makes possible not only France's withdrawal from the NATO command structure, but the development of a diplomacy designed to strengthen links between France and Eastern Europe.

EAST-WEST EXCHANGES AND TRANSACTIONS

All major NATO countries have adopted policies designed to increase the volume of East-West trade, credits, technical assistance, travel, and cultural exchanges.[11] Although the pace of agreements has increased since 1960, the idea of expanding East-West contacts has long found favor in Western Europe and the United States. The Soviet-Yugoslav dispute of 1948 produced Western agreements with Yugoslavia, which became the recipient of military and economic aid from West European countries and the United States, as well as of expanded cultural and trade relationships with the West. Subsequently, as other communist regimes indicated, in one way or another, a measure of autonomy in foreign relations or underwent internal liberalization, they too became objects of increased attention from the West, although none received aid on a scale of that accorded Yugoslavia.

Shortly after the death of Stalin, Western governments began to reduce restrictions upon the sale of strategic materials to communist countries and to conclude economic and cultural agreements with East European regimes. Although the expansion of contacts between Eastern Europe and the West received its greatest impetus in the 1960's, many agreements had been signed and high level delegations exchanged in the years following the death of Stalin, especially in the latter half of the 1950's.

President de Gaulle set forth his vision of Europe in which barriers between East and West would be lowered in his press conference of March 25, 1959, when he discussed the idea of a Europe extending from the "Atlantic to the Urals," whose peoples might engage in collaborative activities, especially in the granting of assistance to less developed areas.[12]

Several subsequent events influenced French policy toward Eastern Europe. The ending of the Berlin crisis after the construction of the Berlin Wall in August 1961 removed the immediate Soviet threat to Western Europe. The establishment of what appeared to French policymakers to be a nuclear stalemate and the growth of French fear of American hegemony in NATO contributed to a rise in French interest in the expansion of contacts with East European countries.

Moreover, the apparent widening of the Sino-Soviet conflict and the perception of change in Eastern Europe led France to step up her efforts to develop new contacts with communist states in Europe and to extricate herself from her commitments to NATO. French foreign policy, especially after 1962, revealed a growing preoccupation with change in Eastern Europe. Between 1963 and

1965, France signed a total of 15 major trade agreements with East European countries and the Soviet Union. She received visits of government officials from all East European countries except East Germany and Albania.[13]

In relationships between Eastern and Western Europe, Germany has always played a role of major importance. The unsolved problem of German reunification, one of the great legacies of World War II, remains a source of East-West contention. For generations, German foreign policy has been designed not only to maintain ties with countries to the West, but to strengthen German links with governments to the East. Although postwar German policymakers gave primacy to the Federal Republic's relations with countries to the West, in the 1960's once again German interest turned toward the East. On June 14, 1961, the Bundestag adopted unanimously a resolution which included the following passage:

> The Federal Government is called upon to pursue with its allies an eastern policy aiming at the restoration of a free and all-German state that maintains friendly and prosperous relations with the Soviet Union and all East European countries. To this end, the Federal Government should grasp every opportunity to bring about a normalization of relations between the Federal Republic and the East European countries without abandoning vital German interests.[14]

In a speech delivered on April 3, 1964, Foreign Minister Schroeder made a detailed statement of Bonn's policy toward Eastern Europe:

> We do not expect our Eastern European policy to yield any spectacular success. But if we continue to steer our course patiently and consistently we will promote understanding for our position in East Europe, too. The Poles, for instance, in particular, should be well able to place themselves in our position, for they know from their own history that a nation cannot remain divided forever. I believe there are indications that in some East European countries there is growing understanding for the German problem and that their judgment is more independent than it has been in the past. It appears to me that our desire for true relaxation of tensions is meeting with more understanding in those countries than with the Soviet government for the time being. Let us not underrate this trend, for the voice of those states is beginning to carry more weight.[15]

According to Chancellor Kiesinger, "Germany was for centuries the bridge between Western and Eastern Europe. We should like to fulfill this mission also in our own time. We are anxious to improve relations with those of our eastern neighbors who share our desire in all fields of economic, cultural and political life and to establish diplomatic relations wherever this is possible under the circumstances."[16]

German officials have stressed the necessity for the Federal Republic "to dispel mistrust and fear and thus to relax tension in Europe."[17] It would perhaps be remarkable had the German government not expressed an interest in the development of links with neighbors to the East more than a generation after World War II. Germany, in many ways like France, has had an historic interest in Eastern Europe. The Federal Republic has encouraged contacts with Eastern Europe in order to reduce fear of a resurgent Germany among Bonn's eastern neighbors, to enhance the prospects for eventual German reunification, and to strengthen commercial links with a region which, before World War II, was a major market for German exports.

The German policy of increased contact with Eastern Europe finds support among members of both the SPD and the CDU. Indeed, the major parties disagree only about the extent to which Bonn should take initiatives to improve relations with Eastern Europe. The advent of the Grand Coalition in December 1966 gave new impetus to the policy, but the Soviet invasion of Czechoslovakia led to a lessening, temporarily at least, of Bonn's initiatives in Eastern Europe. Because such a policy is based upon a widespread consensus, however, it is likely to receive priority attention, whichever political party governs the Federal Republic.

Dependent upon trade to a greater extent than most other nations, Britain has sought to obtain markets for her exports in Eastern Europe. Moreover, the British have seen in trade a device for the "normalization" of relations with communist states. Especially since 1962, British officials have noted in the communist world trends which may hold implications of considerable importance for the West: the widening of the Sino-Soviet split; internal pressure for higher living standards, greater freedom of expression, and the introduction of certain Western organizational techniques; the growth of nationalism in Eastern Europe; and the existence of an East-West nuclear stalemate. British foreign policy objectives in Eastern Europe do not differ greatly in many respects from those of other West European countries. However, unlike French policymakers, British leaders have not given expression to a grand vision of Europe's future. Unlike the German Federal Republic, the British have no pressing national interests related to developments in Eastern Europe. Instead, Britain has stressed the importance of an expansion of trade to the British economy and the prospects for "normalization" of East-West relations supposedly afforded by the proliferation of contacts.[18]

The United States has also placed itself in the forefront of those nations of the West engaged in the expansion of contacts with communist countries in Europe. In 1964 U.S. officials initiated a policy of "building bridges" to communist regimes in Europe.[19] In a speech on February 25, 1964, Secretary of State Rusk gave evidence of changing official U.S. perceptions of communist regimes in Europe:

> The smaller communist countries of Eastern Europe have increasingly, though in varying degrees, asserted their own policies. We have always considered it unnatural for the diverse peoples of Eastern Europe, with their own talents and proud traditions, to be submerged in a monolithic block. We have wanted these peoples, while living in friendship with their Russian and other neighbors, to develop in accordance with their own national aspirations and genius. And they seem to bear a strong nostalgia for their traditional ties with the West. Most of them are increasing their trade and other contacts with Western Europe and, to some extent, with us.[20]

By the second half of the 1950's patterns of interaction similar to those between the West and Yugoslavia had begun to develop between the West and other communist countries in Eastern Europe. In the first half of the 1960's, especially after 1962, there was an acceleration of official contacts between East European countries and Western Europe and the United States. The year 1963 appears to have been most notable for the rise in such contacts. Conceivably, the breakdown of the Brussels negotiations and the failure of the Kennedy Administration's "grand design for Atlantic partnership" contributed to a shift of focus in Western policymaking. According to French statements, it was the lifting by the Soviet Union of its threat to West Berlin after the building of the Berlin Wall in August 1961 which marked the beginning of a new period of East-West relations and relaxation of tensions in Europe. Or perhaps the Cuban missile crisis of October 1962 gave impetus in the West to renewed interest in contacts with East European countries. Certainly it was widely held in the West after the Cuban missile crisis that the Soviet Union sought to encourage a relaxation of East-West tensions. Also the Soviet Union appeared to be loosening its grip upon Eastern Europe. Hence opportunities abounded for effecting beneficial changes in East-West relations. This interest was shared no less by the United States than by most West European leaders. West European and U.S. policies toward the expansion of trade, the establishment of cultural exchange agreements, and the exchange of high-level visits moved along parallel paths, although the objectives of certain NATO countries, notably the United States and France, differed.

Although visits of Cabinet ministers and other official exchanges between Eastern Europe and the West have increased over the past decade, there has been a similar increase in official contacts among the communist states of Europe. For every country except Albania, face-to-face meetings of politburo members of East European countries increased by 75 percent between 1962 and 1965. There was a marked increase in agreements concluded among East European countries. In 1962, for example, fifty percent more agreements were concluded than in 1960, and in 1965, eleven percent more agreements were signed than in 1962. For the most part, agreements among communist states were commercial in nature, although scientific and technical agreements accounted for about 25 percent of the accords signed between 1960 and 1965.[21]

EAST-WEST TRADE PATTERNS

The rise in contacts between Eastern Europe and the West has contributed to a growth in East-West trade. Between 1957 and 1964 exports from East European countries to the major states of the West (Britain, France, the German Federal Republic, Italy, and the United States) more than doubled, rising from $607 million to $1.33 billion. During the same period, exports from major Western countries to Eastern Europe increased at a less rapid rate —from $954 million in 1957 to $1.65 billion in 1964. A major proportion of trade from Eastern Europe to the West consists of agricultural products. For several East European countries—Poland, Romania, Yugoslavia, Bulgaria, and Hungary—the bulk of exports to the West, especially to Western Europe, consists of agricultural products. Hence, the future of agricultural trade with

Western Europe and Common Market policies on agriculture are of great importance to most East European countries.

Viewed from the perspective of total world trade, however, trade between Eastern Europe and the West has not increased greatly over the past decade. In fact, the trade of Yugoslavia, Czechoslovakia, East Germany, Poland, and Hungary with major Western countries, namely, France, the German Federal Republic, Great Britain, Italy, and the United States, has declined as a percentage of their total trade. In contrast, Bulgaria and Romania have registered a steady increase in trade with major Western countries since 1955 and 1959, respectively. In the case of Bulgaria, trade with major Western countries increased from one percent of total Bulgarian world trade to 20 percent in 1964. For Romania, trade with the West rose from 18 percent of total trade in 1959 to 27 percent in 1964. Of East European countries, Bulgaria and Romania before this period ranked lowest in trade with the West as a percentage of total world trade. Thus the increases which they registered brought them to a level of trade more or less similar to that of other East European countries. Although all of these countries showed a slight increase in trade with the West, as a percentage of their total world trade, between 1961 and 1963, they did not attain as high a percentage of total trade as they enjoyed in the late 1950's. At the same time, trade among East European countries, as a percentage of their total world commerce, has increased.[22]

Since 1955 none of the East European countries has traded more with the West than with the Soviet Union. Yet, throughout the period, all East European countries, except Albania and Bulgaria, maintained a greater percentage of their trade with the major countries of the West than did the Soviet Union. In fact, the bulk of the trade of East European countries with non-communist states is with the major nations of the West.

Despite the rise in East-West trade, the communist countries remain heavily dependent economically upon each other. Between 1957 and 1964, the contribution of communist bloc trade to national income increased in every East European country. In Romania, the increase was lowest (only one percent); whereas in Czechoslovakia, East Germany, and Hungary it rose by almost 10 percent. Moreover, in this period the proportion of each country's trade conducted with the Soviet Union increased significantly.

There is a correlation between an East European country's dependence upon bloc trade and its conformity to Soviet policy. Those East European countries for which bloc trade accounts for the lowest percentages of national income are Albania, Romania, and Poland. Each of these countries has adopted policies which display a measure of independence from the Soviet Union. In the early 1960's, Albania left the Soviet bloc. Especially in domestic affairs, Poland has manifested independence from the Soviet Union. In foreign policy, Romania has not always followed completely the Soviet line. Conceivably, the willingness of an East European government to adopt a stance independent of that of Moscow depends in part upon its relative immunity to economic pressure from the Soviet Union.[23] Given this correlation, a reduction in the trade dependence of East European countries upon the Soviet Union could increase their willingness to adopt policies less aligned with those of the Soviet Union. This development, in turn, is dependent upon a reversal in trade trends which even the major Western powers, with their efforts to increase East-West commerce, have proven unable thus far to effect.

In recent years there has been a rise in interest in Eastern Europe in the "normalization" of relations with the West. In particular, De Gaulle's ideas find acceptance there. According to a poll conducted by Radio Free Europe in the spring of 1967, a large percentage of respondents believed that France, to a greater extent than other Western states, had adopted policies designed to promote better East-West relations.[24] Among East European countries whose policies might lead to improved East-West relations, Romania ranked high, although in the Czech sample, Yugoslavia received an even higher rating. The German Federal Republic was most frequently cited as the Western country, and China as the communist power, whose policies placed the greatest obstacles in the way of better East-West relations. Interestingly, in all cases respondents ranked the Soviet Union just behind China as the communist country whose policies stood in the way of improved relations between East and West. Among the problems which posed the greatest obstacles to better East-West relations respondents listed, in that order, the Vietnam conflict, the existence of nuclear weapons and other armaments, the legacies of World War II, and conflicting ideologies. In order to achieve peace and unity in Europe, the largest number of persons interviewed agreed, there was great need for "good will and contacts" between East and West.

In the Czechoslovak and Hungarian samples, 19 percent, respectively, saw the need for a solution to the German problem in order to achieve peace and unity in Europe. In the Czechoslovak, Hungarian, and Polish samples, 18, 19, and 12 percent, respectively, expressed the view that general and complete disarmament was needed in order to achieve peace and unity in Europe.

Those persons who responded affirmatively to the question as to why East European leaders sought to increase transactions with the West were in general agreement that their governments saw such contacts as an economic necessity, particularly profitable because they earned needed foreign exchange. The largest proportion of the minority of persons interviewed who responded negatively to this question believed that their government was not interested in increasing contacts with the West because the government "follows Soviet orders." Of greater significance, however, is the fact that by a ratio of nearly five to one respondents expressed the view that their governments sought greater contacts with the West and did so because of their economic importance. Finally, the sample revealed an interest among East Europeans at the non-governmental level in the expansion of transactions with countries of the West and in the development of more "normal" East-West relations.

For the most part, both the leaders of East European countries and leaders in the West have expressed an interest in the "normalization" of relations through the dismantling of barriers between Eastern and Western Europe. Leaders and important non-governmental elites in the West favor the development in Eastern Europe of "national" governments whose dependence upon the Soviet Union will be diminished.

The efficacy of East-West interaction as a means for accelerating trends toward desired kinds of change in Eastern Europe depends in part upon the receptivity of the leadership elites of communist countries. East European communist leaders, as the RFE opinion poll suggests, appear to place great emphasis upon the development of economic, especially trade, relationships with the West, which they hope will enable their regimes to attain desired economic goals. Especially, they seek access to certain advanced Western technologies. They have turned to the West for imports of computers and equipment for automation, pulp and paper plants, steel mills, chemical production facilities, and factories for the manufacture of synthetic fibers. For their programs of economic development, the countries of Eastern Europe need Western products to a greater extent than the West needs exports from Eastern Europe. The idea of trade as an avenue towards collaboration on a wide range of problems—economic and perhaps political—is not in the foreground of official East European thought. In fact, "peaceful engagement," the idea of an ever-increasing web of relationships which one day will lead to a form of unification, or entente, between Eastern and Western Europe is seen as a Western strategy designed to sow disunity in the communist world and to lead to the disintegration of communist regimes.[25]

Perhaps an indication of the priorities of East European governing elites is to be found in a comparison between trade agreements and cultural exchange accords concluded over the last decade. Trade agreements far outnumber cultural accords. In fact, many of the cultural agreements signed between communist regimes and the West provide for the exchange of scientific data and appear to have been designed primarily to obtain information vital to East European economic programs. In sum, the proponents of "peaceful engagement" and convergence are far more numerous and vocal in the West than in communist countries of Eastern Europe.[26]

Soviet policy, sensitive to West European interest in bridging cold war barriers, has included proposals for greater East-West interaction. In his speech of April 24, 1967, at Karlovy Vary, Czechoslovakia, Brezhnev declared:

> Under pressure from a broad strata of the working class, in a number of European socialist and social democratic parties, the desire is growing to get rid of the ballast of the "cold war" and to join in the search for a constructive solution in the field of consolidating security in Europe. We can see these new trends. They show that at present more favorable conditions are being created for widening contacts with the social democratic movement for purposes of a joint struggle of communists and social democrats against the old division of Europe into military blocs, and for peace and social progress.
>
> The Communist Party of the Soviet Union, for its part, is willing to develop contacts with those social democratic parties which wish to march with us in the interests of struggle against aggressors, for peace, and for the security of the peoples of Europe.[27]

In the same speech, Brezhnev suggested that the Soviet Union still saw "socialism and communism" in Western Europe as the "historic aim" of the communist movement:

> We are convinced that the working class and peoples of West Europe will sooner or later set out on the road to socialism. The communist parties selflessly struggle for this very thing, for the only correct road guaranteeing the triumph of democracy, peace, and the full development of the creative forces of each people.[28]

Although the gap between Soviet and Western policy remains unbridged, in recent years there has been a rise in interest in Eastern Europe in a "normalization" of relations with the West. In particular, De Gaulle's ideas find acceptance among some in Eastern Europe. Especially among non-communist groups, De Gaulle's initiatives, together with his vision of Europe's future, represent an effort to break the "stalemate" in East-West relations in Europe, even if it is not possible to achieve complete liberation from communist rule. But the Soviet invasion of Czechoslovakia is indicative of the limitations upon the maneuverability, in both domestic and foreign policy, available to East European countries.

EUROPEAN ECONOMIC INTEGRATION AND EAST-WEST RELATIONS

It was not until 1962 that the European Economic Community attracted great attention in Eastern Europe. In 1962, during the negotiations for British Common Market entry, the leaders of the Soviet Union and other communist states stressed anti-EEC arguments which were primarily ideological in nature. The EEC was condemned as a vestige of capitalism. It was argued that the Common Market would lead to German "revanchism." Moreover, the EEC was criticized for its allegedly detrimental effect upon less developed countries.

Since 1962, however, communist governments have altered their policy toward the Common Market. Instead of outright condemnation, they have sought solutions to some of the problems posed by the EEC. In general, East European countries stress the importance of minimizing the effect of EEC commercial policy upon Eastern Europe. Certain features of the EEC have been of principal concern in Eastern Europe. As early as February 1963, Community regulations on cereal grains, poultry, eggs, and pork were put into operation. Subsequently, agricultural regulations governing imports of other farm goods were adopted. Imports of agricultural commodities from Eastern Europe have been treated in the same way as such imports from all other third countries. Such commodities must pay taxes established by the Community to raise the price of farm imports to levels set by the EEC. Thus far, the EEC agricultural policy has not seriously affected agricultural imports from Communist countries because the EEC has only begun to place into operation those features which are likely to have a major impact on Eastern Europe.[29] Moreover, the economic growth which Western Europe experienced in the last decade has contributed to an expanding, rather than contracting, market for foodstuffs, thus lessening the potentially adverse effect of the EEC upon East European agricultural exports. Nevertheless, East European countries share with non-communist countries, including the United States, an interest in agricultural trade with the EEC.[30]

During the coming decade EEC trade policy is likely to exert a greater influence upon East-West trade than in the past, especially if EEC countries take measures designed to restrict imports of mineral fuels and agricultural products from Eastern Europe. The EEC, concerned about the potentially harmful effects upon the Common Market of the dumping of agricultural products by communist countries, has adopted regulations designed to prevent such dumping. According to these regulations, if the sales of any communist state to any Common Market country increase to a level 20 percent above the average annual sales of that product in 1960 and 1961, the EEC Commission can act to halt additional imports. The Commission can take such action if "the market, in one or several member states, is being disrupted, or is threatened with serious disturbances."

Although they have attempted to avoid the granting of formal diplomatic recognition to the Community, two East European countries, Yugoslavia and Poland, have conducted technical discussions in Brussels on the development of trade with the Community. The Yugoslav talks, in January and May 1965, were designed to permit both parties to explore the prospects for the "balanced development" of trade. According to a press release after the May meeting,

> The Yugoslav delegation pointed out that it was important that Yugoslavia maintain her sales of farm produce at a level that would enable her to buy more in the EEC, and also to increase her indus-

> trial exports. The Commission delegation expressed the hope that sales to Yugoslavia—particularly in industrial products—would expand steadily.[31]

Apparently, the EEC sought to encourage the expansion of industrial imports from Yugoslavia and perhaps other communist countries as a means of compensating for anticipated losses of agricultural markets in Western Europe. The discussions with Yugoslavia, the most detailed talks undertaken by the EEC with any communist country, did not yield agreement, however, either for Yugoslavia's association with the Community or for the expansion of trade.

Barring a drastic curtailment of agricultural and fuel imports under a quota system, present trends do not suggest the likelihood of a diminution of East-West trade over the next decade.[32] Thus far internal tariff reductions in the Common Market have not drastically affected EEC trade with the communist states. In part, this may be explained by the fact that the pricing of exports from communist countries often bears little relation to actual production costs. In many cases goods produced in communist countries can be sold or bartered by East European governments depending upon the economic or political needs of the day.

East European leaders have expressed a preference for bilateral trade agreements with the West. Whenever possible, they have shunned formal contacts with West European integrative institutions such as the EEC. Instead, depending upon their economic needs, East European leaders have preferred to expand contacts with certain Western countries, including Britain and France, more than with others. As the Common Market moves toward the end of its third transitional period, East European countries will find it necessary to conclude agreements with the EEC rather than with individual countries, since the development of commercial policy will become the responsibility of the EEC Commission. The EEC will then face the need to work out a common policy on trade with Eastern Europe.

WESTERN EUROPE, THE ATLANTIC ALLIANCE, AND THE COMMUNIST STATES

Not a few in the West have questioned the priorities which ought to guide foreign policy. Should the strengthening of the Atlantic Alliance and the movement toward West European integration take precedence over the development of new relationships between Eastern and Western Europe? Given Western perceptions of change in Eastern Europe, the question has arisen whether Atlantic security arrangements established in the early postwar period are relevant to the major East-West problems of today. Does the existence of NATO enhance or hinder the prospects for accelerating change in Eastern Europe? Would a politically integrated Western Europe make more or less promising the prospect of strengthening political and economic links between Eastern and Western Europe?

The future of relations between Eastern and Western Europe preoccupies not a few Europeans. Yet the strengthening of West European integration within an Atlantic framework need not be incompatible with, and may even be vital to, the "normalization" of relations between the West and Eastern Europe. Whatever the form which relations between the West and Eastern Europe assume, the need for integration in Western Europe is likely to become increasingly urgent in a world of superpowers. Should the opportunity eventually arise, an integrated Western Europe might enter various forms of association with certain of the countries of Eastern Europe. With products of advanced technologies needed by East European countries and potential markets needed for East European exports, the EEC will possess considerable leverage in negotiations with these countries. In fact, after its third transitional period, the Common Market will probably conclude a series of commercial agreements with them. To the extent that integration contributes to technological development and economic growth in Western Europe, the position of the West vis-à-vis Eastern Europe will be strengthened. Technologically and economically, the West will possess, in even greater abundance, the products and processes which East European peoples seek to obtain. As a result, Western Europe will gain bargaining advantages in concluding agreements with the East designed to speed desired change.

West European integration within an Atlantic framework bears an important relationship to the future of Germany. Since the founding of the Federal Republic, German leaders have focused attention primarily upon the development of close links with the West. To a considerable extent, German dynamism, in the generation following World War II, was harnessed to the formidable task of regaining German international respectability. Moreover, close identification with the West was held to offer the most promising prospects for Germany to achieve reunification.[33]

In recent years, the idea of unilateral German approaches to the Soviet Union on the issue of reunification has gained adherents in Germany as well as elsewhere in the West. The Federal Republic, it is suggested, should be encouraged in such efforts. But this policy is fraught with serious implications both for Germany and the West. Left to make her own settlement with the Soviet Union, the Federal Republic would be tempted to offer concessions in the interest neither of other Western countries nor of Germany itself in order to attain reunification. Psychologically, the Germans would find it difficult not to accept from the Soviet Union a proposal which gave promise of reunification. The communists would find attractive the prospect of exploiting German vulnerabilities on reunification as a means of detaching the Federal Republic from its Western moorings. The position of the Federal Republic on the reunification issue is strong politically, however, since Bonn has important bargaining points vis-à-vis the Soviet Union, of which perhaps the greatest is German membership in NATO. Thus the bargaining position of the Federal Republic on the reunification issue, is strong politically but weak psychologically. The political strength is likely to be maintained and the ability of the Soviet Union to exploit German sentiment favoring reunification diminished so long as the Federal Republic has strong Atlantic links.

At this point in time, it is not possible to foresee a Europe in which Germany would be reunified on terms mutually satisfactory to all of the major victors of World War II. Although the prospects are far from promising, however, the eastern and western parts of Germany could be rejoined one day as part of a broader European framework in which East European states would have gained greater autonomy and perhaps have undergone a considerable measure of internal liberalization. The strengthening of West European integration would hold important implications for the peoples of Eastern Europe. If progress toward an integrated Western Europe within an Atlantic framework led East European peoples and their governments to explore the prospects for closer ties with the West, the German Federal Republic, by maintaining its ties with the West, could contribute to the integration of Western Europe and hence to the "pull" which the West might exert upon Eastern Europe, including East Germany.

Prospects for effecting such a major change in Eastern Europe are slim indeed. In fact, German reunification, if it were possible in the absence of evolutionary change in Eastern Europe, would not necessarily serve the interests of the West unless a reunified German state were to become part of a West European counterpoise to the Soviet Union. Without Germany, the ability of Western Europe to perform such a function vis-à-vis the Soviet Union in Europe would be dubious. Although the United States should not abandon the vision of eventual German reunification, the German question is related to the broader issue of Germany's place in Europe and in Atlantic relationships.[34]

The Soviet Union has not altered its policy to such an extent that an Atlantic Alliance no longer remains necessary. For the foreseeable future a great disparity will remain between Soviet and West European military strength. Nor is it likely that Soviet influence in East European countries will diminish markedly. On many important political questions East European countries, including Romania, can be expected to adopt policies similiar to or compatible with those of the Soviet Union. East European countries will retain strong trading links with the Soviet Union despite their new commercial relationships with the West. They will continue to look to the Soviet Union for defense and for markets for many of their exports. The prospects for fundamental changes in the alignment of East European countries are less promising than the prospects for West European integration.

According to the official French conception, a strong, independent Western Europe could assume a major burden of its own defense and be freed from U.S. "hegemony." Eventually, Western Europe might be able to achieve a "union" of all European peoples.[35] The prospects for a European equilibrium such as that desired by France are not promising unless West European countries are prepared to create a West European political union and technological community. Within such a framework, Western Europe might assume a greater burden of its own defense than has been possible within NATO as presently constituted. If Western Europe could provide more adequately for its own defense, reductions in U.S. forces in Western Europe could be made in return for reductions in Soviet forces in Eastern Europe, assuming a military equilibrium in Europe. Such changes, in turn, could increase the maneuverability of East European governments in their relations with the West, even hasten the movement toward internal liberalization. The expansion of contacts between Eastern Europe and Western Europe could contribute to the creation eventually of that "wider Europe," of which Europeans increasingly speak. Conceivably, Europe west of the eastern Polish frontier would become a more "European" Europe. Although an integrated Western Europe would retain a "special relationship" with the United States and East European countries would still have important links with the Soviet Union, economic, cultural, and perhaps political ties between Eastern and Western Europe would be strengthened. Hence, West European integration is not incompatible with the ultimate formation of a "wider Europe," in which East European countries would eventually enter into a variety of forms of association with Western Europe. But the question remains as to whether the Soviet Union, given the experience of Czechoslovakia in 1968, could tolerate the emergence of a "wider Europe" in which Soviet influence was diminished.

NOTES

1. The term "Eastern Europe," as used in this chapter, includes the following countries: Poland, East Germany, Czechoslovakia, Hungary, Yugoslavia, Albania, Romania, and Bulgaria.
2. The Harmel Report, reprinted in *Atlantic Community Quarterly,* Vol. 6, No. 1 (Spring 1968), pp. 115–116.
3. In an interview with Henry Shapiro of United Press International on July 27, 1966, Premier Kadar declared that over the past decade Hungary had achieved greater cultural freedom. Most political prisoners had been released. Discussing the Hungarian economic system, Kadar suggested that "The economic mechanism must be changed in order to comply with the new demands. That is why our Party's Central Committee had commissioned the drafting of a reform and has confirmed and resolved the implementation of this reform. An essential feature of this reform is the fact that in the future we will not insure the planned development of the people's economy by central instructions prescribing even details, but by economic means, by providing for increased material incentives for enterprises and the working people. More independence will be extended to enterprises and there will be more scope for initiative and a prevalence of the democratic rights of the working people." Text of Kadar Interview. *Nepszabadsag* (Budapest), August 2, 1966.
4. Romania protested that the draft of the Non-Proliferation Treaty

circulated early in 1968 "discriminates profoundly" against the non-nuclear powers. Romania sought a "precise" security guarantee to non-nuclear signatories and the requirement that both the United States and the Soviet Union be subject to the same inspection to be imposed on non-nuclear countries. *New York Times,* February 7, 1968, p. 8.

5. See, for example, Sydney Gruson: "Action in Prague," *New York Times,* January 29, 1956, p. 1; William J. Jorden, "Soviet Army Plans to Quit Rumania in Near Future," *New York Times,* May 27, 1958, p. 1; "Text of Statement of the Warsaw Pact Members Issued after Moscow Meeting," *New York Times,* February 5, 1960, p. 4; "Soviet Proffers a Pact with NATO at Geneva Talks," *New York Times,* February 21, 1963, p. 1; Seymour Topping, "Moscow Asserts NATO Atom Force Threatens Peace," *New York Times,* April 10, 1963, p. 1; "Reds Renew Bid at Geneva for Nonaggression Accord," *New York Times,* May 18, 1963, p. 2; Seymour Topping, "Kennedy and Khrushchev Call Pact a Step to Peace But Not a War Preventive," *New York Times,* July 27, 1963, p. 1.

6. *New York Times,* May 14, 1966, p. 4. He declared: "The military blocs and the existence of military bases and of . . . troops on the territory of other states is one of the barriers in the path of collaboration among the peoples. The existence of blocs as well as the sending of troops to other countries is an anachronism incompatible with the independence and national sovereignty of the peoples and normal relations among states."

7. See the *New York Times,* May 14, 15, 19, 1966.

8. *New York Times,* July 7, 9, 1966.

9. *New York Times,* January 25, 1967, p. 1.

10. Ambassade de France, *Speeches and Conferences,* No. 247, p. 2.

11. Although most NATO countries have sought to expand their contacts with Eastern Europe, attention in this chapter is focused upon Britain, France, the German Federal Republic, and the United States. For a list of contacts between NATO and East European countries in 1965 and the first four months of 1966, see NATO Press Service, *East-West Contacts,* Press Release (1966), Paris, June 21, 1966.

12. See *Major Addresses, Statements and Press Conferences of General de Gaulle.* New York: French Embassy Press and Information Service, p. 45.

13. During his press conference of September 4, 1965, De Gaulle noted that France was strengthening her links with East European countries: "Thus our contacts and our exchanges are multiplying with the countries of the East, each of them, of course, being treated only in consideration of its national personality. In this respect, we attach great importance to the new trend of our relations with Russia. We are pleased with the results achieved on the occasion of President Maurer's visit with respect to French-Rumanian relations. With great

pleasure we are going to receive President Cyrankiewicz, hoping that his presence here will serve the practical rapprochement of the French and Polish peoples, friends and allies at all times in their history. We do not hesitate to envisage that the day will come when, in order to achieve a constructive entente from the Atlantic to the Urals, all of Europe will wish to settle its own problems and, above all, that of Germany, by the only means that will make it possible to do so—that of a general agreement. On that day, our continent could once again assume in the world, for the good of all men, the role which is worthy of its resources and capacities." Ambassade de France, Speeches from Press Conference No. 228, September 9, 1965, *International Relations,* pp. 3–4.

14. Quoted in Gerhard Schroeder, "Germany Looks at Eastern Europe." *Foreign Affairs,* October 1965, p. 16. See also Diane A. Kressler, "Germany, NATO and Europe." ORBIS, Vol. X, No. 1 (Spring 1966), pp. 223–239.

15. Quoted in Zbigniew Brzezinski, *Alternative to Partition.* New York: McGraw-Hill, 1965, p. 95.

16. *The Bulletin:* A Weekly Survey of German Affairs Issued by the Press and Information Office of the German Federal Government. Bonn, December 20, 1966.

17. Gerhard Schroeder, "Germany Looks at Eastern Europe," *Foreign Affairs* (October 1965), pp. 18–19.

18. Although concerned with economic gains from trade with Eastern Europe, Britain has often been prepared, because of the potential political utility of trade, to permit an East European country to correct a trade deficit with one member of the sterling area by its surplus with another. Thus, Poland might balance a trade surplus with Australia and a trade deficit with Britain.

19. According to Under-Secretary of State Averell Harriman, in a statement on March 10, 1964, before the Subcommittee on Europe of the House of Representatives: "We hope to see, and are trying to encourage, a progressive loosening of external authority over East European countries and the continuing reassertion of national autonomy and diversity. We believe such evolution is a slow but sure way toward freedom and national independence. . . . Our policy is to encourage the evolution now in progress by using every kind of peaceful contact available." Quoted in Zbigniew Brzezinski, *Alternative to Partition.* New York: McGraw-Hill, 1965, p. 122.

20. "Why We Treat Different Communist Countries Differently." Speech by Secretary of State Dean Rusk, February 25, 1964. Department of State Publication 7999. Washington: U.S. Government Printing Office, 1964.

21. Foreign Policy Research Institute, *Changing Trends in East Central Europe.* Book of appendices, A-E (Mimeographed) June 1967, Appendix B, pp. 10–12.

22. *Ibid.,* Appendix E, pp. 4–6.

23. This finding is contained in the study entitled *Changing Trends*

in East Central Europe: Implications for U.S. Security. Foreign Policy Research Institute, University of Pennsylvania, 1967.

24. A total of 892 nationals visiting the West from Czechoslovakia, Hungary, and Poland were interviewed. Most of the interviewing was conducted by an independent opinion research institute in Vienna. Specifically, the sample consisted of 314 Poles, 292 Hungarians, 184 Czechs, and 102 Slovaks. The samples are by and large representative of the major population groups included in them. Nevertheless, the urban population, the well educated, and men are over-represented in all three national samples.

25. For example, in Poland, the pro-regime journal *Slomo Poszechne* (Warsaw, January 6, 1966), attacked Western proposals for Polish-German reconciliation: "Under the cover of 'aid and cooperation;' under the excuse of 'European integration' and 'reconciliation' with West Germany, Washington is attempting to influence Polish public opinion, to loosen the ties uniting Poland with the Soviet Union and with the other socialist countries and gradually to lure our country into the sphere of influence of the imperialist camp. To put it plainly, it is suggested that Poland, in return for some unspecified benefits, should change sides in the present day world." "The Dangers of 'Peaceful Engagement.' " *East Europe,* March 1966, p. 31. In East Germany, fears are expressed that the Federal Republic will increase its political ties with East European countries. For example, Walter C. Weicht, addressing the Romanian Party Congress in July 1965, declared himself in favor of the establishment of diplomatic relations between Bucharest and Bonn in the interest of "peaceful coexistence." However, he suggested, "Ruling West German circles are trying to attain a change in the status-quo by means of diversified tactics, vis-à-vis various socialist countries. They should not overlook, however, that their double-dealing policy has been recognized by the fraternal parties of the socialist countries and will be answered unequivocably by common actions against West German militarism and revanchism as well as by further expanding the cooperation between the socialist countries." *Neues Deutschland,* July 21, 1965.

26. Brzezinski has suggested: "The communist elites would like to lift the Iron Curtain in economics while leaving it down in cultural-social affairs. They demand closer economic contact with the West, and even credits, while still preaching the economic superiority of their own systems, maintaining political restrictions on the development of contacts between European peoples, promising the developing countries that with communist aid they will surpass the West, and aiding Cuba or North Vietnam in their revolutionary measures." Brzezinski, *op. cit.,* p. 69.

27. "The Soviet Views of NATO." Speech by Leonid I. Brezhnev, April 24, 1967. Prepared for the use of the Subcommittee on National Security and International Operations, Committee on Government Operations, United States Senate. Washington, U.S. Government Printing Office, 1967, p. 13.

28. *Ibid.*, p. 14.

29. See "The Common Market Looks East," *East Europe*, October 1963.

30. East Germany has constituted one trade loophole in the Common Market. According to EEC regulations, East Germany is considered to be part of a German trading unit which includes the Federal Republic. Products originating in East Germany and shipped to the EEC are treated as part of the internal trade of the Common Market. Since East Germany is also a member of COMECON, some trade between East and West European countries, especially in agricultural commodities, passes through East Germany. Ironically, the policy of treating German "intrazonal" trade as intra-EEC trade helps to undermine the Federal Republic's policy of isolating East Germany.

31. *European Economic Community*, Press Release, Brussels, May 25, 1965, IP (65) 100.

32. Between 1958 and 1962 total trade among Common Market countries increased by 98 percent, while the external trade of the European Community grew only by 35 percent. However, in the same period EEC trade with Eastern Europe, including the Soviet Union, rose by 80 percent—that is, more than twice as rapidly as trade between the Six and the rest of the world. See Lawrence B. Krause (ed.), *The Common Market: Progress and Controversy*. Englewood Cliffs, New Jersey: Prentice-Hall, 1964, pp. 11-12. In the computation of the percentage figures, both imports and exports were totaled in order to arrive at the total value of trade. While the percentage increase in East-West trade appears quite large, this trade accounts for a small amount of total Western trade.

33. See the statement of Chancellor Adenauer to the Bundestag on May 27, 1965, in *Verhandlungen des Deutschen Bundestages* (Bonn, 1955), Vol. 24, p. 4599.

34. According to President Johnson, "A united Western Europe can move more confidently in peaceful initiatives toward the East. Unity can provide a framework within which a unified Germany can be a full partner without arousing fears." *New York Times*, October 8, 1966, p. 12.

35. During his press conference of February 21, 1966, President de Gaulle suggested: ". . . the Union of the Six, once achieved—and all the more if it comes to be supplemented then by new European memberships and associations—can and must be toward the U.S. a valid partner in all areas, I mean powerful and independent. The union of the Six can and must also be one of the piers on which will gradually be built first the equilibrium then the cooperation and then, perhaps one day, the union of all Europe, which would enable our continent to settle its own problems peacefully, particularly that of Germany, including its reunification, and to attain, in as much as it is the main hearth of civilization, a material and human development worthy of its resources and its capacities." Ambassade de France, *Speeches and Press Conferences*, No. 239, February 21, 1966, p. 11.

VI. The United States and Western Europe in the 1970's

IN THE POSTWAR PERIOD, IT WAS A CARDINAL PRINCIPLE OF U.S. foreign policy that the United States and Western Europe, despite differing perspectives on decolonization, shared essentially similar foreign policy objectives. It was to the interest of the United States not only to safeguard Western Europe from attack, but to provide massive aid to achieve West European economic recovery. Moreover, it was assumed that the rehabilitation of Western Europe after the devastation of war would enhance the prospects for European integration, in itself a major U.S. policy objective. A unified Western Europe would have objectives largely compatible with those of the United States and would become a partner in the sharing of worldwide burdens and responsibilities.

In recent years, however, such assumptions have been questioned.[1] The policies adopted by the French Fifth Republic, the growing preoccupation of West European countries with exclusively European affairs, an increasing European predilection to confine interest in extra-European affairs to vocal criticism of U.S. policy, the rise of European apprehensions about U.S. "hegemony," and cleavages on economic questions as manifested during the protracted discussions on international monetary reform and the Kennedy Round of trade negotiations, have all contributed to a reassessment of the presumed identity of interest between the United States and Western Europe. To what extent are U.S. and European interests—East-West and North-South—likely to diverge or converge in the 1970's? Will the United States and Western Europe develop conflicting or compatible foreign policies? On economic questions, are their interests and objectives likely to be more dissimilar than similar? Would the achievement of European integration in one form or another enhance the prospects for transatlantic collaboration, or exacerbate existing tensions and even contribute to the emergence of new differences between the United

States and Western Europe? To answer such questions is to provide an answer to another question: to what extent is an Atlantic consensus on major foreign policy issues likely to develop in the 1970's? Upon the development of such a consensus depends the building of new and effective Atlantic institutions capable of attracting the support of peoples in Western Europe and North America, for NATO found acceptance among its members so long as it reflected an Atlantic consensus on major political and military issues.

Answers to such questions depend upon several other imponderables: Does Europe wish to share responsibility with the United States for world leadership, or does Western Europe wish to become preoccupied only with specifically European problems? Can Western Europe take the steps needed to escape U.S. "hegemony" in economic, military, political and technological affairs? Is the United States prepared to take the lead in building a new Atlantic consensus, or will the United States find agreeable an Atlantic hegemony in which a fragmented Europe will be subordinated to the United States in decisions of major importance? To ask such questions is to ask to what extent Europe is prepared to move toward political integration, for a unified Europe would have the potential to develop relationships with the United States based on greater equality than can the existing nation-states of Western Europe. Moreover, to ask such questions is to inquire to what extent the United States is willing to use its own great potential to resolve major problems of U.S.-European relations.

THE STATE OF EUROPEAN INTEGRATION

The integration movement in Western Europe has been characterized by periods of forward momentum followed by periods of little progress and even great setbacks. Between 1950 and 1954, for example, there were major strides toward European integration, with the formation of the European Coal and Steel Community (ECSC) and discussion about the creation of the European Defense Community (EDC). Although the failure of EDC in 1954 represented a setback to European integration, it was followed by an effort to "relaunch" the unification movement. The Messina Conference of 1955 led to the signing, in March 1957, of the Rome Treaties for the EEC and EURATOM. In the period from the formation of the EEC until the failure of the Brussels negotiations for

British entry into the Common Market in January 1963, not only did the EEC move on schedule toward the achievement of goals set in the Rome Treaty, but its members even agreed, in the Hallstein Plan of 1960, to accelerate the transition. The Six reached agreement upon the framework for a Common Market agricultural policy and held discussions, although unsuccessful ones, on political unification. The high economic growth rates of its major members increased the attractiveness of the Common Market to countries on its periphery and contributed to the decision of Britain and other European governments to apply for admission.

If the period from 1955 to 1963 was notable for the apparent progress in European integration, it was followed by a period of setback and consolidation. In fact, some writers have seen a halt, or at least a slowing, in the European integration movement.[2] Judgment as to the course of European integration in the 1960's depends upon the criteria upon which evaluation is based.[3] Nevertheless, the period following the failure of the Brussels negotiation was a testing time for existing European institutions rather than a time for the extension of integration to new sectors. Although the refusal of President de Gaulle to agree to British entry into the Common Market evoked opposition to France in the capitals of all other members, no government was prepared to withdraw from the EEC in protest against French policy. The durability of the European Community, despite the periodic crises which have confronted it, bespeaks the commitment of its members to economic integration and their belief that they have more to gain by remaining signatories than by renouncing the Rome Treaty. Yet psychologically the rejection of the first British application was damaging to the cause of European integration. Although the admission of so important a new member as Britain, as President de Gaulle warned, would have added to the already formidable problems of achieving a European consensus, the momentum created by the British application would probably have spurred Western Europe to seek new institutions, especially in the political sector. After the failure of the bid, however, the European political climate was not conducive to major new initiatives toward European integration.

In 1965–66, the European Community faced still another major crisis, which pitted France against the Commission and threatened to destroy the EEC. The dispute concerned the nature of supranationality within the institutions of the EEC, especially the position of the Commission; the strengthening of the European Parliament; and the completion of arrangements for the Common Market agricultural policy. For several months during the latter part of 1965 the future of the EEC was uncertain, with France having withdrawn from the deliberations of the Council. France opposed the efforts of the Commission to link the financing of the Common Market agricultural policy to the strengthening of the European Parliament. According to the proposal put forward by the Commission, levies collected on imports of agricultural products into the Common Market from third countries would have gone directly to the EEC to be used in the financing of the Common Market agricultural policy. The effect of this proposal would have been to give the EEC a major new source of revenue which would have reduced its financial dependence upon the member governments. Although France pressed for the completion of the Common Market agricultural policy, she refused to link the financing of agricultural policy, as the Commission wanted, to the strengthening of the institutions of the EEC.[4] But the French government, like the other member governments at the time of the failure of Britain's first Common Market application just two years earlier, was not prepared to press its opposition to the point of destroying the European Community. As the price for returning to the Council, France insisted upon the completion of the EEC financial regulations for agriculture. Moreover, France obtained from her partners agreement that the Commission, in preparing proposals for the consideration of the Council, would henceforth "make the appropriate contacts with the Governments of member States." In the future, the Council would undertake to ensure that in cases where majority decisions can be taken solutions will be sought "that could be adopted by all members of the Council in respect of their mutual interests and those of the Community."[5]

Several months later, on May 11, 1966, the EEC Council reached agreement on the Common Market financial regulations. Ninety percent of the revenues collected from levies upon imports of agricultural products from third countries are to be paid to the EEC Fund for Agricultural Modernization and Guaranty. From this fund subsidies will be paid to Common Market countries for the modernization of their agriculture. Although France will be the chief beneficiary of modernization subsidies, the principle was established that the major portion of EEC levies on imports of agricultural products would be paid to the EEC, not directly to the member governments. This agreement represented a victory for the proponents of a strengthened European Community. However, the successful French effort to reduce the independence of the Commission in developing proposals for submission to the Council and to restrict majority voting clearly dampened the prospects for the emergence of a truly supranational EEC. Such regulations, which keep decision-making power at the national level, make more difficult the task of European integrationists.

Despite the formidable problems which faced the Six after the failure of the first British application, the Six continued to make progress toward the achievement of objectives set forth in the Rome Treaties. Unlike the period immediately following the failure of the EDC in 1954, however, when decisions were taken to form the Common Market, this period produced no major new initiative toward European integration. Instead, the Six diverted their energies to the consolidation and completion of the integration they had begun in the EEC. Far from halting after 1963, the European integration movement made great gains. Not only did the Six demonstrate an ability to reconcile their differences. They reached agreement on the merger of the executives of the European Communities and on the pricing and financing of agricultural policy, and developed for the first time in their history a level of consensus on commercial policy adequate to enable them to negotiate as a unit with the United States in the Kennedy Round. Without the development of European institutions with novel patterns of collaboration beyond the nation-state, these achievements would hardly have been possible.

The evolution of the institutions of the European Community provides still further evidence of the vitality of the European integration movement. In addition to reducing the number of European institutions, the merger of the executives of the European Community enhanced the prospect for greater coordination in the development of European policies in such sectors as energy and transport. The Kennedy Round furnished evidence not only of the attainment for the first time of a European position on major commercial issues, but of the ability of the Six, having worked out common policies among themselves, to negotiate as a unit with outside powers. They had made substantial progress since 1963 toward the achievement of objectives set forth in the Rome Treaty. In addition to reaching agreement on an EEC agricultural policy, they made spectacular progress toward the completion of the customs union in industrial products, worked out a new agreement for the association of overseas states, and completed arrangements for the admission of several new states as associate members. If European integration is equated with the attainment of objectives set forth in the Rome Treaties, then the movement toward European integration made substantial progress after 1963, even if its accomplishments were less spectacular than those registered in the preceding years.

This conclusion is further strengthened by the revival and upsurge in British interest in the European Community. In the postwar period the countries which formed the Common Market passed through a period of disillusionment with the nation-state as a unit adequate to their needs both in the security field and in economic affairs. The defeat and destruction of World War II contributed to a rise in interest in an alternative. Britain, however, appeared immune to this crisis of confidence in the nation-state, so long as she felt herself, as a victor of World War II, to be a world power. Only in the decade after the Suez crisis of 1956 did Britain pass through a period in which traditional foreign policies and world outlooks were tested, found wanting, and discarded. The growth of the European integration movement in Britain stems from the belief that Britain's only alternative to becoming an appendage of the United States or an insignificant, economically stagnating offshore island lies in European integration. The fact that such dissatisfaction reached Britain almost a generation after it reached continental Western Europe helps to explain the greater interest in European integration displayed by British political leaders than by many of their continental counterparts in the late 1960's. As a result of a long period of economic prosperity, together with De Gaulle's efforts to restore national pride, on the Continent, especially in France, the nation-state appears more adequate today than it did a generation ago to many of the tasks facing it, however unfounded such sentiment may prove ultimately to be.

Support for European integration derived from an emotional commitment to a conception of Europe. But European integration attracted support for another reason: it would provide a framework more adequate than the nation-state for specific groups in Western Europe to achieve specific objectives, such as greater markets, lower costs of production, and higher income levels. Politically, an integrated Europe held appeal because it could enhance the international position of either the participating national units or Europe as a whole or perhaps both. The base of support broadened as elites, governmental and non-governmental, developed expectations of gain from participation in a unit beyond the nation-state.[6] However, integration sentiment based upon expectations of gain is likely to wane once the interests which gave rise to it have been satisfied. Thus an emotional attachment to "Europe" may be a more durable base for integration than interest-inspired support.[7]

Further progess toward European integration depends both upon the growth of expectations of gain and the strengthening of emotional commitment to "Europe." The continued British interest in Common Market membership bespeaks not only the attractiveness of the EEC to states on its periphery, but the increase, since the failure of the first British application, of expectations of gain—economic and political—inside and outside the British government. These expectations, especially in the economic sector, are similiar to those which initially gave impetus to economic integration on the continent. In contrast, as a result of the great prosperity which accompanied the EEC, the need for further economic integration appears to its continental European members less urgent than it did a generation ago. Thus, if integration in one sector provides satisfactory solutions to the problems which gave rise to it, it does not necessarily lead to "spill-over," to the growth of support for integration in other sectors. In fact, within the framework of the European Community, the satisfaction of demands may contribute to a reduction in support for further integrative efforts even in that sector. Because demands upon the EEC are channeled essentially through the national governments, the national governments are able to benefit from the successes of the European Community.

The experience of Western Europe does not provide evidence that economic integration will necessarily lead to political integration. The EEC does not necessarily provide a catalyst to political integration as long as the objectives envisaged in the Rome Treaty can be achieved largely by coordination among member governments, with a bureaucracy charged with the task of developing proposals for Community policy for submission to member governments and the execution of policies upon which member governments have agreed. Notwithstanding the impressive development of European Community institutions, the locus of decision-making power remains at the national level. Although it may be argued that the decisions taken within the European Community have been essentially political in nature, even though related specifically to economic issues, they have not yet given rise to a feeling of need for European political institutions to carry them out.

If previously held expectations, especially in the economic sector, have been satisfied, the extension of European integration to other sectors depends upon the development of new expectations of gain. In another sector, technology, European expectations of gain from the formation of a unit beyond the nation-state have increased. In recent years the growth of apprehension about the existence of an Atlantic technological imbalance has led to discussions not only about the future of European technology but also about the inadequacy of the European national unit for the development and production of advanced technology. One alternative to a further widening in the imbalance between Western Europe and the United States—in aircraft, space exploration, computers, electronics, and communications equipment—lies in technological collaboration within Western Europe. Support for a European technological community derives from several European expectations of gain, such as the more effective allocation of resources to the building of advanced technologies and the development of large-scale markets comparable to those of the United States. Related to the technological imbalance has been the revival of European interest in a defense community for the development and production of armaments. As in the case of the Atlantic technological imbalance, European support for a defense community rests to a considerable extent upon apprehensions of U.S. "hegemony" in the NATO armaments market.[8]

The European integration movement has never stemmed primarily from motivations based upon military considerations. Since the failure of EDC, it has been the assumption of proponents of European integration that defense is the last sector likely to be integrated and that such progress must await the development of attitudes favorable to political integration. Given diminished perceptions of an attack by the Soviet Union, European integration will obtain even less momentum than in the past. To a considerable extent, however, the apprehension of U.S. hegemony in military affairs, the development of advanced technologies, and the control of European industries through direct investment has replaced the fear of a major Soviet military attack. Given existing trends, the imbalance between the United States and Western Europe in the closely related military and technological fields is likely to persist and to continue to be the cause of considerable European concern.

With the completion of the Common Market, new momentum toward European integration is likely to occur in the fields of advanced technology, including defense. The utility of technological collaboration in military R&D as a catalyst to political integration depends upon the salience of defense to European elites in the 1970's. In particular, it depends upon the extent to which West Europeans conclude that advanced armaments industries are vital in the light of a perceived military threat from the Soviet Union or a perceived political-economic-technological threat from the United States. In the case of the latter, West European elites could be motivated to joint programs of production in order to assure their independence from the United States in foreign policy and to preserve their industries from U.S. penetration.

The rise to prominence of armament production as an issue area for joint action at a level beyond the nation-state is fraught with implications for integration not present in the case of integration in the economic sector. To a far greater extent than economic issues, armaments development and production are directly related to the political independence of national units. In agreeing to collaborate in developing and producing armaments, national governments not only tacitly acknowledge their inability to maintain a full range of nationally produced weapons systems, but limit their freedom of action to the extent that they become dependent upon other nations for a part of their weaponry. Agreement among national units to produce jointly a series of weapons systems either presupposes or makes necessary the development of common foreign policies. The institutional arrangements needed for an effective European armaments community far exceed both in scope and power those of the European Economic Community, since it would be necessary to vest in a central authority the power to develop a "European" research program, to establish priorities for R&D, to allocate research tasks and contracts, and to evaluate performance.

Unlike the technical sectors which functionalist theory stresses, joint armaments production as a technical sector would confront national governments with the need to take essentially political decisions about their future. So in contrast to the experience of the EEC, centralization at the European level of armaments development and production is likely to affect or to "spill over" into another sector. In fact, even the development of a European technological community, given the military implications of such fields as space research, rockets, electronics, and aircraft, is likely to contribute to European integration and thus *ipso facto* to one form or another of political union. European national units would have agreed, in effect, to the formation of such a European political unit, because large-scale armaments collaboration would make necessary the development of a European consensus as to strategic doctrine and the nature of European foreign policy objectives. The lack of such agreement has undoubtedly hampered efforts over the past decade to achieve higher levels of European collaboration in armaments development and production.

Whether or not, then, they turn their energies to new forms of integration after the attainment of economic objectives set forth in the Rome Treaty depends upon several factors; notably, European elites' perception of the adequacy of existing institutions and their expectations of gain from integration in other sectors. In particular, the need to reduce the several imbalances between the United States and Western Europe is likely to give new impetus to the European integration movement. Support for and impetus toward European integration is likely to come, therefore, from the industrial-technological-managerial elites of Western Europe.

If such is the case, what kinds of interests will an integrating Europe and the United States have in common? Will it still be to the interest of the United States to encourage the movement toward European integration, or would it even serve the U.S. interest to thwart the European integration movement and seek to perpetuate the dependency relationship between Western Europe and the United States? The answers to such questions are dependent upon such factors as the foreign policy outlook of an integrating or integrated Western Europe. Would Western Europe become in world politics a "third force" which would take independent initiatives toward an increasingly responsive Soviet Union and make major concessions in order to achieve a European settlement? Would an integrated Western Europe attempt to exclude the United States not only from the negotiations for such a settlement, but also from European affairs generally? Would an integrated Western Europe find little in common with U.S. foreign policy in Asia, Africa, and Latin America, and even place itself in opposition to U.S. policy, as France under De Gaulle has done in the case of Vietnam?

The answers to such questions depend upon several factors, including the institutional framework within which an integrated Europe would be developed, the extent to which Gaullist or post-Gaullist elites control the decision-making apparatus, and the balance of forces both nationally and internationally within an integrated Europe. The balance of forces is related to the role which Britain can be expected to play in an integrated Europe. By the 1970's Britain in all likelihood will have drawn closer economically, militarily, technologically, and politically to continental Europe. Whatever the short-run problems facing Britain in entering the Common Market, the commitment of major British elites to a European policy has produced a momentum in Britain which can be expected to endure. Although Britain, as a participant in an integrated Europe, would no longer retain a "special relationship" with the United States, Britain would exert a major influence upon European foreign policy. The balance of forces among the national units in an integrated Europe would affect its outlook on major foreign policy issues. But the balance of forces within, as well as among, West European political units will be affected greatly by the foreign policy decisions which the United States takes. As in the past generation the influence of the United States upon Western Europe will be enormous.

The foreign policy outlook of European national units will undoubtedly reflect the prevailing balance of domestic forces. For example, post-De Gaulle France may not be subjected to political instability comparable to the Fourth Republic, although if such were to occur, it would divert French interests from foreign policy issues to domestic problems. As an alternative to the multiparty system of the Fourth Republic, France could evolve an essentially two-party system. If this political system included the Gaullists and a popular front embracing the socialists and communists, the result could be an exacerbation of Franco-American tensions. If the Gaullists remained in power as the only alternative to a government based upon a popular front, in order to attract supporters from the opposition they would probably be obliged to give even greater emphasis to anti-American policies. To the extent that France, under such circumstances, played a major or even predominant role, the foreign policy of an integrated Europe would largely reflect French foreign policy. But an integrated Europe in which Britain, France, and Germany were the major units would provide such a balance of forces that the prospects for French dominance would be reduced considerably—a consideration of which President de Gaulle was undoubtedly aware when he vetoed the British EEC bid.

Although it is not possible clearly to foresee the organizational form, the foreign policy outlook, or the balance of forces of an integrated Europe it is possible to postulate the economic, political, and military interests which an integrated Europe will have with the United States in the 1970's.

Western Europe has achieved a large enough measure of economic integration to make it possible to assess the nature of transatlantic harmony or conflict on issues of major economic importance. European economic integration has had several implications for transatlantic economic relationships. Although European economic growth since 1957 cannot be attributed solely to the Common Market, the European Community nevertheless has contributed to the unprecedented prosperity which its members have experienced.[9] Economic growth in Western Europe has led to increases and changes in patterns of consumption and to a major expansion in trade not only within the European Community, but between the EEC and non-member countries. Since the formation of the EEC, U.S. markets in Western Europe have grown rapidly.

But European economic integration has had an adverse effect, in several respects, upon the United States. The policies which the Common Market has developed, most notably in agriculture, do not serve U.S. interests, at least in the short-run. The EEC agricultural policy is protectionistic to the extent that it encourages the expansion of higher-cost European farm production and imposes restrictions upon imports of lower-cost farm products from major agricultural exporters such as the United States.

Against U.S. losses in overseas markets, however, must be weighed the longer-run implications of EEC agricultural policy, which are not necessarily incompatible with other U.S. interests.

As a result of agricultural modernization and the expansion of output spurred by the Common Market, Western Europe is likely to become on balance an agricultural surplus region. Together with the United States, Canada, and Australia, Western Europe would constitute a major contributor of agricultural aid to less developed countries, many of which over the next generation will probably experience severe food shortages. West European agricultural production could be vital to a Western effort to reduce the world "food gap."

As a result of the EEC, Western Europe has developed bargaining power vis-à-vis the United States which would not have been available to individual European countries. In the absence of an EEC negotiating unit, Western Europe would hardly have been able to obtain concessions from the United States in tariffs on chemicals, of considerable importance to European exporters. Undoubtedly, the United States would have had fewer problems in safeguarding specifically U.S. economic interests in trade negotiations with individual West European countries than with the EEC as a unit. The formation of the Common Market, together with the growth of U.S. trade with Western Europe, provided the incentive to U.S. policymakers to formulate the Trade Expansion Act and press for the successful conclusion of the Geneva trade negotiations. In the absence of the European Community it is unlikely that trade legislation so far reaching as the Trade Expansion Act would have been proposed and then pushed with such vigor by two U.S. administrations. Moreover, the existence of the Common Market made it necessary for the United States to agree to major reductions in its own tariffs in return for hard won advantages overseas. But the general effect of the U.S.-European economic confrontation in the Kennedy Round was to reduce the importance of the tariff as a barrier to international trade. This, in turn, serves the general interest not only of the United States and Western Europe, but of less developed countries, whose economic future depends heavily upon access to markets in the West.

An examination of the impact of the Common Market upon transatlantic economic relations is important for the substantive problems it created. The formation of the Common Market led not only to a "European" position on commercial issues, but also to a certain rigidity in the negotiating posture of the EEC. Because it must accommodate the often diverse interests of several nations, the development of a Common Market policy has been a formidable undertaking upon the success of which the future of the Community has sometimes depended. So great have been the problems of achieving a Common Market policy that Europeans have not been prepared to risk the weakening of a carefully constructed European consensus in order to reach agreement with third countries, including the United States. In fact, the EEC policy in certain economic sectors, for example agriculture, was worked out at the expense of interests of third parties, such as the United States. But the significance of the "Community method" extends beyond its implications for U.S.-European economic relations. To what extent would the policy-forming process of a European political unit resemble that of the EEC? Would a European political unit have in its negotiating posture on foreign policy and defense issues a rigidity comparable to that of the Common Market?

Even though there is a declining interest in Western Europe in regions outside Europe, along with an increasing interest in relations among European states and concern about U.S. "hegemony," there is no "European" policy on major political, military, or technological issues. The extent to which a common European foreign policy and defense policy would serve U.S. interests would depend upon several factors.

For example, the organizational form of an integrated Europe would affect the flexibility of Europe in accommodating itself politically to the interests of the United States and other third countries. The structure of the EEC is more akin to that of a confederal Europe, which would be based organizationally, but not necessarily in policy orientation, upon Gaullist proposals for European integration. The rigidity of U.S. foreign policy would undoubtedly be greater if it represented the amalgam of the separate foreign policies of the fifty states. A federal decision-making unit in Western Europe would have considerably greater flexibility in foreign policy than a European unit in which the locus of power in foreign relations remained at the national level. A West European political unit based upon a confederal structure would, therefore, have greater built-in rigidity than a Europe organized as a federal unit.

For the United States this problem would be of great importance only if the "European" foreign and defense policies were likely to be widely at variance with those of the United States. Whether this situation develops depends upon the nature and outlook of the elites which gain ascendency in Western Europe over the next decade and upon the foreign policy orientation of the United States itself. Most particularly, it is related to the extent to which Gaullism is likely to survive De Gaulle and to the form which it will take. Although these questions cannot be answered definitively at this stage, it is possible to identify several general trends which can be expected to persist whatever the fate of Gaullism. Given the presence of these trends, the objective of U.S. foreign policy should be to develop a framework at the European and Atlantic levels, within which European goals can be reconciled with general U.S. policy goals.

First, the United States faces a declining European interest in problems of developing areas. This trend probably cannot be reversed; at best it can be modified. In a Western Europe in which there is no political integration beyond the nation-state, this trend cannot be reversed, since it derives from the belief that no West European nation-state has the resources to remain deeply committed in regions outside Europe. Instead, European countries will concentrate upon influencing developments within Europe. Their foreign policy behavior will resemble that of a regional rather than a world power.

This trend could be modified by the creation of an integrated Western Europe, which would have greater capabilities than are available to any single West European national unit. In contrast to the European nation-states, an integrated Europe would not necessarily be precluded by the lack of resources from the assumption of major responsibilities in one or more regions outside the North Atlantic area. But it is by no means certain that an integrated Europe would choose to develop new political or economic interests outside Europe. For a long period in its own history, the United States, even though it had the capabilities for an internationalist foreign policy, clung to isolationism. It is unlikely that even the United States, with its vast capabilities, will be prepared to remain committed to the tasks of defense and modernization in scores of countries around the globe, especially if it is alone in assuming such burdens. Nor can it be certain that Western Europe, if it developed a European policy in regions outside Europe, would have interests compatible with those of the United States.

To a considerable extent, again, this depends upon the future configuration of political forces in Western Europe. A revival of European interest in regions beyond the North Atlantic area would most likely be focused upon the Middle East and Africa because of their greater geographic proximity and economic and strategic importance as compared with Southeast Asia or the Far East. West European leaders share with the United States the objective of assuring the security of these regions from a force which menaced the security of the North Atlantic area.[10]

Psychologically, it would be important for Western Europe to collaborate, even on a limited scale, with the United States in regions where the West shares common objectives. In Southeast Asia, the United States has sought to retain at least a symbolic British presence so that the United States will not become the only non-Asian power committed to the defense of that region. A greater European interest in at least one region outside Europe would not only lessen burdens borne by the United States, but would make less likely the development of isolationism based upon disillusionment with the large-scale diversion of U.S. resources to the attainment of overseas objectives.

The second major trend in West European foreign policy is the interest in evolving new relationships between Eastern and Western Europe. Not only is this trend likely to continue; it could become the only major foreign policy interest of West European governments. In the absence of European integration, each West European government is likely to make its own attempt to achieve objectives, some of which, such as reunification in the case of Germany, are national goals, and others of which, such as the "normalization" of East-West relations, are shared by all West European governments and the United States. The question arises, however, whether the United States would face the risk of an integrated Western Europe combining with the Soviet Union in opposition to the United States. As in the case of other questions about the potential orientation of the foreign policy of an integrated Europe, the answer depends upon the balance of forces within Western Europe and in the United States and upon the strength of transatlantic links. Never in its history, except for short periods as a result of conquest, has Europe—east and west—been unified. Although it is doubtful that the peoples of Western Europe would develop policies and interests more compatible with the

Soviet Union than the United States, the strengthening of links between the United States and a unifying Europe renders such a prospect even more unlikely.

To be sure, dangers inhere in the development of an integrated Western Europe capable of reducing U.S. influence in Europe and even entering negotiations on its own with the Soviet Union. But nation states in a fragmented Western Europe might be no less willing to make separate settlement with the Soviet Union. It is likely that the Soviet Union, for its part, would seek wherever possible to exacerbate tensions among states in a fragmented Western Europe and between a fragmented Western Europe and the United States. Although the development of West European integration is fraught with uncertainties for the United States, there is considerable risk in the perpetuation of the status-quo in Western Europe as it affects relations with the Soviet Union and with the United States.

In the postwar period, one of the most persuasive reasons for European integration was the need to provide a framework within which German energies and attention could be turned from reunification, a goal attainable at best on terms unacceptable to most NATO countries, including the United States. As a result of its westward orientation, the Federal Republic, to a greater extent than preceding German political systems, has been integrated into the fabric of Western civilization. Although the goal of reunification on terms mutually acceptable to both the Soviet Union and the United States remains remote, the need for the strengthening of German links with the West and with the European integration movement is still great. A West European unit with greater capabilities than the separate national units would enhance the prospects for the formation of a broader European framework in which a variety of policy objectives could be reconciled.

A third major trend in West European foreign policies relates to transatlantic relationships and, in particular, the European perception of the need to reduce Europe's dependence upon the United States. The widening of the Atlantic imbalance in technology, GNP, and military capabilities would, of course, increase the dependency status of Western Europe vis-à-vis the United States. Especially in a fragmented Western Europe, anti-American sentiment is likely to rise as perceptions of U.S. hegemony in major areas of European life increase. A fragmented Western Europe is likely to give rise to greater European perceptions of U.S. hegemony. Moreover, it is illusory to expect that the United States could ensure the subservience of individual European national units even if it chose actively to attempt to do so. Elsewhere in the world, governments with far fewer resources than those of Fifth Republic France have opposed U.S. policy and extricated themselves from what they perceived to be U.S. "hegemony." At least some states in a fragmented Western Europe are likely not only to attempt to reduce U.S. influence, but also in the pursuit of greater independence to develop policies which diverge from those of the United States. Thus the United States cannot preserve the status-quo or even benefit from its preservation if this were possible.

In technology, as in military and economic affairs, an integrated Western Europe would enhance the prospects for the success of West European efforts to reduce the Atlantic imbalance. It would accord as well with broad U.S. interests, even though in technology, for example, an integrated Europe would probably become a competitor in certain fields where the United States is now predominant. Moreover, the development of a European technological community would lead to European protectionism in the products of certain advanced technologies such as aircraft. The idea of protectionism, at the early stages at least, is inherent in the building of a European technological community, for one of the major problems facing Western Europe is the disparity in size between the assured domestic markets available respectively to the United States and West European countries.

The importance of such factors to the United States may be diminished by the fact that the United States is likely to develop new technologies which will place us ahead of Western Europe in the next decade. But rising costs of R&D may make it difficult, if not impossible, even for a country with the capabilities and resources of the United States to maximize the potential inherent in advanced technology. An integrated Western Europe, with a strengthened technological base, could become a more equal partner for technological collaboration than a fragmented Western Europe with several smaller, less advanced technological capabilities.

The strengthening of European technological capabilities bears a direct relationship to the future of European military programs.

Militarily, the creation of a European defense framework based upon an integrated Western Europe could provide a sense of security which is lacking in NATO as presently constituted. Within a European framework, major European countries could contribute more effectively to the defense of Western Europe and gain a greater measure of influence in Atlantic military relationships. Those smaller NATO countries whose governments preferred to rely exclusively upon the U.S. nuclear guarantee provided by the Atlantic Alliance could continue to do so. In fact, the United States would maintain its guarantee for the defense of Western Europe, for even in the best of circumstances an integrated Europe would not fully replace the United States as the guarantor of European security.

The major changes in transatlantic relationships which have occurred over the past generation have not obviated the need for Western Europe to attain a higher level of integration than achieved thus far. Nor have such changes as have taken place rendered obsolete the notion that, on balance, an integrated Western Europe is in the interest of the United States. In fact, the future course of the integration movement in Western Europe will have important implications for transatlantic relationships. To the greatest extent possible, it should be the objective of U.S. foreign policy to enable Western Europe to move toward greater unity. The extent to which such a course of action is possible depends upon future developments in Western Europe and even more upon policy decisions taken in the United States.

NOTES

1. See, for example, Ronald Steel, *The End of Alliance: America and the Future of Europe*. New York: The Viking Press, 1964; "Moscow, Washington, and the Two Europes," *Interplay*, Vol. 1, No. 1 (June/July 1967), pp. 15-18.

2. For an analysis which suggests that the European integration movement since the 1950's has slowed, see Karl W. Deutsch, "Integration and Arms Control in the European Political Environment: A Summary Report," *American Political Science Review*, Vol. LX, No. 2 (June, 1966), pp. 354-65, and by the same author, *Arms Control and the Atlantic Alliance*. New York: John Wiley and Sons, Inc., 1967, pp. 17-29. Karl W. Deutsch, Louis J. Edinger, Roy C. Macridis, and Richard L. Merritt, *France, Germany and the Western Alliance: A Study of Elite Attitudes on European Integration and World Politics*. New York: Charles Scribner's Sons, 1967. For a contrary interpreta-

tion of trends in the European integration movement, see Ronald Inglehart, "An End to European Integration?" *American Political Science Review,* Vol. LXI, No. 1 (March, 1967), pp. 91–105; Ernst Haas, "Technocracy, Pluralism and the New Europe," in Stephen A. Graubard (ed.), *A New Europe?* Boston: Houghton Mifflin Company, 1964; Leon N. Lindberg, *The Political Dynamics of European Economic Integration.* Stanford University Press, 1963.

3. For example, Deutsch bases his conclusion that the European integration movement has slowed upon an examination of increases in trade, travel, postal correspondence, and the exchange of students among West European countries. Increases in these transactions were greater in the 1950's than the 1960's. *Arms Control and the Atlantic Alliance,* pp. 17–29.

4. Explaining France's withdrawal from the work of the EEC Council, President de Gaulle, in his press conference of September 9, 1965, declared: "In Brussels, on 30 June, our delegation came up against a serious stumbling-block concerning the final definition of the financial regulation, as previously agreed upon. Shortly before, the Commission had suddenly abandoned its political discretion and formulated terms in connection with this financial regulation whereby it would have a budget of its own, possibly of up to 20,000 million new francs ($4 billion), the states having made over into its hands the levies and customs receipts which would literally have made it a great independent financial power. And then those very states, having fed these enormous amounts to it at the expense of their taxpayers, would have no way of supervising it."

5. Ambassade de France, *Arrangements Made in Luxembourg between the Foreign Affairs Ministers of the Six on January 31, 1966.* (French Affairs—No. 188).

6 See, for example, Ernst B. Haas, *The Uniting of Europe.* Stanford: Stanford University Press, 1957, especially Chapter I.

7. See Ernst B. Haas, "*The Uniting of Europe* and the Uniting of Latin America," *Journal of Common Market Studies,* June 1967, pp. 315-331.

8. See, for example, Alastair Buchan, *The Implications of a European System for Defense Technology.* London: Institute for Strategic Studies, 1967.

9. See, for example, Lawrence B. Krause, *The Meaning of European Economic Integration for the United States.* Washington, D.C.: Brookings Institution, 1967 (Mimeographed).

10. To be sure, French policy, at the time of the Arab-Israeli conflict of 1967, diverged sharply from that of the United States. But De Gaulle's policy of opposition to Israel, which bore many similarities to Soviet policy, aroused considerable opposition in France, even among members of the UNR and within the French Cabinet. In contrast to many other French policies under De Gaulle, this policy reflected the personal views of the French President rather than a more broadly based consensus which De Gaulle had helped to mold and whose views were not greatly different from De Gaulle's.

VII. Toward a New Atlantic Relationship

AT THE ROOT OF U.S.-EUROPEAN DISCORD ARE SUCH PROBLEMS AS conflicting strategic doctrines, differing conceptions of the role which West European countries, singly or jointly, should play in the Alliance, disagreement about the command and control of nuclear weapons, and European apprehension about U.S. hegemony in fields in which an imbalance exists between U.S. and West European capabilities. France rejects "subordination" to the United States within NATO. Other problems confront the countries of the North Atlantic area: divergent policies regarding change in the non-Western world; the Atlantic technological imbalance; economic questions, such as the role of the dollar and pound sterling as international reserve currencies; the future of trading relationships; and the proper role for U.S. investment in Western Europe. Western Europe faces difficult problems of adjustment to meet needs which cannot be satisfied within a national political framework. Finally, tensions between the United States and Western Europe are related to European perceptions of American dominance in technology and military affairs, together with the apparent inability of the United States to solve its major economic problems or to stem a rising tide of domestic disorder. Despite its great technological and military strength vis-à-vis Western Europe, the United States does not project the image of a nation capable of responding effectively to the problems facing it.

If the United States and Western Europe have contributed to the deterioration of Atlantic relationships, both have a major role to play in reshaping them to meet the needs of the 1970's. For the United States the most immediate task is to restore European confidence in U.S. leadership both in domestic and foreign affairs. At the same time, the United States faces the formidable challenge of collaborating with Western Europe to develop a framework adequate to both Atlantic and European problems of the 1970's.

In U.S. policy discussions in recent years there has been a tendency to place upon Western Europe primary responsibility for formulating proposals for changes in the Atlantic Alliance. Undoubtedly, such sentiment is the result of frustration in official U.S. circles with the inability of the United States to achieve an Atlantic Partnership or to create the U.S.-proposed MLF. Although Europeans often voice opposition to U.S. dominance in NATO, it is suggested in official U.S. circles, they have not been prepared to make major changes in their own economic, social, and political structures needed to give Western Europe a more effective role at the Atlantic level. Such criticism of Western Europe is not without justification, but it must be realized that the United States itself bears a major part of the onus for the impasse in Atlantic relationships, and must bear a major part in their remolding to the needs of the 1970's.

For Western Europe, the main task remains, as writers and policymakers in the United States have often suggested, the development of more effective institutions and political practices beyond the nation-state. Given the many obstacles to integration at the international level in a region which was the birthplace of modern nationalism, it seems likely that Western Europe will achieve at best in the 1970's a form of political unity based upon organizational principles put forward by Gaullist France, although not necessarily embodying Gaullist policies on major economic, defense, and foreign policy issues. As De Gaulle suggested, Europe has no "living reality if it does not include France and her Frenchmen, Germany and its Germans, Italy and its Italians."[1] Whatever its inadequacies, the nation-state remains the primary focal point of loyalty in Western Europe.

In the 1970's, expectations of gain from integration, based upon a recognition of needs which the national unit can no longer satisfy, will contend, almost in dialectical fashion, with residual, but powerful, loyalties to the nation-state. Conceivably, one form or another of emotional commitment to "Europe," together with a growing preoccupation with European affairs, will gain strength, but these forces will also face countervailing loyalty to the nation state.

Even if the peoples of Western Europe were able to reach agreement upon a political federation, as they are unlikely to do in the 1970's, the problems facing such a political unit would be formidable. Only after long periods of political unrest and civil conflict have existing national units, including the United States, overcome separatist tendencies and established high levels of cohesion. Even in Western Europe today the deep cleavages between Flemings and Walloons in Belgium, the conflict between German- and Italian-speaking peoples in the Alto Adigio region of Italy, separatist movements in Wales and Scotland in as old a nation-state as Great Britain, do not augur well for a smooth transition to a political unit composed of far more diverse peoples. Conceivably, conflicts such as those which trouble existing national units could be sublimated by the formation of a still larger European unit which embraced French-speaking peoples in Belgium and France, and German-speaking peoples in the Alto Adigio region of Italy. But the process of political development wherever it has occurred has been accompanied by vexing problems of transition.

It is difficult to envisage the development of an integrated Western Europe which does not rest upon Franco-German solidarity and, more broadly, upon strengthened links among Britain, the German Federal Republic, and France. These three powers form the core members of a larger West European unit. Although there is great temptation to seek to isolate a recalcitrant France, perhaps even some justification in such a policy from short-run U.S. interests, in the longer run the United States can better achieve its objectives by avoiding policies which deepen cleavages between individual West European countries. By forcing West European governments to choose between commitments to the United States and closer links with their West European neighbors, the United States may not only weaken the European integration movement, but also deepen transatlantic tensions.

STRATEGY, WEAPONS SYSTEMS, AND ALLIANCE STRUCTURE

The Atlantic Alliance is in need of strategic concepts which reconcile U.S. and European conceptions of defense. With the passage of time and the erosion of NATO, the strategy of "flexible response" will be even less relevant to the evolving NATO force posture or European strategic concepts. In such circumstances, the credibility of this strategy either to West European countries or to the Soviet Union will diminish. Thus the development of strategic consensus which gives a greater role to advanced weapons systems is urgent if the Atlantic Alliance is to reflect European perceptions of interest in the 1970's.

Although in the next decade strictly military problems may be of less importance to Western Europe than such other issues as Atlantic technological imbalance and development of new economic and political relationships with countries to the East, concern about European defense will persist. But the military issues of importance in transatlantic relations are likely to differ from those of the recent past. With both Britain and France having developed their own nuclear technologies, U.S. legislation against the exchange of nuclear information will have less importance as an irritant than was once the case. Given the high costs of R&D, however, Western Europe is likely to encounter substantial difficulty in acquiring a new generation of weapons and even delivery systems, despite the progress registered by France in the 1960's in the development of aircraft, nuclear submarines, and missiles. Therefore, so long as they seek to retain a defense capability in their own hands, Europeans will find it necessary to collaborate among themselves and with the United States in fields other than nuclear energy, i.e., delivery systems, aircraft, and early warning systems.

If there are major breakthroughs in the United States and the Soviet Union, neither Britain nor France may find it possible in the next decade to sustain the scientific-technological establishment needed to maintain a credible national nuclear force. The military value of the separate Anglo-French nuclear forces is likely to decline. In this case France and Britain will face essentially three alternatives: to maintain obsolescent nuclear forces, to rely exclusively upon the United States for nuclear defense, or to develop a nuclear force more broadly based than the existing British and French forces. It is possible to envisage a variety of forms which an Anglo-French nuclear force might assume. Initially, Britain and France might retain separate command structures; yet the two countries could join in detailed planning as to the circumstances in which their forces would be used. Agreement could be reached on strategic doctrine and the kinds of weapons systems to be developed in the 1970's. Although retaining separate nuclear forces, Britain and France could extend technological collaboration to include other projects in order to strengthen the R&D base of Western Europe. In many of those fields where the

Atlantic technological imbalance is greatest—aircraft, rocketry, electronics—Anglo-French collaboration could profitably be undertaken. Considerable potential exists for technological collaboration in fields vital to the future of European defense industries which have a variety of kinds of non-military spin-off.

A strictly Anglo-French collaborative effort, in either defense or other fields, will not suffice if Europe is to narrow greatly the Atlantic military technological imbalance. Even a strictly French-British nuclear consortium would have dubious value as a credible guarantee for the defense of any other European country, even perhaps of France and Britain. A European nuclear force which included Britain, France, and the German Federal Republic as principal members would have greater credibility, since together these countries might find the resources needed to develop advanced technologies which no European country by its own national efforts is able to produce. Within such a consortium, greater specialization of effort could be achieved. Even though the Federal Republic would continue to abide by the WEU Protocols prohibiting the manufacture of atomic, biological, and chemical weapons on its soil, Germany would become part of the European R&D base vital to the development of advanced technologies. Britain and France together would exercise greater influence than the Federal Republic over the use of such a force.

Especially if Britain and France decide to coordinate or merge their nuclear forces and thereby form the nucleus of a broader European atomic capability, the need will increase for changes in the Atlantic Alliance in order to accord Western Europe formally a greater nuclear role in the Alliance. Such changes could be made in recognition of collaborative arrangements which the Europeans had already worked out among themselves. Or the United States could hold out the prospect of a greater European role in return for the formation of collaborative arrangements within Western Europe deemed compatible with U.S. interests. In fact, the United States should make available to a European, rather than national political authority, data on certain advanced, defense-related and non-defense-related technologies.

The United States should furnish Western Europe technical information designed to reduce the likelihood of war by accident or miscalculation. Efforts should be made to assure that Europeans have continuing access to U.S. technologies for the maintenance of centralized command and control of weapons systems. A program of technological collaboration should be conceived, in part, as a means whereby Western Europe will be granted technologies not merely for the production of advanced weapons systems but also for their control. Safeguards similar to those designed to enable the United States to retain centralized command and control of its nuclear capabilities should be built into a European force or a British-French force.

The United States should be prepared to make other adjustments in U.S.-European relations. Not always without justification, Europeans have objected to U.S. efforts to dominate the Atlantic market for armaments. To many in Western Europe, the ability of the United States to retain a dominant position as supplier of arms reflects and contributes to U.S. "hegemony" in NATO and the Atlantic technological imbalance. The Alliance is in need of an agency for the more systematic examination of Atlantic weapons needs. Such an agency should provide for the allocation of contracts in such a manner that a European firm whose weapons system proved superior to that of the United States might be assured a market within NATO for its product.

The United States should reduce European suspicions that it seeks to dominate the market for NATO arms by indicating a willingness to consider a greater degree of international specialization of effort. Under such a scheme, more orders for tactical weapons systems could be given to European industry. For the production of tanks, anti-tank weapons, rifles, and certain kinds of advanced aircraft, European firms should receive an appreciably greater share of contracts than they have in recent years, even though U.S. industry would continue to supply a large part of the NATO arms market, especially that part requiring advanced research and development, where scarcely any competition exists outside the Soviet Union. Yet Western Europe, as a result both of more equitable procurement policies and of the strengthening of the European R&D base, would gain a greater share of contracts for the development of advanced weapons systems than at present.

Western Europe, in turn, should develop a European armaments community either as part of or separate from a European technological community. The objective of a European armaments community should be to achieve weapons standardization as well as agreement upon the joint procurement of weapons systems. Several or all member countries would share the costs and the planning for the development of weapons systems, which would then be purchased by all participating countries. Such a community would presuppose substantial West European agreement upon strategic doctrine and even foreign policy. The community might stem inroads of U.S. weapons manufacturers into the European armaments market and reduce West European military dependence upon the United States.

Although West European strategic thought has not placed great emphasis upon defensive capabilities, the development and deployment of an ABM by the Soviet Union is likely to reduce the credibility of European national nuclear deterrent forces. In fact, the deployment of ABM systems by the United States and the Soviet Union may have as profound an effect upon U.S.-European relations in the 1970's as the development of intercontinental missile capabilities had in the 1950's. The defense of Western Europe would become more difficult. The military imbalance between Western Europe and the Soviet Union—and between Western Europe and the United States—would increase. Defense links with the United States would become less relevant to West European security. Instead, Western Europe, at best, would undertake a massive effort to provide a more adequate political framework for a European defense policy; at worst, Western Europe would choose a policy of neutrality guaranteed by the Soviet Union in exchange for the withdrawal of U.S. forces from Europe and the termination of the Atlantic Alliance. In this event, the Soviets would have achieved a long-range policy objective and the United States would have been excluded from whatever political settlement is eventually reached in Europe.

In the construction of a European ABM system lies one possible solution to such problems. A European ABM system could not be criticized, as proposals for national nuclear forces in Europe have been, as constituting unnecessary duplication of U.S. strategic capabilities. Nor would a European ABM system, give rise to the problem of Germany's role, as would a European nuclear capability. An ABM system designed to protect Western Europe would necessarily be located in Western Europe and operated by Europeans themselves. Unlike a European nuclear force, an ABM system could not be construed as offensive in nature, for it would be technologically feasible to provide an ABM system with electronic controls to restrict the use of warheads to their intended purpose. By obtaining physical custody of an ABM, the Europeans would gain a voice in their defense which they have been denied thus far in NATO. In an ABM system, however, the need for a more integrated defense of Western Europe would become apparent. An ABM could hardly be utilized effectively except in conjunction with an early-warning system operative on a European or Atlantic level.

The deployment of an ABM system in Europe would have important technological and economic implications. To be sure, the United States could sell a U.S.-built system to Western Europe, thus easing the U.S. balance of payments problem and assuring export orders for many U.S. corporations. But such a solution would not accord with the European interest in avoiding an excessive technological dependence upon the United States. Hence, a decision to deploy an ABM system in Western Europe, if it were taken, could be linked to a program of technological collaboration. Under appropriate agreements with the United States, West European industries could be assigned the production of certain component parts of the ABM system. In addition to the financial consideration, the United States, in return for making available ABM technologies, could obtain from Western Europe agreements designed to strengthen the prospects for European integration and for future technological collaboration at both the European and Atlantic levels. However, the negotiations for the building of a European ABM system would have to be conducted with the utmost skill, for decisions about which urban complexes or military installations to protect or leave exposed could lead to new frictions both within Western Europe and between West European countries and the United States. Yet the prospects for the deployment of an ABM system in Western Europe are not promising unless West European governments are prepared to allocate greater funds to such defensive systems than they have indicated thus far.[2]

The future of U.S.-West European collaboration in both defensive and offensive weapons systems is related to the question of the Non-Proliferation Treaty between the United States and the Soviet Union. The Non-Proliferation Treaty will limit the ability of the United States to assist Western Europe to acquire an antiballistic missile system, since nuclear warheads are crucial to ABM defense. But the Non-Proliferation Treaty is likely to have other effects on NATO. First, it will take from the United States the option of providing nuclear assistance to non-nuclear nations or to a European nuclear force. Since Britain and France already possess nuclear weapons and nuclear technologies are available to other European countries, the Non-Proliferation Treaty will not necessarily prevent the dissemination of nuclear weapons in Western Europe. It will only limit the ability of the United States to influence the shape which future European nuclear forces assume. Moreover, the unwillingness of France to sign the treaty would place Britain in the difficult position of having to choose a policy favored by the United States or to demonstrate the British commitment to "Europe" by accepting the French position. By becoming a signatory, Britain would foreclose the possibility for nuclear collaboration with other West European countries. Also, she would be likely to incur the displeasure of France and thus postpone once again the date of her entry into the European Community.

Finally, the Non-Proliferation Treaty may increase the German sense of isolation at a critical period in the development of the Federal Republic. Although Germany under a WEU Protocol renounced the right to produce ABC weapons, the Federal Republic sought to gain a greater voice in NATO strategy both through "hardware" and "non-hardware" solutions to the problems of nuclear sharing. With the signing of the Non-Proliferation Treaty by the United States, the Federal Republic may be forced more than ever to rely either on its own resources or on other West European countries for the development of advanced military capabilities. The West European nuclear powers, i.e., Britain and France, rather than the United States, will hold the key to Germany's place in a European nuclear force. In return for agreement to German participation, France could extract important concessions from the Federal Republic, including the revision of Germany's status in NATO. In short, the Non-Proliferation Treaty is fraught with potentially serious implications for the Atlantic Alliance.

Although efforts over the past generation to extend the Alliance to non-military collaboration, in keeping with Article 2 of the North Atlantic Treaty, have not been successful, it is increasingly difficult to treat certain transatlantic problems in isolation from others. More than ever, the distinction between military and non-military problems seems blurred. Decisions in the military field have important implications for Atlantic technological collaboration. Decisions on military and technological questions affect options, priorities, and decisions in Atlantic economic matters, and vice versa. Although the Alliance is not likely to be broadened to include the many non-military issues of importance to Atlantic countries, the Alliance should afford greater opportunity for an examination of them.

Within the Atlantic Alliance a series of operations analysis groups should be established for the examination of problems other than military strategy. For example, East-West trade, joint space exploration, the choice and development of weapons systems, arms control, international monetary problems, Atlantic trade policy, and other problems of vital concern to Atlantic countries could be examined. Despite some progress within the Alliance to develop study groups of experts, more traditional procedures still predominate, and much of what is "decided" by the experts attached to SHAPE is not acted upon by member governments. An Atlantic Committee on East-West European relations should be created, in which the question of German reunification could be studied. By subjecting the German question to examination in an Atlantic committee, the Federal Republic and its Western allies might gain a greater understanding of their respective national policies and the relationship between German reunification and broader European-Atlantic problems.

Each of the proposed committees should be structured to provide the European members, especially the Common Market Six and Britain, with the opportunity to develop a common European position in advance of consultations with the United States and Canada. In fact, for each of the proposed Atlantic committees, a series of parallel European committees should be created. The ability of European countries to reach a consensus among themselves would contribute to the emergence of a "European" viewpoint on many important policy problems and to the strengthening of Europe's bargaining position vis-à-vis the United States. Britain and the Common Market Six could form a European secretariat, to be charged with the development of study papers and policy recommendations—and ultimately a "European" position on major issues. Such a Secretariat could provide assistance to the proposed European committees. In many fields of endeavor, intergovernmental European collaboration such as that envisaged in the committees might prove inadequate to the solution of problems facing Western Europe. Conceivably, such inadequacy would contribute to the eventual strengthening of sentiment in favor of supranational institutions at the European level.

At least twice a year, the NATO Council should devote a week-long session to the exploration and discussion of problems outside the North Atlantic area. Additional procedures for joint consultation should be developed. Periodic meetings should be held of Atlantic heads of government, as well as foreign, defense, and finance ministers, as proposed by President de Gaulle in his model for European integration. Such a procedure would strengthen systematic communication among members about problems within as well as outside the geographic perimeter of the Alliance.

The prospects for Atlantic collaboration would be enhanced by the ability of national delegations to pass data quickly to their governments and to receive instructions based upon available information. At the time of the Cuban missile crisis, SACEUR rather than the Secretary General had a "hotline" to Washington. The construction of a series of "hotlines" between NATO capitals and between the NATO Secretary General and member governments would speed the process of consultation both in crisis and non-crisis situations.

At the very least, it has been suggested, extra-European problems should be subjected to more systematic examination at the Atlantic level, either within the Atlantic Council or in operations analysis groups. West European governments should make an effort to develop a common position among themselves on major issues before engaging in discussions with the United States. In the absence of such agreement within Europe, however, operations analysis groups at the Atlantic level should be so designed as to include those European countries which have a continuing interest in a given problem or region. If European consensus on problems outside the North Atlantic area could be developed, a series of European bases, or staging areas, could be built and, depending upon the level of agreement at the Atlantic level, could be used jointly by the United States and Western Europe. For example, although Britain plans before 1975 to have withdrawn practically all of her military forces from regions east of Suez, the British are expected to join with the United States in financing and maintaining a few key bases and staging areas.

EUROPEAN AND ATLANTIC TECHNOLOGICAL COLLABORATION

The future of European technology is important because of the implications of technological breakthroughs for defense and economic growth. Although the imbalance is the result of several factors, the formation of a European technological community endowed with resources and authority far greater than are available to existing European technological organizations, would provide a powerful stimulus to the reduction of the imbalance. Such a community should include as founding members both Britain and the Six. In addition to assuming the tasks in space research which European countries have already undertaken in ESRO and ELDO, a European technological community should develop a coordinated program for European R&D in a broad spectrum of technological efforts. European requirements in computers, aircraft, communications equipment, and even weapons systems should be harmonized. Within such an organization, levels of R&D expenditure necessary for member countries to achieve agreed goals should be set. A technological community should be charged with the task of assessing European needs over the next decade in scientific personnel, laboratory facilities, and institutions for scientific and technological education. An examination of such needs should be related to the long-range program of R&D which was set by the technological community. The United States should make available know-how which it was not prepared to give to purely national programs, and make its programs of collaboration contingent upon European contributions and other efforts designed to enhance the prospects for European integration in forms compatible with U.S. interests.

As part of a European technological community or as a separate organization, a European information and documentation center in science and technology should be created. The center could make available as quickly as possible information on advanced technologies to major research centers throughout Western Europe. Criteria could be developed for the selection and acquisition of information in order to reduce the likelihood of collecting irrelevant or trivial data. The European center would work closely with similar centers elsewhere in the world. The center could become a useful device for the exchange of information at the Atlantic level between the United States and Western Europe.

The strengthening of the European technological base is dependent upon other decisions taken in Western Europe. They relate to the development of European company law, common legislation regarding patents, provisions for the free movement of capital, and a European fiscal policy. The creation of a European market for the products of advanced European technology would contribute to the growth of corporate enterprises, for example in aircraft and computers, more comparable to U.S. firms. The merger of firms within European countries, especially across national frontiers, would not only strengthen the position of Western Europe vis-à-vis the United States, but would contribute to a more European company law. A harmonized fiscal system would enhance the prospects for transnational corporate mergers in Western Europe. The creation of "European" firms in place of national corporate enterprise would not only increase European companies to a size nearer that of their American competitors. It would also reduce the problems of coordination and increased costs resulting from duplication in management which face separate national European companies in competing with larger, more integrated U.S. competitors. In sum, the completion of the Common Market would contribute to the reduction of the Atlantic technological imbalance.

Western Europe's technological future depends upon the changing of attitudes toward careers in applied science, as well as upon the expansion and democratization of higher education not only to add to the numbers of technically competent persons, but to increase mobility within industry and between industry and other fields. The increase in such mobility would enhance the prospects for information transfer within Western Europe. Increased emphasis should be placed upon training in advanced managerial techniques. Western Europe has no educational institution comparable to the business schools which have long been established at several leading American universities.

Despite the growth of "Europeanism" over the past generation, parochial national outlooks still characterize much of the thought in Western Europe about research and development. In order to counteract such tendencies, young engineers, scientists, and technicians, upon the completion of their education, should be urged to accept positions or take training courses for short periods in other countries, even in the United States. Although some persons undoubtedly would choose to remain in the United States, those who returned to Europe would carry back a fund of knowledge and experience and thus would contribute to the future growth of European technology. In order to provide advanced training at the European level, a European Institute of Science and Technology should be created.[3] The Institute would be composed of an international faculty and student body and would have a curriculum including the basic sciences, economics, sociology, and psychology, as well as all subjects concerned with technical progress.

Even while West European collaborative efforts in technology are being strengthened, a more effective technological partnership at the Atlantic level should be created. Of particular concern during the first decade of NATO's existence was the problem of cooperation in the field of aeronautics. In 1952 an Advisory Group for Aeronautical Research and Development (AGARD) was established, under the NATO Standing Group.[4] AGARD made possible the exchange of unclassified information among NATO members about specific problem areas in aeronautical research, such as aircraft performance at supersonic speeds, flight testing, aero-medicine, electronics in air defense, meteorology at high altitudes, the aerodynamic problems of placing guns and rockets on a high performance air frame, and operation from improvised runways. With a small permanent secretariat, as well as periodic meetings of persons engaged in aeronautical research, AGARD increased the flow of technical information between the United States and its allies.

AGARD could be refurbished, or a new Atlantic agency created, to assume major tasks of technological collaboration so that more unified planning for R&D in the North Atlantic area could be undertaken. Such an agency would be charged with the task of advising the Secretary-General and the NATO Council on both the civilian and military aspects of R&D in the North Atlantic area. In particular, an Atlantic technological agency is needed to provide a forum for discussion of allocating tasks of research, development, and production in certain weapons systems. Depending upon the level of technological collaboration European countries achieved among themselves, European NATO members could be represented in an Atlantic technological agency either as national units or by the delegation of a European technological community.

An Atlantic technological agency should be given the assignment not only of coordinating respective European and U.S. efforts in certain fields of R&D but of placing controls upon research, development, and production in member countries. Techniques of inspection, drawn from the experience of the Agency for the Control of Armaments of Western European Union and EURATOM, could be worked out in order to assure that member countries adhere to the guidelines set for them by the NATO technological agency. Recipients of R&D in an Atlantic program of technological collaboration could be required to agree in advance not to engage in certain kinds of national efforts and to subject themselves to a system of inspection.

The strengthening of European technology would enhance the prospects for transatlantic technological collaboration, for Western Europe would become for the United States a more attractive partner. At the same time, Europeans would have less cause for fear that in programs of Atlantic technological collaboration, European firms would become inevitably the junior partner in vast U.S.-dominated efforts in research and development. The United States and Western Europe could engage in a variety of forms of collaboration in many fields, including, for example, the exploration of outer space and oceanography. Over the next generation, the cost of many technologies, for example, space technology, will make increasingly attractive some specialization of effort between the United States and Western Europe, especially if Western Europe creates a technological community within which the European contribution to space technology can be maximized. In oceanography may lie the solution to many problems which face both developing and developed areas. The desalinization of water for use in the urbanized West and in regions of the world in need of irrigation and the development of new sources of food supply and energy are representative of the benefits which might issue from the exploration and study of the ocean depths. The United States and Western Europe together could make great strides, should they join in a program of oceanography.[5]

One alternative for Western Europe is to develop a European R&D program in selected fields. In a few carefully chosen sectors of advanced technology, Europe could achieve levels of collaboration and R&D expenditures needed to narrow the Atlantic technological imbalance. In the chemical industry, for example, where no technological imbalance exists, total European expenditures for R&D do not differ greatly from those of the United States.

Rather than attempting to develop technologies in fields where the U.S. lead is greatest, Western Europe could emphasize those technological sectors which have been most neglected in the United States, including, for example, urban transportation and shipbuilding. But such a choice would have important implications for Western Europe's future. The Atlantic technological imbalance is greatest in several technologies which are vital to the U.S. defense effort. Thus for Western Europe the Atlantic technological imbalance has political and strategic as well as economic implications. If Western Europe is unable to develop and build its own weapons systems, it may not be possible to reduce greatly her military dependence upon the United States. But Atlantic technological collaboration is related to problems which are not merely of a military nature. Even in the absence of an Alliance between the United States and West European countries, Western Europe would still face the need for a concerted effort to narrow the imbalance.

The relationship between technological collaboration and economic integration—like the relationship between economic and political integration—is not clear. Proponents of functionalist theories of integration posited a close relationship between technology and integration. Especially during World War I, advances in technology had hastened the development of governmental centralization within nation-states. It was anticipated that technological advances which made necessary the development of functional cooperation beyond the nation-state would lead eventually to centralization at the international level.[6]

In the aftermath of World War I, technology, of course, did not lead to the development of international integration anticipated by proponents of functionalism. Especially over the past generation, though, changes in technology have heightened the need for a wide range of collaboration, especially in Western Europe. Numerous commentators have argued that Western Europe must attain one form or another of political integration in order to reduce the U.S. hegemony. The perception of the imbalance in technology could lead Europeans to develop the will to make needed decisions about their political future in new steps toward integration. So long as military affairs are perceived within a primarily national framework, however, nations are likely to look upon the development of defense-related technologies primarily as national undertakings. The very importance which certain nation-states attach to such fields as nuclear energy, electronics, and aero-space activities as contributing to national prestige diminishes the prospects for fruitful technological collaboration at the international level.

Essentially, Western Europe has several options: to embark upon more collaborative ventures among existing national units; to continue to emphasize specifically national R&D programs; to join, if the United States were willing, in the creation of an Atlantic federation with a large-scale technological base; or to create an integrated Western Europe with its own large-scale technological base. If the first, or even the second, option is chosen, it is likely that Western Europe will become even more heavily dependent upon the United States and the Atlantic technological imbalance will widen. In turn, European perceptions of U.S. hegemony may become more widespread in Western Europe. Hence the third option is more adequate than the others to the needs and the mood of Western Europe.

THE RESOLUTION OF ATLANTIC ECONOMIC PROBLEMS

In contrast to its great strength vis-à-vis Western Europe in technology and military capabilities, the Untied States appears unable to find solutions to major economic problems. The persistent balance of payments deficits, together with domestic inflationary pressures unmatched by adequate fiscal and monetary policies to reduce spending, have already diminished confidence in the dollar as the leading reserve currency of the international monetary system. In response, the United States has chosen to emphasize controls over the export of U.S. capital, restrictions on tourist spending, and cuts in foreign aid, rather than adequate fiscal and monetary policies at home. The effect of such a choice has been to reenforce European doubts about the ability of the United States to exercise international economic leadership. The importance of effective U.S. policies designed to restore confidence in the dollar lies as much in their psychological effect upon other nations as in their implications for the future orderly evolution of the international monetary system.

In part, the resolution of major economic problems confronting the United States depends upon the success of U.S. efforts to obtain a more equitable formula for the sharing of aid and defense burdens. This in turn is related to changes in the framework for Atlantic collaboration to take account of changes in the capabilities of Western Europe since the founding of NATO. In return for concessions sought by Western Europe, the United States should seek a greater European commitment in sectors in which the U.S. has borne the major burden, in particular, a commitment to provide aid and capital to developing areas.

In some cases the resolution of Atlantic economic problems, as in the case of the U.S. and British balance of payments deficits, calls for domestic policies which will restore international confidence in the world's two most important reserve currencies, as well as systematic consultation at the international level. In addition, if the existing international monetary system is to be preserved, there is clearly the need for new reserves or increases in credits which can supplement existing reserve currencies in the settlement of international accounts.

In the trade negotiations of the 1960's great progress was made in the reduction of tariff barriers to the flow of international commerce. Given the persistence of protectionist sentiment both in the United States and Western Europe, the prospects for further tariff reductions in the immediate future are not great. However, the reduction of non-tariff barriers to trade should be a priority consideration for Atlantic countries. In fact, the United States has an interest in the removal of such impediments as one means of increasing U.S. exports and reducing the balance of payments deficit.

The great increase in U.S. investments in Western Europe has been the object of concern both to European governments and the United States. European fear of the control of its most important industries by the United States has been matched by official U.S. concern about the adverse effect of capital exports upon the balance of payments. Although restrictions on the export of U.S. investment capital to Western Europe will dampen the trend toward U.S. dominance in European industry, it will also lead U.S. corporations to borrow more heavily abroad, with the effect of raising European interest rates and increasing European resentment.

Because of the importance of Atlantic investment patterns to the technological and economic future of Western Europe, as well as to U.S.-West European relations, there is need for systematic consultation at the Atlantic level and among West European governments. If a European technological community is created, it should have the task of formulating a European policy regarding investment. Such a policy should be designed to reconcile the European interest in investment as a means of gaining access to advanced U.S. technology and managerial skills with the European concern about the control of its major industries by Americans. Historically, Europe has been a net exporter of capital. Europeans hold portfolio investments in U.S. corporations which almost equal the total U.S. direct investment in Western Europe. The growth in West European direct investment in the United States could increase access to and participation in the development of U.S.-based advanced technologies and perhaps reduce European fears about U.S. dominance in the industries of Western Europe. Either as separate national units or as a delegation from the proposed European technological community, Western Europe could join with the United States in the examination, on a systematic basis, of Atlantic investment problems, as well as the future of European and American investment in less developed areas.

EAST-WEST RELATIONS

The growing West European preoccupation with European affairs has already contributed to a marked rise in West European interest in the "normalization" of relations with East European countries. Given the prospect that the "European" orientation of the policies of West European governments will increase rather than diminish in the 1970's, there is likely to be an intensification of effort to develop new links with Eastern Europe. Since the U.S. is interested in lessening Soviet influence in this region, the Western countries will be engaged simultaneously in the pursuit of policies designed to achieve increased economic and political ties with communist states in Europe.

However desirable coordination might be, the nations of the

West have not enjoyed notable success in the development of common policies toward Eastern Europe. For Atlantic countries to engage in discussions on the details of policies to be adopted individually or jointly is a cumbersome and time-consuming process. To add such a dimension to the complex process of policy-formulation at the national level, with its competing executive agencies and departments, is to impose a new burden upon decision-makers and to complicate the decision-making process. Moreover, the expansion of the decision-making process to include other governments creates problems of security. An allied government whose leaders do not find themselves in agreement with a policy under discussion may leak its details prematurely in an effort to torpedo it. For these reasons, Western governments are likely to pursue their policies toward Eastern Europe individually. Only the European Community will have leverage in dealings with Eastern Europe beyond that possessed individually by West European member states.

If Western Europe moves toward political integration, a common foreign policy vis-à-vis Eastern Europe is likely to emerge. Even in the absence of such a policy, however, Western Europe, together with the United States, should make a continuing effort to develop common guidelines for policies toward Eastern Europe. Discussions of such could be conducted within one of the operations analysis groups proposed in an earlier section of this chapter. Individual governments would then be free to pursue specific policies within commonly agreed guidelines.

The objective of Western policy should be the diminution of the cohesiveness of the communist bloc and the encouraging of processes of internal liberalization in East European countries. In particular, such policies should be designed to increase the scope for the effective articulation of popular pressures and to reduce further the ideological commitment of communist elites.

Each major Western country has attempted to expand cultural interaction with East European countries. The objective of communist elites has been to maintain such contacts at a low level. By increasing vastly the numbers of scholarships and travel grants to East European students to attend Western institutions of higher learning, for example, the countries of the West could increase pressures upon East European governments for greater freedom of movement to the West. At the same time, larger numbers of

East European students would be exposed to the economic, cultural, and educational benefits of the West.

Greater interaction among larger numbers of persons in professional and business fields in conferences and seminars of at least several days' duration should be arranged. Western governments could permit the cost of such programs to be written off as tax deductions. Wherever possible, an expansion of cultural exchange programs should be linked to the conclusion of economic agreements sought by East European governments. In the conclusion of trade agreements, Western countries should have as another objective to lessen the dependence of East European economies upon the Soviet Union. For example, Western countries should offer to buy from and sell to East European countries products which the Soviet Union trades with them at prices substantially above those prevailing in the world market. Moreover, the West should attempt to purchase goods that are in short supply in the Soviet Union or in another East European country, thus confronting a communist government with a choice between economically advantageous trade or bloc solidarity. Finally, by seeking markets in Eastern Europe for consumer goods, Western countries could contribute to a rise in pressures for higher living standards.

In order to promote economic decentralization as well as greater interaction, Western governments should press their East European counterparts to extend the scope for trade and business contacts at the non-governmental level. In fact, such action should be linked to the conclusion of trade agreements sought by East European governments.

To the extent that West European integration contributes to the strengthening of Western Europe economically and technologically, it will exercise a magnetic attraction upon East European peoples. In addition to making it necessary for East European countries to deal with the institutions of an integrated Western Europe, the development of West European integration would provide advanced technologies and attractive markets. East European peoples would be attracted to participation in organizations at the European level. At this stage, West European peoples would face the difficult choice between maintaining West European institutions or altering and perhaps diluting them to accommodate diverse peoples from the East.

If Western and Eastern Europe evolved more "normal relationships with each other, each would retain security links respectively with the United States and the Soviet Union. The development of a Western Europe less dependent militarily upon the United States would make possible a major reduction in U.S. forces stationed on the Continent, in exchange for Soviet troop reductions in East European countries. Thus the respective security links would remain, although West European aspirations for broader contacts with Eastern Europe would be partially satisfied.

* * *

The problems which have beset U.S.-European relations in the past decade are attributable to a great extent to the inadequacy of existing institutions and political practices at both the Atlantic and European levels. The United States and West European countries face the difficult task of developing a framework which can accommodate their common and individual policy objectives. But the problems which have been the object of examination in this study are also the result of policy decisions taken in Western Europe and the United States, often in response to changes in the international environment.

Trends within the major Atlantic countries do not augur well for the development of policies responsive to the problems confronting the West. Britain faces formidable economic problems, which not only have made impossible the preservation of a British presence East of Suez, but have delayed her admission to the European Community. Having withdrawn from overseas commitments, France stands as the critic of U.S. policy and the proponent of a European grouping from which U.S. influence would be largely excluded. Despite great strides in the postwar period, the psychological alienation of Germany from the West has by no means been ended, and Germany, a generation after World War II, seeks not only to attain a position of equality but to pursue policies which do not subordinate her to other Western nations. In the United States, domestic demands compete with international commitments for the attention of U.S. policymakers and the far from inexhaustible supply of U.S. resources and treasure. The multitude of problems which press upon the United States makes ever more difficult, yet ever more urgent, the development of a broadly based consensus about foreign policy priorities. The very growth of U.S. commitments around the world increases the likelihood that the United

States will become unable to shoulder vast new international burdens. Yet in the Middle-East—whose future intertwines with that of Europe—the U.S. may find it necessary to make a greater U.S. commitment of resources.

For the United States, the challenge of creative statesmanship is to develop a policy which is responsive to European conceptions of Atlantic technological, military, and economic imbalance; European visions of a "wider Europe;" European sensitivity to U.S. hegemony; and European misgivings about the adequacy of U.S. leadership to solve major problems at home and abroad. For Western Europe the need is equally urgent to effect attitudinal and institutional changes without which effective European action to gain a more powerful voice in Atlantic relations will be next to impossible. Europeans as well as Americans need to remember they are part of a larger world and turning inward may not solve their problems. That the United States and its European allies will overcome the formidable problems which face them is by no means certain. Whether or not the peoples of the West develop a framework adequate to the problems of the 1970's depends upon political decisions taken in Western Europe and, above all, the ability of the United States to match U.S. dynamism in those fields where Atlantic imbalances exist with the creativity in policy needed to minimize their adverse repercussions upon Western Europe, to reconcile emergent "Europeanism" with the Atlantic problems of the 1970's, and to restore European confidence in the United States.

NOTES

1. Press Conference of May 15, 1962. *Major Addresses, Statements, and Press Conferences of General Charles de Gaulle,* May 19, 1958–January 31, 1964. New York: French Embassy Press and Information Division, p. 175.

2. According to reports about discussions within the NATO Nuclear Planning Group in April 1968, an ABM system in Western Europe would cost about $40 billion. The *Times* (London), April 20, 1968, p. 4.

3. This proposal received the endorsement of participants at the Conference on Trans-Atlantic Technological Imbalance and Collaboration, held in Deauville, France between May 25–28, 1967. The Conference, which brought together a group of 30 U.S. and Canadian participants, and 40 Europeans, was co-sponsored by the Scientific Technological Committee of the North Atlantic Assembly and the Foreign Policy Research Institute, University of Pennsylvania.

4. It was announced in 1965 that AGARD would change its name to Advisory Group for Aerospace Research and Development. *NATO Letter,* Vol. 13, No. 2 (February 1965), p. 21. The NATO Standing Group was abolished in 1966.

5. For an examination of the potential inherent in oceanography, see Victor Basiuk, "The Oceans—A New Frontier for America's Public Policy?" ORBIS, Vol. X, No. 2 (Summer 1966); E.W. Seabrook Hull, "The Political Ocean," *Foreign Affairs,* Vol. 45, No. 3 (April 1967), pp. 492–502.

6. See David Mitrany, *The Effect of War in Southeastern Europe.* New Haven: Yale University Press for the Carnegie Endowment for International Peace, 1936, especially pp. 96–97 and 131–137; Ernst B. Haas, *Beyond the Nation State.* Stanford: Stanford University Press, 1965, pp. 2–85.

Index